GEOGRAPHY

Curriculum Bank

KEY STAGE TWO
SCOTTISH LEVELS C-E

THEMES

SIMON ASQUITH, BILL CHAMBERS AND KARL DONERT

Published by Scholastic Ltd,
Villiers House,
Clarendon Avenue,
Leamington Spa,
Warwickshire CV32 5PR

2 3 4 5 6 7 8 9 0 7 8 9 0 1 2 3 4 5

AUTHORS
SIMON ASQUITH,
BILL CHAMBERS AND KARL DONERT

EDITOR
LIBBY RUSSELL

SERIES DESIGNER
LYNNE JOESBURY

DESIGNER
SUE STOCKBRIDGE

ILLUSTRATIONS
PAT MURRAY & THE DRAWING ROOM

COVER ILLUSTRATION
JONATHAN BENTLEY

INFORMATION TECHNOLOGY CONSULTANT
MARTIN BLOWS

SCOTTISH 5–14 LINKS
MARGARET SCOTT AND SUSAN GOW

Designed using Aldus Pagemaker
Printed in Great Britain by Ebenezer Baylis,
Worcester

British Library Cataloguing-in-Publication Data
A catalogue record for this book is available from the
British Library.

ISBN 0-590-53408-4

Contents

ACKNOWLEDGEMENTS

The publishers gratefully acknowledge permission to reproduce the following copyright material:

Ordnance Survey for the use of symbols from the *Landranger* series of maps © The Controller of Her Majesty's Stationery Office. Reference number 82816M.

Introduction

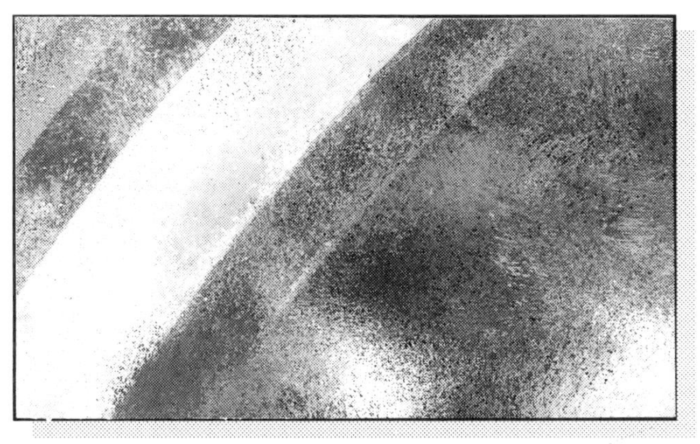

Scholastic Curriculum Bank is a series for all primary teachers, providing an essential planning tool for devising comprehensive schemes of work as well as an easily accessible and varied bank of practical, classroom-tested activities with photocopiable resources.

Designed to help planning for and implementation of progression, differentiation and assessment, *Scholastic Curriculum Bank* offers a structured range of stimulating activities with clearly-stated learning objectives that reflect the programmes of study, and detailed lesson plans that allow busy teachers to put ideas into practice with the minimum amount of preparation time. The photocopiable sheets that accompany many of the activities provide ways of integrating purposeful application of knowledge and skills, differentiation, assessment and record-keeping.

Opportunities for formative assessment are highlighted within the activities where appropriate, while separate summative assessment activities give guidelines for analysis and subsequent action. Ways of using information technology for different purposes and in different contexts, as a tool for communicating and handling information and as a means of investigating, are integrated into the activities where appropriate, and more explicit guidance is provided at the end of the book.

The series covers all the primary curriculum subjects, with separate books for Key Stages 1 and 2 or Scottish Levels A–B and C–E. It can be used as a flexible resource with any scheme, to fulfil National Curriculum and Scottish 5–14 requirements and to provide children with a variety of different learning experiences that will lead to effective acquisition of skills and knowledge.

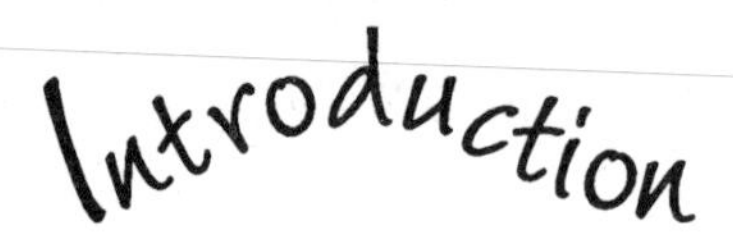

SCHOLASTIC CURRICULUM BANK GEOGRAPHY

The *Scholastic Curriculum Bank Geography* books aim at providing teachers with a comprehensive coverage of Key Stages 1 and 2 of the Geography National Curriculum. Activities are designed to stimulate the learning and practice of geographical skills according to a range of themes and in the context of a range of places. The books aim to help focus teachers in planning learning in and about their own school's local area as well as the contrasting localities which have to be taught in these key stages. There is one book for Key Stage 1 which provides coverage of early geographical skills, using your own school grounds and local area, studying a contrasting locality and the thematic study on environmental quality. There are two books for Key Stage 2. This one concentrates on the themes of Rivers, Weather, Settlement and Environmental Change, the other focuses on place study and concentrates on using the local area and learning about contrasting UK and overseas localities.

Bank of activities

This book provides a bank of learning activities which may be used in a number of ways. It can be used to supplement existing schemes of work in geography; to supplement a block of work or topic, or to help form the framework for a new geography scheme of work (in conjunction with the *Curriculum Bank Geography: Places* book).

Themes to be studied

During Key Stage 2 children are expected to learn about four themes which are identified in the programme of study. These can be studied as discrete blocks of work (or topics), in conjunction with each other or as a part of work on localities as defined in the places section of the programme of study. It is important that children study the themes in the context of real places and according to a range of scales and contexts. Studies will involve them in learning through first-hand experience about their own locality and then through either first or second hand experience about other localities with which they can contrast their own. They will learn best if you help them research real issues which affect real people in these places.

Each of the themes lends itself to different opportunities within the realm of geography. The theme of 'Rivers' provides the teacher with a particularly good opportunity to involve the children in learning about the physical environment. Children can examine how physical processes can lead to the development of specific landforms. The theme provides good opportunities for fieldwork within physical geography.

The theme 'Weather' is particularly suited to study by primary children as weather is something that all children have direct and meaningful first-hand experience of. It provides the teacher with excellent opportunities for involving the children in gathering primary (first-hand) data and in studying patterns through time as well as across space.

The theme 'Settlement' lends itself well to study about the human environment. It should be used to help the children develop an understanding not only of their own settlement but of other settlements, of why these settlements exist and about how and why land is used in these settlements.

The theme 'Environmental change' allows the teacher to teach 'about, in and for the environment' (NCC, 1990). This theme offers an excellent opportunity for children to develop in their understanding of the relationship between people and the human and physical worlds, to use the outdoor environment as an extension of the classroom and importantly, to support children in recognising their own potential to affect change in the environment.

Fieldwork

An essential component of children's learning about rivers, weather, settlement and environmental change should be through fieldwork. Any geographical learning will be more meaningful if it is based on direct experience and it is important that children are provided with experiences which give them opportunity for direct observation and the collection and recording of primary data.

Fieldwork should underpin thematic study in the local area and occasional visits to other localities is to be encouraged. If your school is able to provide a residential curriculum fieldwork experience during the key stage then you may find an excellent opportunity for tackling one or more of the themes in conjunction with a contrasting locality study. Consider how you ensure progression through all of the fieldwork experiences you offer.

Safety has to be paramount when studying geographical themes beyond the school gate. Make sure that you have a clear understanding of safety procedures and your obligations by discussing this through with your headteacher and consulting policy and local authority guidelines. Consult senior colleagues and guidelines, conduct a risk assessment, but importantly ensure that children do get the quality fieldwork experiences that should be at the heart of a good geography curriculum. Activities where children will be working outside the classroom are flagged with the icon, and those where they will be outside the school grounds have the icon.

Lesson plans

Detailed lesson plans, under clear headings, are given for each activity and provide material for immediate implementation in the classroom. The structure for each activity is as follows:

Activity title box

The information contained in the box at the beginning of each activity outlines the following key aspects:

Introduction

▲ *Activity titles and learning objective* – For each activity, a clearly-stated learning objective is given in bold italics. These learning objectives break down aspects of the programmes of study into manageable, hierarchical teaching and learning chunks, and their purpose is to aid planning for progression. These objectives can be easily referenced to the National Curriculum and Scottish 5–14 requirements by using the overview grids at the end of this chapter (pages 9 to 12).

▲ *Class organisation/Likely duration* – Icons and signpost the suggested group sizes for each activity and the approximate amount of time required to complete it.

▲ *Safety* – Where it is necessary in activities, safety considerations are flagged with the ▲ icon.

Previous skills/knowledge needed

Information is given here when it is necessary for the children to have acquired specific knowledge or skills prior to carrying out the activity.

Key background information

This section is intended to help the teacher understand the context of the activity within geographical learning and the geographical concepts under-pinning it. The information should give the teacher greater confidence in teaching the activity.

Preparation

Advice is given for those occasions where it is necessary for the teacher to prime the pupils for the activity; to prepare materials; to set up a display or activity ahead of time.

Resources needed

All of the materials needed to carry out the activity are listed, so that either the pupils or the teacher can gather them together easily before the beginning of the teaching session.

What to do

Easy-to-follow, step-by-step instructions are given for carrying out the activity, including (where appropriate) suggested questions for the teacher to ask the pupils to help instigate discussion and stimulate investigation.

Suggestion(s) for extension/support

Ideas are given for ways of providing for easy differentiation where activities lend themselves to this purpose. In all cases, suggestions are provided as to how each activity can be modified for the less able or extended for the more able.

Assessment opportunities

Formative assessment suggestions have been included in the 'Assessment opportunities' section. In some of the activities the photocopiable sheet can be used in a summative way. These sheets are indicated by the icon.

Opportunities for IT

Suggestions are made as to how IT might enhance the activity or be directly utilised within it. Regular use of the computer is encouraged for the collection, handling and presentation of data collected as a part of geographical work. Every activity includes suggestions in this section but activities which are particularly relevant to the application of IT are marked with the icon, and indicated by the bold page numbers on the chart. The chart on page 159 presents specific areas of IT covered in the activities, together with more detailed support on how to apply particular types of program.

Display ideas

Where they are relevant and innovative, display ideas are incorporated into activity plans and illustrated with examples.

Other aspects of the PoS covered

Geography has one Programme of Study (PoS) and one Attainment Target for Key Stage 2. Geographical skills will often be taught through the study of geographical themes in the context of different places; therefore, there is an inevitable (and intended) overlap between different parts of the PoS. The most obvious links are highlighted under this heading.

Reference to photocopiable sheets

Where activities include photocopiable activity sheets, small reproductions of these are included in the lesson plans, together with guidance notes for their use and, where appropriate, suggested answers.

Assessment

The assessment chapter provides assessment activity ideas with accompanying summative assessment sheets. The activities have all been designed to allow the children to do them individually and with little introduction. There are also some photocopiable sheets from the other chapters which can be used for assessment purposes (see 'Assessment opportunities').

Photocopiable activity sheets

Most of the activities are accompanied by at least one photocopiable activity sheet. Some of these sheets are in direct support of the activity, some form part of the activity, some provide necessary information or techniques and others provide introductory or follow-up opportunities. Many of the sheets have been designed to be generic, allowing any teacher in any school to use them within the context of their own school's local area and the contrasting localities that they decide to study with their pupils.

Cross-curricular links

Strong links between Geography and the Programmes of Study for other subjects of the National Curriculum and Religious Education are identified in a grid (see page 160). Geographical skills in the study of themes, thematic maps, rivers, weather, settlement and environmental change are all examined with respect to each subject.

GEOGRAPHY AT KS2: THEMES

Geography is an essential part of every child's curriculum. If taught well it should encourage and develop the natural sense of wonder that all children have about the world in which they live. It should help children find answers to their questions about the world and it should stimulate a desire for ever-increasing knowledge and understanding of the world and the people in it.

The subject is concerned with places, with the people who inhabit those places and with the interaction between people and place. In the primary school, it should involve children in asking questions and exploring real issues surrounding the human and physical worlds and how those worlds inter-relate. Work organised along a thematic line can often provide children with the structure necessary to enable them to answer these questions and explore such issues.
Although geographical learning can be organised into a wide range of different topics or thematic areas, within Key Stage 2, there are four themes which must provide the 'backbone' of the child's experience however they are arranged into a school's curriculum. These are Rivers, Weather, Settlement and Environmental change. (See the section on 'Themes to be studied' page 6).

Geography is concerned with the spatial dimension and with the patterns and processes operating within space. It is concerned with the spaces between places and how these places are linked together. It is a vehicle for improving empathy between peoples and understanding why the world is as it is.

In learning about geography children will be observing, recording, analysing, and presenting and communicating their findings to others. This will lead to the development of their interpersonal and group work skills.

This book encourages the teacher to truly 'involve' the children in their world and in the issues operating within it. It enables children to move out of the classroom and to examine the world first hand and it encourages teachers to help children make sense of their world by developing their skills and providing as meaningful a range of experiences of other places through the vehicle of the four themes as possible.

The book aims to show that with a little forward planning, places can be presented to children as 'real' and not simply abstract areas of knowledge beyond their direct experience. It asks that teachers recognise the opportunities offered by teaching along a thematic line so that a structure or framework exists against which children can study different places.

It is important to support the development of children's attitudes and values as well as their knowledge, skills and understanding. The activities provided in this book can be used to provide children with as accurate an understanding as possible about what it would be like to live in the places that they study closely and to provide them with an overview of the world as a whole.

Learning objective	PoS/AO	Content	Type of activity	Page
Skills and themes				
To describe and interpret surroundings with reference to a theme (weather).	3a. *Physical and built environment: P3.*	Recording temperatures around school. Interpreting differences.	Paired walks around school. Discussion and simple data collection.	14
To develop children's use of vocabulary in the context of thematic work in geography (settlement).	3a. *As above: P3.*	Generating lists of theme-related words. Writing poems.	Group/class poetry activity.	16
To recognise the importance of accurate measuring in fieldwork. To be able to make, record and interpret measurements as a part of thematic work in the field.	3b. *Making and using maps: P3.*	Making a map by surveying a large area using measurement skills.	Paired work within groups. Measuring and mapping work in school playground/field/hall.	18
To encourage the use of a wide range of sources about an area. To use the 'Yellow Pages' and other service directories to inform the study of settlement.	3e. *Collecting evidence: P3.*	Searching for information using a service directory.	Individual/paired work using a service directory and a worksheet.	20
To devise a questionnaire and to handle its results using a computer spreadsheet.	3f. *Collecting evidence; Record and present: P3.*	Carrying out questionnaire in area near to school. Inputting results onto spreadsheet.	Individuals/pairs in a group. Fieldwork questionnaire. Data handling using computer.	21
Thematic maps				
To be able to make maps of your local area at different scales.	3c. *Making and using maps: P4–P6.*	Mapping school and local area at different scales.	Individuals. Making four-page atlas of school/ local area at four different scales.	24
To use symbols and a key when making a thematic map.	3c. *As above: P4–P6.*	Mapping river features and designing appropriate symbols.	Game played in pairs.	26
To be able to make a thematic map which has a scale, symbols and a key.	3c. *As above: P4–P6.*	Mapping/identifying opportunities for reuse, recycling and disposal of waste around school.	Small groups. Mapping activity in school buildings/grounds.	28
To use a globe to identify information of a thematic nature.	3d. *As above: P3.*	Making a thematic papier mâché globe.	Small group research/ papier mâché work.	30
To use and interpret weather maps which show the weather at different scales.	3d. *As above: P4–P6.*	Mapping the weather at regional and national scales.	Individual worksheet mapping/map interpretation activity.	31

Learning objective	PoS/AO	Content	Type of activity	Page
To use and interpret a map of a town using co-ordinates.	3d. *As above: P4 P6.*	Using co-ordinates to plan on maps.	Small group worksheet village planning activity.	33
To use and interpret a thematic settlement map of the UK using four-figure grid references.	3d. *As above: P4–P6.*	Using four-figure grid references in interpreting a map.	Individual UK map activity.	35
To measure distance and direction using a linear scale and a compass rose on a thematic river map.	3d. *As above: P4–P6.*	Using a compass rose and linear distance scale on a map.	Individual/paired worksheet map activity.	37
To make a thematic building materials map of the local area and then to use it to follow a route.	3d. *As above: P4–P6.*	Designing and following maps in the local area on the theme of building materials.	Small groups as part of a whole class activity. Map design and route following in local area.	39
To use, interpret and add to a thematic map showing settlements in high and low places in the UK using atlas skills.	3d. *As above: P4–P6.*	Mapping land height and settlements on a UK map.	Small group mapping/ atlas research activity.	41
Rivers				
To identify where river water comes from and how it gets into the river.	7a. *Physical and built environment: P3.*	Interception, infiltration and evaporation of water, and porosity and permeability of ground.	Class and group practical activities in school grounds.	44
To identify and learn appropriate vocabulary for the parts of a river.	3a; 7a. *As above: P3.*	Learning rivers terminology through practical model.	Group practical sand tray activity.	48
To be aware that most rivers flow downhill to the lowest point which is a lake or the sea and that most lakes have rivers flowing into and out of them.	7a. *As above: P3.*	Identification of rivers and lakes in UK and where they flow from and to.	Individual/paired map interpretation.	50
To understand that rivers erode, transport and deposit materials.	7b. *As above: P4–P6.*	Experiments concerning erosion, transportation and deposition.	Group practical experiments.	54
To be able to recognise river landforms, the materials they are made of, the processes which cause them and that they change through time.	7b. *As above: P4–P6.*	Recognise erosional, depositional, bedrock and sediment river landforms.	Individual worksheet and discussion activity.	57
To develop awareness of the potential dangers associated with rivers. To understand how to act in a safe and sensible manner when working in rivers.	1b; 3b; 7. *Health and safety in the environment: P4–P6.*	Assessment of risks associated with working in and near rivers.	Group and class discussion and worksheet activity.	60

Learning objective	PoS/AO	Content	Type of activity	Page
Weather				
To measure and record the weather at one site.	3b; 8a. *Physical and built environment: P3.*	Measure temperature, wind speed, wind direction and rainfall and analyse data.	Class/small groups on rota. Practical observation and recording of weather.	64
To understand that different places within a small area can experience variations in weather conditions.	8a. *As above: P3.*	Comparison of weather at two sites around the school grounds.	Class/group. Practical recording in school grounds and worksheet activity.	66
To recognise patterns in how weather varies over the course of a year.	8b. *As above: P4–P6.*	Comparison of weather data for different times of the year in your region.	Paired worksheet and data interpretation activity.	69
To recognise that seasonal weather patterns vary around the world.	8c. *As above: P4–P6.*	Research into five climatic zones around the world.	Class/small groups. Research using secondary sources.	71
To recognise that weather conditions vary around the world and that they can be extreme in nature.	8c. *As above: P4–P6.*	Research into extreme weather conditions/ presentation of findings.	Class/small groups. Research using secondary sources. TV documentary-style presentations.	73
Settlement				
To recognise that settlements vary in size.	9a. *As above: P3.*	Identification of settlements of varying size and calculation of land area they cover.	Paired road atlas and worksheet activity.	76
To understand that the characteristics and locations of settlements reflect the types of economic activity which caused them to grow.	9a. *As above: P4–P6.*	Identifying settlements which show evidence of their origin.	Individual map interpretation and worksheet activity.	78
To recognise that land in settlements is used in different ways.	9b. *As above: P4–P6.*	Surveying ground floor land use in the local area.	Groups carrying out a land use survey in the local area.	80
To consider how changing land use affects people and some of the issues that arise out of changing land use.	9c. *As above: P4–P6.*	Issues surrounding proposed redevelopment of an urban park.	Class, divided into groups for role-play and worksheet activity.	82
To study a possible real land use issue within your own school grounds.	9c. *As above: P4–P6.*	Planning for a land-use change in the school grounds and considering environmental impact.	Class/group planning and environmental impact activity using school grounds.	84

Learning objective	PoS/AO	Content	Type of activity	Page
To recognise the main settlements in the region, and their size and location.	9a. As above: P4–P6	Identifying and mapping features of settlements within the local region.	Group 'photo montage' mapping work using a wall map.	87
Environmental changes				
To understand that people affect their environment.	10a. *Ways people affect their environment: P3.*	Collection of data on traffic noise in local area.	Class/group fieldwork activity in local area and discussion.	90
To recognise that environments change through time and that sometimes careful observation is needed to understand changes.	10. *As above: P3.*	Interviewing as a fieldwork technique. Change in a local parade of shops.	Paired interview design. Performing interviews at local shops.	92
To understand how and why people seek to manage and sustain environments.	10b. *As above: P4–P6.*	Identifying 'nice' and 'nasty' features in the school grounds.	Groups. Following a 'nice' and 'nasty' map trail around the school grounds.	94
To understand how change in the environment has good and bad effects.	10a, 10b. *As above: P4–P6.*	Positive and negative effects of a proposed reservoir scheme.	Class/group discussion and 'public enquiry'.	96

Entries given in italics relate to the Scottish 5–14 Guidelines.

Skills and Themes

The aim of this chapter is to provide the teacher with a bank of activities that will help the children improve their geographical skills. It sets the development of these skills within the context of activities based on the four themes at Key Stage 2.

It is essential that geographical themes are studied in the context of real places and using a full range of geographical skills. These skills include:

▲ the appropriate use of geographical vocabulary;

▲ the ability to work in the field gathering primary (first hand) data;

▲ the ability to use simple instruments for collection of this data;

▲ the appropriate use of secondary sources where direct and practical experience is impossible;

▲ the use of IT in geographical work.

Some of the most important skills of the geographer are those surrounding the making and using of maps. These skills are dealt with fully in a separate chapter, 'Thematic Maps'.

Although the activities here are each set in the context of one of the themes, they could be applied to any of them. Most of the activities can be used in any locality being studied although all, and particularly the last one, are suited to thematic work in the school's local area.

The chapter cannot cover every single geographical skill relevant to the study of the Key Stage 2 themes but does concern itself with some of the most centrally important.

WEATHER AROUND OUR SCHOOL

To develop the ability to describe and interpret surroundings with reference to a theme (weather).

Whole group, then pairs.

20 minutes for group discussion; 30 minutes for plotting information.

Previous skills/knowledge needed

Children should have had experience of exploring their school buildings and grounds in an informal way. It is important that children know the extent of the school grounds and where is 'within bounds'. Some discussion about the weather and the recording of it should have already taken place, and children need to have been introduced to using and reading thermometers.

Key background information

Exploration for exploration's sake should have been encouraged in children, and indeed opportunities for exploring the school buildings and grounds should be provided at an early opportunity. It is now important that children can describe and interpret their surroundings and particularly that they can do so within a thematic context. We are now saying 'Don't just look, but describe and explain what you find out according to...'. Here we make the thematic context the weather. Other themes could be used.

Children will have heard of the term 'greenhouse effect' and they will realise that windows can be areas which lose heat and can also magnify heat. The glass of a window pane will transmit low air temperatures from outside on a cold day and can be responsible for increasing the temperature in a room on a sunny day. In very simple terms, the 'greenhouse effect' is where energy being reflected back from within a greenhouse (radiated heat) is absorbed more easily than the solar energy which has been transmitted through the panes of glass. The temperature therefore rises inside the greenhouse.

Preparation

Walk around the school in order to identify a range of places with different temperatures and amounts of sunshine. It might be helpful to prepare a large version of the photocopiable sheet to refer to with the children while introducing the activity.

Resources needed

One or more simple thermometers, one or more magnetic compasses, simple, large-scale map of the school and grounds, one copy of photocopiable page 104 for each pair.

What to do

Discuss with the children that some parts of the school, both inside and outside, are warmer and sunnier than other parts. Encourage them to come up with reasons why we might like to know where such places are, or, on the other hand, where cooler, less sunny places are. The children might suggest that reasons include knowing where to put certain types of plant. They might suggest that books, posters and computers are best kept out of direct sunlight. You could discuss why we tend to locate television sets with their backs to windows (so that sunlight does not spoil our view of the picture). Talking about the effects of windows (both in terms of heat loss and a 'greenhouse effect') will prove useful.

Ask the children to walk around the school in pairs and to plot the temperatures in two different places on a copy of the photocopiable sheet (if limited resources are available, pairs will need to do this at different times). The sheet also asks them to fill in information on whether there is artificial light, some natural light, natural light, or strong natural light. The blank spaces at the bottom are for the children to add sections, if they wish to. They might, for example, look at wind (still, draughty, windy) and dampness (dry, damp, wet). You can decide how children should record this information, but a simple written comment is probably the simplest method. The children could experiment with a compass as they visit different locations to see which way the windows that supply strong sunlight are facing.

Once the children have completed the sheet, they should transfer the information in a way of their choosing to a large-scale map of the school. They could devise, for example, a colour key for different temperature bands and a shading key for the different qualities of light and then map their findings. Finish the activity with a reporting back session so that the whole class can benefit from the various reasons children have put forward for differences in temperature and light in different parts of the school.

Suggestion(s) for extension

Other ways in which the weather affects our lives both indoors and outdoors could be plotted. Children could look for windy places outdoors and draughty places indoors. They could look for places which are prone to puddles and flooding outdoors and parts of buildings that suffer from having damp carried into them, such as entrance halls.

There are obvious extensions into map work. The children are being asked to make thematic maps. One very good activity is to ask different pairs or small groups of children to plot different aspects of the weather and then for them to compare the maps made and to look for patterns.

Suggestion(s) for support

It is advisable to limit the activity to one weather variable (for example, temperature) per pair if this is the most that they can reasonably be expected to cope with. Similarly, if you decide on the locations to be used there will be less decision-making needed by the children in the early stages. Children can be grouped able with less able. The idea of using compasses with this type of activity is quite demanding and is useful as an 'optional extra' in the exercise.

Assessment opportunities

If the teacher makes comments against a class list at the time when the children are reporting back, evidence may be gained as to the children's ability to use appropriate geographical vocabulary to describe and interpret their surroundings.

If the children have used thermometers (and compasses), the photocopiable sheet will contain evidence as to whether the children can undertake fieldwork, including the use of instruments to make measurements.

Evidence might be obtained from comments on the photocopiable sheet and/or the map of the children's understanding of how site conditions can influence the weather and its effects.

Opportunities for IT

The children could use the weather records they have made to create a simple database. They might use the following fieldnames:

Day	Thursday
Place	back of hall
Temp inside	19
Temp outside	17
Position	SW
Time	1430

The children could then sort the information to find the hottest or coldest locations, plot graphs to show the temperatures or look at the differences between the temperatures indoors and outdoors. The same information could be used in a spreadsheet. The statistical functions of the spreadsheet can be used to work out average temperatures. The spreadsheet can be sorted and graphed and pie-charts drawn using the data.

The children could also use a data-logger to automatically record the temperature at a particular location in the school. Various sorts of data loggers are available, some handheld and others linked directly to the computer. Two sensors could be linked to the computer, one inside and the other outside and the data used to plot graphs of the change in temperature over time. This activity will give children an opportunity to watch the graphs being drawn as the temperature changes throughout the day.

Display ideas

A large display plan of the school labelled with specific locations and annotated with the children's findings about the locations that they studied, could form a central part of a display of some of the photocopiable sheets and any maps that the children have completed.

A wall thermometer could be incorporated into the display and daily readings can be taken from it and entered on to a chart or even a graph. This provides the display with an interactive component and makes it of continuing interest to the children.

Other aspects of the Geography PoS covered

3b; 8a.

Reference to photocopiable sheet

This is a recording sheet. The rows for *temperature* and *light* are provided and there are blank spaces for the children to add sections if directed by the teacher. Suggested extra sections might be wind (for example: still, draughty, windy) and dampness (for example: dry, damp, wet).

Weather around our school

Name ______ Date ______

Location 1...

Aspects of weather we are finding out about	Comment/measurement
Temperature	
Light (eg. artificial light, natural light, some natural light, strong natural light).	

Location 2...

Aspects of weather we are finding out about	Comment/measurement
Temperature	
Light (eg. artificial light, natural light, some natural light, strong natural light).	

RHYMES OF REASON

To develop the use of geographical vocabulary in the context of thematic work.

Groups or whole class.

5 minutes introduction; 25 minutes introductory (or follow-up) worksheet poem writing; 10 minutes group discussion; 20 minutes poem writing.

Previous skills/knowledge needed

Children should be studying a geographical theme from the Programme of Study in the locality being studied. They will benefit from having had some experience of writing poems.

Key background information

Each different theme in geography, as in any subject area, has its own set of subject-specific vocabulary which is important to know if communication is to be effective. For example, within the theme of 'settlement' words to do with different types of settlement (village, city, resort, port, industrial area), words concerning the human features which make up settlements (building, road, warehouse, junction, accommodation, factory), and words to do with people in settlements (resident, teacher, shop assistant) are all important vocabulary.

A list poem is a collection of words or phrases, all connected by a theme, and arranged in simple list form.

Preparation

Depending on the place that your children are currently learning about and the theme you have taken within the work, prepare yourself by brainstorming a range of connected words. Make copies of photocopiable sheet 105 for the children to use either as an introductory exercise or as a follow-up.

Resources needed

Copies (as above) of photocopiable sheet 105 for each child, writing and drawing materials.

What to do

Gather the group or class together and start a discussion about the theme you are studying. It might be that you are studying green space within your local town. It might be that you are studying traffic in your local village. It could be that you are studying places where people work in a contrasting overseas suburban area.

You can either provide the children with a copy of photocopiable sheet 105 at the outset, so as to give them an idea of what is expected, or you can ask them to complete the sheet as a follow-up exercise. The sheet provides one example of a list poem and starts the children off with two others.

Explain to the children that they will be creating a poem

based on the theme you are studying. As a group, brainstorm as many words connected with your theme and your place as you can. Encourage the children to think in as divergent a manner as possible. Note the words on a wall board as the children think of them.

Once the group or class have generated a good list ask the children to start writing their own poems. These are best written on A4 or A5 paper. The children can then illustrate around the edge of the piece of work.

End by asking the children to read their poems back to the rest of the group.

Geography list poems

Name ____ Date ____

▲ Poem 1 is a list poem made of words which are all to do with traffic in London. Poems 2 and 3 need you to finish them. Poem 2 is about the weather on the highest mountain in the world, poem 3 is about the River Rhine.
▲ Write in the title to each of the poems.

Poem 1.
Title ....
Marble Arch
Beeping horns
Notting Hill Gate
Red double-deckers
Waterloo
Whooshing tube trains
Escalators
Circle, Northern, Jubilee
Traffic jams
Parking meters
Baker Street
Fraying tempers
Smoking exhausts
Taxi cab
River boatmen
Landing jetties
Island Gardens
Capital

Poem 2.
Title ....
Highest mountain
Scary feeling
Summit blizzard...

Poem 3.
Title ....
Swiss stream
Mountain torrents
Growing slowly. .

Suggestion(s) for extension
Children who are capable of doing so could try to rhyme their poems. They could be encouraged to include place and street names or even the names of people who live in the area.

Suggestion(s) for support
Provide the children with books, maps and other materials about the area. These can be used as reference for the words in the poems. Emphasise that some of the most effective poetry does not rhyme and that the structure which will make their poem a poem is the list itself.

Assessment opportunities
The completed poems will help provide evidence of the children's success at using appropriate geographical vocabulary, but the process of thinking of the words is also important. You might log who thinks of what words in the group discussion by putting each child's initials beneath words as you write them up. This will have the added benefit of encouraging the children to contribute.

Opportunities for IT
The children could use a word processor to create their list poem. Children could create either their own or group lists of words connected with your theme and place and save these in an initial list. Words could then be picked and arranged to make individual poems, each child saving their poem as a separate document and then printing it out. The end product could be a class desktop published poetry book.

Display ideas
Each list poem could be mounted onto strips of stiff card and hung from the ceiling. Using dowelling frames or hoops as suspended frameworks from which to hang the individual poems is often effective. The suspended poems could be hung over a display table with books, maps and other materials about the place studied.

Other aspects of the Geography PoS covered
3e; 4; 5a; 6.

Reference to photocopiable sheet
Photocopiable sheet 105 can be used to help children understand the idea and form of a list poem and to support them in writing one. It can be used by way of introduction or it could be used as follow-up. Each child reads the first poem and gives the poem a title. They then complete their own versions of the remaining three poems and entitle them.

MEASURE AND MAP

To recognise the importance of accurate measuring in fieldwork. To be able to make, record and interpret measurements as a part of thematic work in the field.

Individuals, then pairs within a group.

10 minutes introductory worksheet; 5 minutes explanation; 20 minutes paired surveying work in school grounds; 15 minutes map making.

Previous skills/knowledge needed

Children will need to be able to use accurately a tape measure and a ruler. They must know what a right-angle is. They should have an understanding of what scaling down means.

Key background information

Accurate measurement is essential in geographical fieldwork. Children doing geographical work at Key Stage 2 might use a wide range of instruments which involve the taking of measurements. These include:

▲ rulers, metre rulers and tape measures;
▲ protractors and clinometers (measure angle of a slope);
▲ rain gauges, thermometers, anemometers (wind speed/strength gauge), wind direction indicators (wind vane) – some primary weather station kits include barometers (air pressure) and hygrometers (humidity);
▲ direction compasses;
▲ soil pH meters, soil thermometers.

A starting point, and one which requires frequent reinforcement and development by the teacher, is assuring that children can accurately use rulers and tape measures for a purpose. Accurate measurement of small areas is an important skill that will help children in work on land and building use when studying settlements and environmental issues. Accurate use of rulers and tape measures will also help children in studying streams as a part of work on rivers.

Preparation

Decide on an open area that the children could survey and map. Preferably, this area should not be larger than 20m x 20m (to avoid problems later in the activity when the children map the surveyed area onto A3 paper). A school playground, an area of school field or a quadrangle would serve the purpose. Alternatively you could use the inside of the school hall. The area would be best suited to this activity if it had some (although not too great an) irregularity of shape about its boundaries.

Immediately before the activity mark a line (using playground chalk or a long rope) right across the middle of the area. This line must run from one edge to the opposite edge and it must be as straight as possible (this is easier achieved using string or rope which you can pull tight).

Resources needed

One (or preferably more) metric tape measure(s) – these should be long enough to stretch from your line at a right-angle to the furthest point of the area's boundary, straight-edged rulers marked in centimetres, a supply of A3 white paper, copy of photocopiable sheet 106 for each child, pencils and set-squares.

What to do

Give each group member a copy of the photocopiable sheet and explain that the points 1–15 in the table refer to the points 1–15 on the map line and that 'A' and 'B' refer to each side of the map line. Tell them that the map will show an imaginary school playground and that the measurements in the table are the distances from the line to the perimeter of the playground. Ask them to use a set-square and pencil and to measure these distances on the relevant side of the map line and mark them. They can then join these marks up. They will be left with a map of the school playground.

Give each pair of children a piece of A3 paper and ask them to draw a line on it. This line should correspond to the line you have marked in the area to be surveyed and should be in the centre of the paper. The line should be at a 1:100 scale to the original (if your original is 12 metres long, the children's paper copy should be 12 centimetres long).

Take the children to the area you have chosen and show them its perimeter and the line you have marked. Unwind a tape measure, lay it along your line and get one of the children to make a mark (with chalk, a peg or a weighted down piece of paper) every metre (or two metres if you are surveying a larger space).

The group now measure the distance from each of these

points to the perimeter along lines which are at right-angles to the original line. They record these measurements in their own rough table similar to the one on the photocopiable sheet (as on this sheet it will be helpful to refer to one side of the line as 'A' and the other as 'B').

Back in the classroom the children map this information using their rulers. One metre on the ground is treated as one centimetre on paper. The children can draw the lines they measured or they can simply make a mark to show where that part of the perimeter is. Finally, the children link up these perimeter marks to make a finished accurate map of the space surveyed.

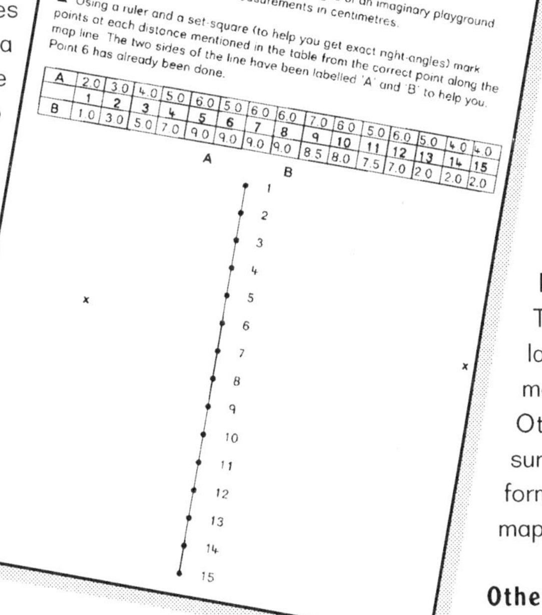

Measure and map

Name ______________________ Date ______________

You are going to draw a map showing the edges of an imaginary playground. The numbers in the table are measurements in centimetres.

▲ Using a ruler and a set-square (to help you get exact right-angles) mark points at each distance mentioned in the table from the correct point along the map line. The two sides of the line have been labelled 'A' and 'B' to help you. Point 6 has already been done.

A	2.0	3.0	4.0	5.0	6.0	5.0	6.0	6.0	7.0	6.0	5.0	6.0	5.0	4.0	4.0
	1	2	3	4	5	6	7	8	9	10	11	12	13	14	15
B	1.0	3.0	5.0	7.0	9.0	9.0	9.0	9.0	8.5	8.0	7.5	7.0	2.0	2.0	2.0

A B

1 2 3 4 5 6 7 8 9 10 11 12 13 14 15

Suggestion(s) for extension

Children could survey the exact locations in the space you are surveying of litter bins, trees, signs, benches, plants or other free-standing objects. If you are working in the hall they could mark PE equipment or the position of peripheral doors.

Suggestion(s) for support

If children are likely to find this activity difficult, start by doing a smaller space. You could limit the number of measurements to the periphery by marking survey points on the line at larger intervals (say every three metres).

Assessment opportunities

Ask children to explain their completed photocopiable sheets and how they made their map. Check that the children have understood how to use the tape measure, the ruler and the set-square.

Opportunities for IT

The children could use a drawing or simple computer-aided design package to create their maps. It is usually possible to create a background grid of squares which can be set at 1cm intervals. Many packages also have a 'snap to grid' facility which helps the children to line up their drawings accurately. A simple template file with the base line and its gradations marked on could be created and saved to disk. The children can then retrieve this file and use it as the basis for their own map.

Display ideas

The children could make a slightly larger scale version of the final map and display it on a table top. Other features in the space surveyed could be added in model form. Display children's completed maps around the model display.

Other aspects of the Geography PoS covered

3c; 4.

Reference to photocopiable sheet

Photocopiable page 106 is best used to help the children understand the main activity before they start. The children measure the distances in the table using a ruler, starting from the map line below it (see 'What to do'). By joining up the marks they make, they end up with the perimeter of an imaginary playground.

'LET YOUR FINGERS...'

To encourage the use of a wide range of resources about an area. To use the* Yellow Pages *and other service directories to inform the study of settlement.

Group, then individuals.

5 minutes discussion; 30 minutes photocopiable sheet activity.

Previous skills/knowledge needed

Some starting knowledge of services in the area being studied will be useful.

Key background information

The *Yellow Pages* and other service directories such as *The Thomson Local* provide a useful source of information about services available in an area. They generally include street maps of the locality and have information on services of all kinds arranged alphabetically by service type. It is worth obtaining copies of these types of directories covering contrasting localities being studied.

The term 'service' is a variously used one. For the sake of this activity we take it to mean any operation which provides people with a service of whatever kind (shops, information, medical services, expertise, repair and so on).

It is important to recognise that different directories cover areas of very different geographical size. Some urban directory regions are surprisingly small.

Preparation

Gather together as many copies as possible of the directory you are going to use for the area you are studying.

Resources needed

Copies of service directories as described in the 'Key background information'section above, one copy of photocopiable sheet 107 for each child, a large scale map of the area being studied will be useful.

What to do

Discuss when and why we use the type of service directory that you have provided. Give the directory/ies out to the children and ask them if they can tell you what geographical area it covers. The title and maps in the directory will help them do this. Now discuss the area that you are studying and ask the children if they can tell you a variety of services which exist or might exist in the area.

Ask the children to explain how the directory works and make sure that they understand that types of service are listed in alphabetical format. The directory might list types of service in an index as well. Explain that once you know what you want to look for, you then have to find which is the most appropriate section.

Give each child a copy of the photocopiable sheet and ask them to look up the nearest of the service types (listed on the left hand side of the sheet) to your school, or to an agreed point on a map if you are studying another locality. The children now fill in the section title, the name of the company they have chosen and the company's address for each service type. Finally they draw and/or write as close a copy of each of the inserts they have used as they can.

It is possible that different children will end up with different results from their interrogation of the directories. If this happens, make this a discussion point. Perhaps the children used slightly different procedures when 'navigating' their way through the directory they used. (Also, some directories can be more specifically local than others and, therefore, this will bring about different results.)

As a follow-up, this information can be mapped map using dots of different colours for each of the different service types and a key.

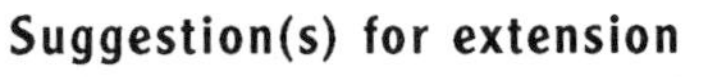

Suggestion(s) for extension

Using additional sheets of paper or copies of the photocopiable sheet, children could expand the number of service categories or research more than one company in each category.

Suggestion(s) for support
If children are likely to have trouble locating the correct sections in the directory, you could mark each section beforehand.

Assessment opportunities
Use the completed sheet and discussion with targeted children to help you decide whether they are able to use the directory adequately as a source of information on the area being studied.

Display ideas
Display one or more copies of the directory on a table and ask the children to help you devise a series of questions to be displayed on stand-up cards or on the wall behind the table which ask observers to find certain services in the area. Copies of the completed photocopiable sheets could be displayed around the directory.

Other aspects of the Geography PoS covered
1b; 2b; 3a; 4; 5a; 9a.

Reference to photocopiable sheet
Photocopiable sheet 107 involves the children in researching a locality using a service directory such as the *Yellow Pages*. The children find the closest (see 'What to do') of six different types of service in the area they are studying. They record the title of the section in which they found the service, the name of the service itself and its address. They then make a drawn and/or written copy of the inserts that they have found.

'Let your fingers...'

Name ____________ Date ____________

Type of directory:

Area covered by directory:

	Title of section in directory	Name of company	Address	Copy of the entry
Doctor				
Supermarket				
Clothing shop				
Furniture shop				
Car repair				
Travel agent				

ISSUES

To devise a questionnaire and to handle its results using a computer spreadsheet.

Individuals in a group.

5 minutes introduction; 30 minutes fieldwork questionnaires; 20 minutes inputting data on computer; 5 minutes interpretation.

Previous skills/knowledge needed
Children should have at least some experience of operating a computer including the use of a mouse to input data. Children should be studying an environmental issue about which people in the area are likely to have opinions.

Key background information
This activity relies on the children using a simple questionnaire where all of the responses are logged as numbers on a scale. Most computers in school have a spreadsheet program loaded on them. Such programs allow the inputting of data into boxes or 'cells' which expand to take the required amount of information, and which can be organised in rows and columns using simple buttons and commands at the head of the screen. Spreadsheets also allow the operator to carry out simple calculations on the data using the computer as a calculator.

The questionnaire is one of the most used data gathering techniques of the geographer but any questionnaire's success depends on how well it is thought out.

Preparation
Ensure that your computer spreadsheet program can perform summation (SUM) operations. This is normally done by clicking a button with the Σ symbol.

Consider the issue the children are studying and devise four simple statements which will gauge any respondent's opinion about different aspects of the issue. All of the statements must be answerable with the response 'strongly disagree', 'disagree', 'no opinion', 'agree' or 'strongly agree'. The following statements are examples:

Issue: Pollution of a local stream (Runny Brook).
1. Runny Brook is polluted.
2. The stream is dangerous to wildlife / children.
3. The stream is polluted by 'LocalCo Ltd'.
4. I would sign a petition to get the stream cleaned up.

Set your computer spreadsheet program up so that the children can create a simple table with five columns and eleven rows. Input a table similar to the main grid on the photocopiable sheet, save it to use as a template.

The issue you are studying may involve the children working outside the school grounds. If this is the case, seek the required permission from parents and arrange adult support in line with your school or authority's policy.

Resources needed

Make copies of photocopiable sheet 108 for each child. The children may require clipboards when they are interviewing people. Arrange any adult supervision the children may need.

What to do

Talk to the children about the need to gather people's opinions about the environmental issue you are studying. Give the children copies of the photocopiable sheet and explain that they are going to ask ten people to comment on whether they strongly disagree, disagree, have no opinion, agree or strongly agree with each of the four statements you have devised. Ask the children to write the four statements in the relevant places on the sheet. Explain the scoring system whereby each person is given a score between 0 and 4 according to their response.

The children go out in supervised groups and ask people to give their responses to the statements. As people respond the children write number 0, 1, 2, 3 or 4 in the relevant boxes on the sheet.

On return to the classroom the children take it in turns to enter their data on the spreadsheet table in exactly the same format as their photocopiable sheet. By clicking on the top response in each column and dragging down to the last, the children can highlight all ten of each statements' responses. If the children do this and then click on the Σ button, they should be provided with the total score for that column.

This done for all four columns, the children can add this new information to their photocopiable sheets inserting it in the 'Total score' boxes provided on the sheet table. They then explain their findings at the bottom of the sheet.

They could pool their results to obtain group data results. If different groups of children have collected different sets of results then there would be a lot of benefit in spending some time as a class comparing the results and discussing why there might be some discrepancies.

Suggestion(s) for extension

The children could be involved in devising the questions. They could write their explanations of the results using a text box below the spreadsheet grid or by using a word processing program. More able children might be encouraged to interrogate further the database to work with and compare data across the groups.

Suggestion(s) for support

Some children will need to be in very small groups while collecting their data. Group children who have not had much experience using computers with those who are more confident.

Assessment opportunities

Ask the children to show you their completed computer spreadsheet files and photocopiable sheets. Discuss their findings with them. This activity will show how capable they are of using a computer to store, handle and present data. Their explanations of their findings will show whether they have understood how a questionnaire works and how to derive information from the results they obtain.

Opportunities for IT

This activity, if completed in full involves children in using IT to store, handle and present data.

Display ideas

Get the children to print out their spreadsheets. Display these with copies of the completed photocopiable sheets and a map showing the sample points where the children interviewed people. Include information on and images of the issue being studied.

Other aspects of the Geography PoS covered

2a–c; 3b; 4; 5a, d; 10a, b.

Reference to photocopiable sheet

Photocopiable sheet 108 is used as explained in 'What to do' to support the children in their collection, organisation and interpretation of data using a simple questionnaire on an environmental theme. It is used to support the children using a computer spreadsheet program and should be used initially by the teacher when setting out the spreadsheet.

Issues questionnaire

Name ______

Issue: ______ Date ______

Statement 1: ______

Statement 2: ______

Statement 3: ______

Statement 4: ______

	Statement 1	Statement 2	Statement 3	Statement 4
Person 1				
Person 2				
Person 3				
Person 4				
Person 5				
Person 6				
Person 7				
Person 8				
Person 9				
Person 10				
Total score				

▲ Using the 'Scores' table below, give each person a score between 0 and 4 for each of the four statements that they comment on.

Scores	
Strongly disagree	0
Disagree	1
No opinion	2
Agree	3
Strongly agree	4

Total score for each column of 10 people
Between 0–7 = generally people strongly disagree
Between 8–15 = generally people disagree
Between 16–24 = generally people are mixed in views
Between 25–32 = generally people agree
Between 33 40 = generally people strongly agree

Using the 'Total score' table above, explain the result of your questionnaire:

Thematic Maps

Maps can be regarded as tools, and just like any other tool, every map is individually suited to a specific job for which it has been designed.

Children are far better motivated into the acquisition of skills in mapping if they are involved in using maps of different types, which have been drawn for a range of purposes and if they are real maps of real places. Just as with a piece of writing, a map should be made with its 'reader', 'user' or 'audience' in mind. The map maker has to consider 'exactly what is this map meant to communicate to those who will use it?' Put the other way round the map user, when examining a map, should enquire 'for what purpose was this map made?' A simple illustration of this would be the London Underground Map which, while being appropriate for helping you navigate your way around London by tube train, would be almost impossible to use as a map to help you walk or drive around the city.

This chapter involves children in making and using a range of maps, many of which are connected with the Key Stage 2 themes of rivers, weather, settlement and environmental change. Some activities involve the children in using maps and atlases of the UK. These could be used to help set localities being studied in a broader geographical context.

For any Ordnance Survey maps that you are going to copy, ensure that your school or LEA have the appropriate Ordnance Survey copyright permission licence.

MAKING MAPS AT DIFFERENT SCALES

To be able to make maps of the local area at different scales.

Individuals working in groups.

5 minutes introduction; 60 minutes practical mapping activity.

Previous skills/knowledge needed

Children should know what an atlas is.

Key background information

During Key Stage 2 it is important that children develop their ability at making maps and appreciate that different scales are appropriate for different mapping tasks. If a teacher is redesigning her classroom then she will benefit from using a plan or map which is at a scale where the plan of the classroom virtually fills a piece of paper. If a town planner is redesigning the traffic flow in a neighbourhood, then he might use a map at a smaller scale which covers the whole neighbourhood on one piece of paper. Atlases contain maps of different scales because as geographers, we want to examine places at different resolutions of detail. We may need to know our local village or district fairly intimately (at large scale), and only need a general geography of our country as a whole (small scale).

Small scale maps are those where on a given size of paper a large area is shown but little close detail. Large scale maps are those where on the same size of paper only a small area is shown but a larger amount of detail is included.

Preparation

Collect one or two atlases for each group and large scale maps of your local area (a local 1:10 000 Ordnance Survey map will be very useful). Make a four-page sugar paper or card booklet for each child where each page is at least A5 (half A4) in size (the children can do this themselves as a part of the activity).

Resources needed

Copies of photocopiable sheets 109 and 110 for each child, at least one atlas for each group and one or more large scale maps of your local area, metre rules and metric tape measures, four-page sugar paper or card booklets.

What to do

Show the children the atlases you have collected and discuss the fact that the atlases contain maps at different scales. Look at a map of a part of the British Isles from near the front of the atlas and then at a map of one of the continents or even the whole world further on in the atlas.

Discuss how you would like the children to make a 'mini-atlas' of their own local area which contains maps at different scales. Show them the four-page booklets you have made which will be turned into their mini-atlases. Explain that their completed atlas will contain maps of their classroom, their school, the school and its immediate surroundings, and lastly the whole of the school's local area.

Distribute copies of the two photocopiable sheets to each child and explain the scales on each sheet. Photocopiable sheet 109 contains blank mapping squares which are at scales 1cm = 2m (10cm = 20m) and 1cm = 10m (10cm = 100m). Photocopiable sheet 110 contains blank mapping squares which are at 1cm = 50m (10cm = 500m) and 1cm = 100m (10cm = 1km). Show the children the scales at the bottom of each of the squares and then get the children to examine the map of the local area. The children draw maps into each of the squares which have their classroom as the central feature.

Square 1 will have their classroom dominating the square. Encourage the children to use the metre rule to measure their classroom (and possibly the area immediately surrounding it) and help them to convert the measurements taken into a drawn version of the classroom in the square. In this square, 1cm will represent 2m on the ground (for example, if the classroom is eight metres long, it will measure four centimetres on the map).

Square 2 will have their classroom as the central feature

in a smaller scale map which is likely to include most or all of their school and its grounds. The large scale map of the local area and the metric tape measure will be of help as the children draw their map which should now have 1cm representing 10m on the ground. It is important that the classroom should be noticeably smaller on this map than on the previous one.

Square 3 will be at a smaller scale still and with 1cm representing 50m should now show the school and its immediate area (bordering streets or the equivalent).

Square 4 will show an even larger area at a scale of 1cm representing 1km on the ground. If you have a copy of the local Ordnance Survey 1:10 000 map, then this square should be mapped at exactly the same scale.

The children cut along the lines indicated on the photocopiable sheets and then stick each of their completed maps (in order of scale) into the four-page sugar paper or card booklet prepared earlier.

Suggestion(s) for extension

In total each 'booklet' will have six potential pages (including the two inside covers). Children who are capable could extend the exercise each way in terms of scale and do a 10cm × 10cm map of their desk top for the front inside cover (making an appropriate scale) and a 10cm × 10cm map of their district or their town for the back inside cover (again, with an appropriate scale).

Suggestion(s) for support

If children are at a very early stage of tackling scale, you could draw the classroom (at each of the scales) on to a copy of each of the squares yourself and then photocopy the sheets. The children could now arrange these maps in scale order starting with the largest scale and moving to the smallest.

Assessment opportunities

Use the children's completed mini-atlases to examine whether they have understood the concept of scale in the context of thematic maps of the local area. Sit with individuals and share their completed atlases. Ask the child to show you the page with the largest scale map, the smallest scale map and so on.

Opportunities for IT

Some children could use a drawing or mapping package to create their maps. They could start by drawing a plan of the classroom which fills the working screen and print this out for the first of their maps. Using the background grid, set to 1cm intervals will help children draw a correctly scaled plan of the classroom.

They can then scale down this plan so that it becomes the centre point of the next scale map. To do this task children will need to know how to create a single drawing object from all of the individual parts of their plan by 'grouping' them together so that they can scale the plan down as a single object. At this stage the children could either print out this map and complete the task freehand or continue using the computer.

Display ideas

Make a display of the atlases on a table top. Attach to the wall behind the table a metre rule, a tape measure, a local map and a smaller scale local map. Position a good example of a child's 'mini-atlas' in the centre of the wall display and use threads to link the metre rule to the largest scale map, the tape measure to the map of the school, the local map to the map of the school and its bordering streets, and the smaller scale map to the last of the maps.

Other aspects of the Geography PoS covered

1a, d; 3b, d; 4; 5e.

Reference to photocopiable sheets

Photocopiable sheets 109 and 110 are used for the children to make maps at four different scales, each based on their own classroom. Each blank map square has a scale below it to which the children should try to adhere. The completed maps are cut out as indicated on the sheets and then incorporated into a sugar paper or card 'mini-atlas'.

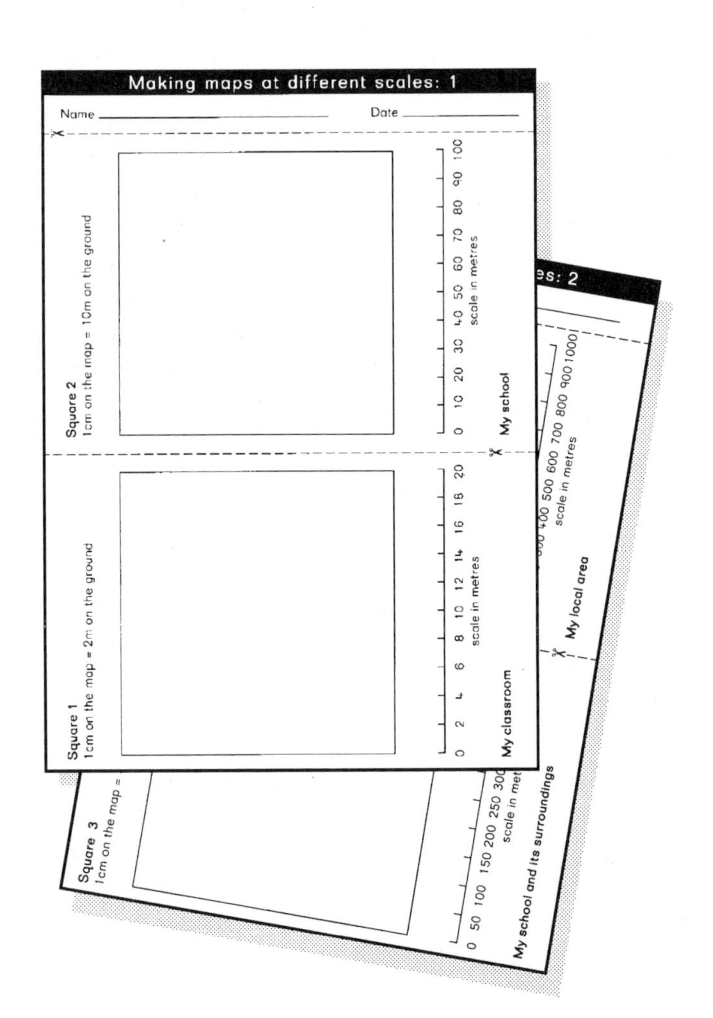

Making maps at different scales: 1

Name ______ Date ______

Square 2
1cm on the map = 10m on the ground

0 10 20 30 40 50 60 70 80 90 100
scale in metres

My school

Square 1
1cm on the map = 2m on the ground

0 2 4 6 8 10 12 14 16 18 20
scale in metres

My classroom

Square 3
1cm on the map =

0 50 100 150 200 250 300
Scale in met

My school and its surroundings

400 500 600 700 800 900 1000
Scale in metres

My local area

SYMBOLS AND KEYS – RIVER BASIN

To use symbols and a key when making a thematic map.

Pairs.

10 minutes introduction; 30–40 minutes paired game; 10 minutes group discussion.

Previous skills/knowledge needed

Children should have studied or be studying the features which make up the parts of a river's drainage basin.

Key background information

We use symbols to represent real life features on a map. This is because to draw everything out as it really is on the ground, at the scale necessary when drawing maps, would mean an impossible degree of complexity.

Symbols can be representational (like the elephant symbol used to represent a zoo) or non-representational (like the red circle used to represent a railway station on an Ordnance Survey map). The use of symbolisation necessarily requires the use of a key which the map reader consults to 'de-code' the symbols.

A river's catchment area (or its basin) is the area in which any rainfall which eventually flows out of the mouth of that river must fall. Rainfall falling outside of this area will eventually flow out at another river's mouth.

Resources needed

One copy of photocopiable sheets 111 and 112 for each pair of children, writing and drawing materials.

What to do

This activity is similar to the popular game 'Battleships'. Each member of the pair has a source map and an empty map on which to record features as described verbally by the other child. Number the children in each pair number one and number two. Give child number one sheet 111 and child number two sheet 112.

Explain that child number one has to use his powers of description to explain where each of the river features labelled on map 1 are located in relation to the pattern of rivers and streams in the river's catchment basin. Child number two has to draw each of the features on map 'A' by designing a symbol. A copy of each symbol has to be drawn into the empty key area of the sheet.

All of this done, child number two now describes where the river features on map 2 are located using a similar process. Child number one now locates features on map 'B', designs symbols and the key on sheet 111.

Suggestion(s) for extension

Children who have a good understanding of the features (human and physical) which might be found in a river catchment area could add these to their maps. Encourage them to use less representational, neatly drawn and appropriate symbols.

Suggestion(s) for support

If children are going to be confused by the 'Battleships' element of the game, ask them to use the two sheets on their own. The locational description part of the activity will not now be necessary.

Assessment opportunities

In a group or class discussion following the activity, ask targeted individuals to explain the symbols they have used for different features. Make your own records of children who have created suitable, appropriate symbolisation.

Symbols and keys – River basin: 1

Name ______ Date ______

Map B

KEY	Mouth	Jetty	Port	Meander	Bridge	River	Tributary	Stream	Rapids	Waterfall	Spring

Map 1

spring, waterfall, stream, rapids, bridge, meander, river, waterfall, port, jetty, mouth, spring, tributary

Map 2

spring, waterfall, rapids, bridge, river, waterfall, port, tributary, meander, jetty, mouth, spring

Display ideas

A fun interactive display which could be located in a general area in the school or in another classroom would be a large scale version of the activity itself. Make multiple copies of the photocopiable sheets and position a pile of each sheet, each side of a screen positioned between two tables. Write instructions on a notice for each player and display them on the screen facing each player.

Other aspects of the Geography PoS covered

3a; 7a.

Reference to photocopiable sheets

Photocopiable sheets 111 and 112 are used in a 'Battleships' style game where two children describe the features from river catchment maps to each other (map 1 on 111 and map 2 on 112). They have to locate each feature on blank maps (map 'B' on 111 and map 'A' on 112) using an appropriate symbol which they design and then record in the key.

MAPPING WASTE

To be able to make a thematic map which has a scale, symbols and a key.

Groups of four.

10 minutes introductory discussion; 25 minutes walk around school and grounds in groups; 15 minutes classroom activity.

Previous skills/knowledge needed

Children should be working or should have worked on environmental issues surrounding their school's environment. They should have some experience of what scale means on a map and of what makes a good mapping symbol. They should know what a key is on a map.

Key background information

Mapping can be used to provide information with respect to a specific theme. Waste materials are those materials which as a society we do not need any more. They fall into two categories, those of managed waste and unmanaged waste. Managed waste includes that which is reused, recycled and sent to be carefully (and hopefully, safely) disposed of. Unmanaged waste includes litter and rubbish which is 'fly-tipped' and left as someone elses problem. (Fly-tipped waste is that tipped illegally, often during the night by people who do not want to pay for or cannot be bothered to use a proper tip site.)

Preparation

Collect large scale maps of your local area and any leaflets, pamphlets or other information which is available about recycling and waste disposal in the local area.

Resources needed

Materials on recycling and waste disposal in the local area (as described above), a copy of photocopiable sheet 113 for each child, pencils, large pieces of art paper and felt-tipped pens to be shared by groups of four.

What to do

Discuss what we do with things when we no longer need or want them. Use the school as an example but then broaden the discussion to include the whole local area.

Discuss how when something is no longer required, it is either stored, given to someone else, used in some other way (reused), recycled or thrown away. Talk about any recycling or similar schemes that the children may know of and ask if any of them have been to a domestic waste disposal centre (or 'tip'). Children generally enjoy discussing waste that they know of which is unmanaged such as litter, 'fly-tipping' and other types of pollution.

Talk to the children about what makes a good map. Encourage those who suggest that such a map will be informative, colourful, and easy to understand. Discuss how important symbols and keys are.

Distribute copies of photocopiable sheet 113 and tell the children to draw in pencil a map of the school and its grounds (tell them to draw the map as lightly as they can as they are going to modify it later). Put the children into groups of four and tell them that they are to walk around the school grounds looking for evidence of any of the types of waste management which are depicted in the key on the sheet. These are as follows:

Reuse

▲ places where paper is stored for reuse (for example classroom 'scrap' paper storage)

▲ clothes bins/collection points for reuse of clothing (often being collected by charities)

▲ unwanted food for reuse by someone else (tuck shop apples unwanted by one person which can be eaten by another)

Recycling

▲ paper recycling bins

▲ glass recycling bins

▲ aluminium/steel can recycling bins

▲ other recycling bins (plastic, for example)

▲ compost heap

Disposal

▲ indoor waste paper baskets / bins

▲ indoor bins for other waste (food bins used when clearing plates at lunch time)

▲ outdoor litter bins

▲ large 'industrial dustbins'

The children operate in their groups of four and mark symbols on the maps to represent places where there is evidence of reuse, recycling or managed disposal of waste in the school grounds. They use the symbols with squares around them as indicated by the key on the photocopiable sheet. Each child completes the scale line on the bottom of the map.

They then return to the classroom and discuss where they see opportunities in the school for even more reuse of materials, recycling of materials or improved collection of waste for disposal. They mark these places on their maps using the symbols with circles around them. All of this done, the children can then go over their map and symbols to make a neater final version.

Once the group of four have done this they can make a larger version of their maps using large art paper and felt-tipped pens (their maps should be the same and, therefore, one group map can be made). An excellent follow up to this activity is for the children to write up how they would improve their school's 'environmental policy'. Children could even make a presentation of their 'recommendations' to the headteacher and/or governors.

Mapping waste
Name
Date
Map of my school and its grounds
scale in metres
m
0
Could be used in school grounds
Present in school grounds
P Paper recycling bins
G Glass recycling bins
A Aluminium/steel can recycling bins
R Other recycling bins (plastic, for example)
C Compost heap
I Indoor wastepaper basket/bins
N Indoor bins for other waste
O Outdoor litter bins
D Large 'industrial bins'
S Places where paper is stored for reuse
L Unwanted food for reuse by someone else
F Clothes bins/collection points for reuse of clothing

Suggestion(s) for extension

Children could design their own symbols for the different types of waste management referred to on the sheet or they could think of even more categories.

Suggestion(s) for support

Some children may find the idea of non-representational symbols difficult to cope with. They could devise representational symbols (for example, a cola can to represent a can recycling bin) or they could make a pictorial map instead by drawing the features that they discover.

Assessment opportunities

As the children are working in groups of four you will have to use discussion with the children or analysis of any written follow up to see whether individuals are fully capable of using symbols, keys and scale in the making of a thematic map.

Opportunities for IT

The teacher could make a plan of the school using a drawing or mapping package and save it to disk. The children could then retrieve this plan and use it as the basis for mapping waste around the school. The teacher could add an appropriate key and the children copy the symbols from this and move them to appropriate parts of the plan, or they could make up their own symbols and keys. The completed map could be printed out for display. Larger versions can usually be made by changing the paper size and re-sizing the map to fit. It may then be necessary to print out the map in A4 parts and joint them together.

Display ideas

Ask the children to help you create a large wall display of the map of the school and its grounds based on their large paper maps. Each child could make one or two enlarged paper versions of the symbols required for the map. Label the finished display, clearly showing where reuse, recycling and disposal of materials is taking place.

Other aspects of the Geography PoS covered

1b; 2a, b; 3b; 4; 10a, b.

Reference to photocopiable sheet

Photocopiable sheet 113 is used by each member of a group of four children to record places where the reuse, recycling and disposal of waste materials are or could be happening in their school grounds. Children draw a simple map of their school grounds in the large box and use the key on the left of the sheet as they draw symbols in the relevant places on the map.

THEMATIC GLOBES

To develop understanding of what a thematic map is. To use a globe to identify information of a thematic nature.

Groups of three.

10 minutes introduction; 2–5 minutes group discussion; papier mâché work taking a number of 10–15 minutes sessions; 20–30 minutes drawing and gluing activity.

Previous skills/knowledge needed

The children should have already been introduced to the globe as a model of the Earth, understand about continents and oceans and be able to locate the British Isles on a globe. They should have experience of using papier mâché in model-making.

Key background information

The globe is a three-dimensional map of our world and as such is the closest we can get to accurately depicting the actual proportions and shapes of the continents and oceans (they are massively distorted on flat map projections). It is important that children have experience in using globes as globes show where different parts of the world are in relation to each other in a way that flat maps never can (for instance the proximity of eastern Asia to Alaska is seldom seen on the flat maps which we tend to use in this country).

A thematic map is one which shows information on a specific theme. Well known examples include the London Underground map and weather maps shown on television. Local maps might include those of your local zoo, supermarket or theme park.

Preparation

Prepare an area of the classroom as a papier mâché modelling area, provide a supply of paper suitable for papier mâché (preferably blank newsprint and supplies of green and blue paper), prepare papier mâché paste, and obtain a supply of round balloons. Gather together source books on different themes and/or software or internet access to computer reference materials (for example, 'animals', 'buildings', 'transport', 'food' and 'clothes'). These themes may relate to general class work you are doing. Make available at least one globe, some felt-tipped pens and some PVA paper glue.

Resources needed

A supply of round balloons (and a balloon pump), white, green and blue, papier mâché paper, papier mâché paste, at least one globe, reference books and computer reference programs on the themes which the children are to work on (see suggestions above). Copies of photocopiable sheet 114 for each group (if required).

What to do

Talk with the children about what a thematic map is. Put the children into groups of three and ask each group to agree on a theme (see suggestions in 'Key background information') which they can find information on all around the world from reference books or computer information sources.

Tell the children that they are going to make a globe using a balloon and papier mâché and that it is going to be a 'thematic globe' which shows picture information on the theme they have chosen. Give each group a balloon to inflate (to a sensible size) and help them to tie if off. Explain that

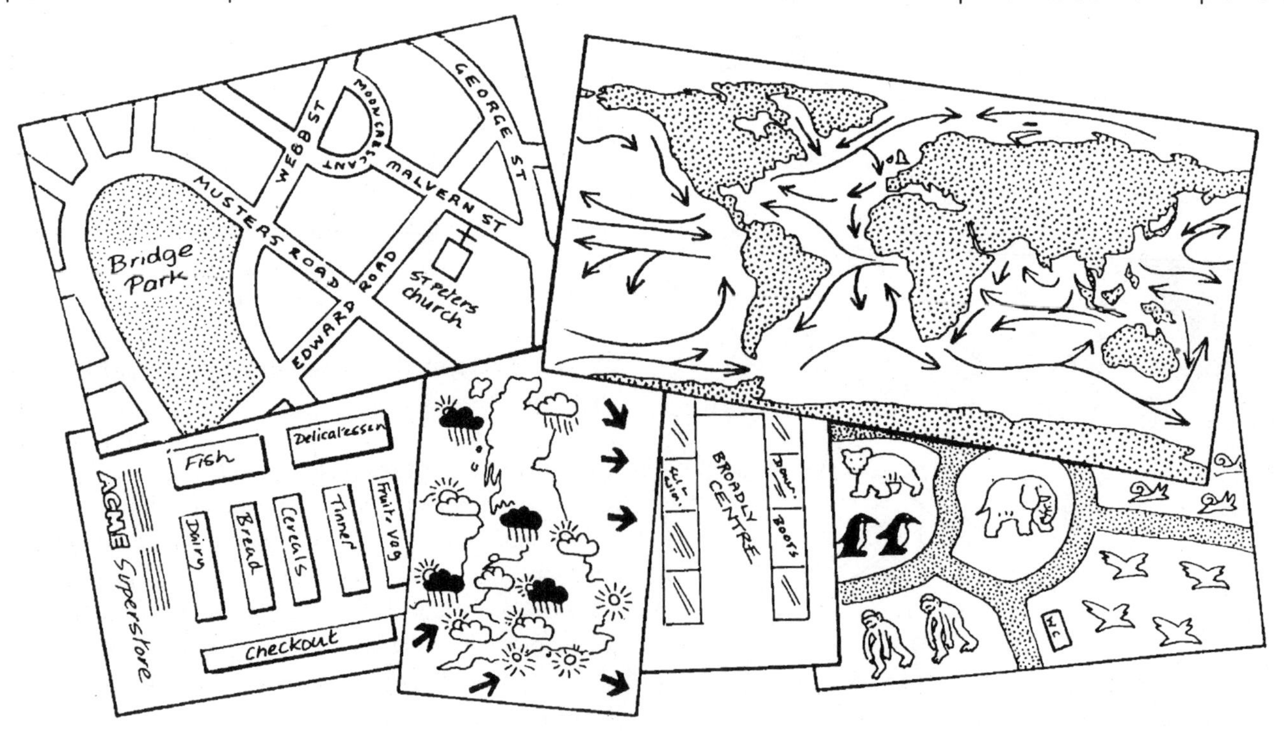

they are to cover the inflated balloon with several layers of papier mâché paper.

The last layers should be in the green and blue paper which should be applied to give the effect of the land masses and the oceans. If children take care at this stage the result can be very effective. They should consult the globe to help get their land masses the correct size and in the correct positions. (If it would help, let them mark on the land masses with pen before they apply the paper.)

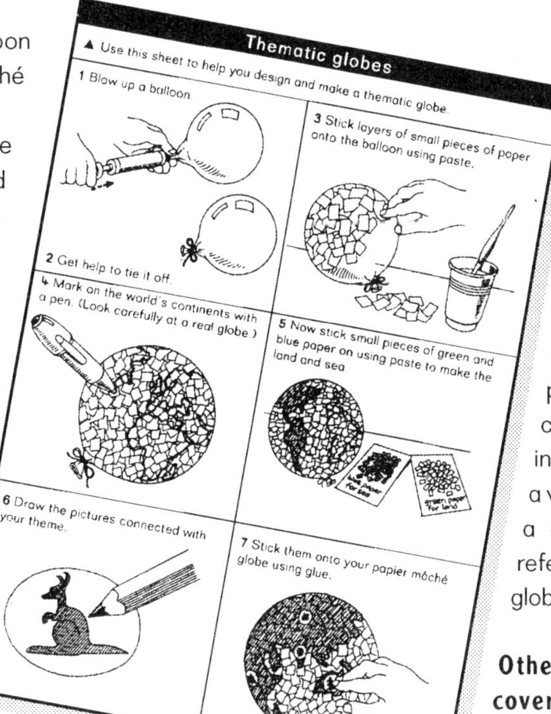

The children now draw small pictures relating to the theme they have chosen which reflect the variations in that theme across the world. An example for the theme 'animals' would be to draw small pictures of a whale for the Atlantic Ocean, a panda for Asia, a giraffe for Africa, a kangaroo for Oceania, a lemur for South America, a bear for North America, a penguin for Antarctica and a squirrel for Europe. Once drawn, these pictures are then stuck on to the dry papier mâché globe using PVA paper glue. Apply a coat of varnish to the finished (dry) globes. This has the effect of helping to preserve them and can be aesthetically pleasing.

Suggestion(s) for extension
Children might like to use symbols on their globes. This will be useful if the theme they have chosen results in them having a lot of detail to add to their globe. If they do this they could make a key to display next to the globe.

Suggestion(s) for support
The difficult part of this activity is the correct mapping of the world's land masses using papier mâché . For children having trouble at this stage, wait for the previous layers to dry and then mark the outlines of the world's continents with pen to guide the children as they add the blue and green papier mâché paper. Photocopiable sheet 114 can be used to provide children with support as to what to do next during the activity.

Assessment opportunities
Look for children who are capable of mapping their group theme in a meaningful way – restricting themselves to mapable information which relates to that theme only and choosing a good cross-section of that information. Assess whether individuals can use the globe and understand its parts by asking them about their finished work.

Display ideas
The finished globes should be fairly hard and rigid. Feed a piece of string through the globe, in through the 'north pole' and out through the 'south pole', using a piece of strong wire or a knitting needle. (The balloon can be burst and removed although this is not necessary.) Attach the string to a paper-clip and hang the globe from the ceiling. Several of these globes hung in a group at varying heights can make a very effective display. Hang them over a central table which houses the reference books used and the original globe.

Other aspects of the Geography PoS covered
1a, d; 3d, e, (f).

Reference to photocopiable sheet
Photocopiable sheet 114 can be used as a guidance sheet for the children as they carry out the activity and is designed to take some of the pressure of explanation off the teacher.

WHAT'S THE WEATHER DOING?

To use and interpret weather maps which show the weather at different scales.

Individuals.

10 minutes discussion; 10–15 minutes for each photocopiable sheet activity.

Previous skills/knowledge needed
Children should ideally be involved in work on the weather and know what a weather forecast entails.

Key background information
Maps at different scales are used by experts in varying fields to show the situation at the wider scale as well as at the large scale, 'zoomed in view'. A small scale thematic map helps them to see the wider view and a large scale map can allow a more detailed and localised study.

Weather maps (or charts as they are often called) are a good example of how different scales can give varying information. A small scale chart, covering a wide area can show a complete weather system (for instance, a high or a low pressure system). A large scale, local chart can show in detail what the weather is doing in a specific area.

Preparation
Collect together drawing and colouring materials.

Resources needed
One copy for each child of photocopiable sheets 115 and 116, drawing and colouring materials.

What to do
Talk to the children about how we forecast the weather. It is important that your discussion includes the problem of forecasting the weather in any accuracy over periods longer than three days. Ask the children if they know how experts (meteorologists) forecast the weather. Stress the importance of regular, scientific data collection from weather stations all over the country and the world. Children may know that satellites are now very important because they can look down from space and see large patterns in the weather (complete weather systems). It is important children recognise that seeing the wider view helps experts to predict what might happen locally.

Give each child a copy of each of the photocopiable sheets. Sheet 115 has a map of the British Isles which has no weather symbols on it, and two maps of parts of the British Isles with weather symbols. These cover:

▲ the Lake District/Solway Firth/Dumfries and Galloway/ Isle of Man

▲ the Isle of Wight /Solent/Southampton/Dorset.

The children have to draw symbols on to the British Isles map to show what the weather might be like across the whole of the country. They must use the two large scale maps' information to make sure they map the weather correctly for these areas. They can use the same symbols as are on these large scale maps or make up their own.

Photocopiable sheet 116 provides the same type of activity but in reverse. This time the local area maps show:

▲ Strangford Lough/Belfast/Lough Neagh/Antrim

▲ Anglesey/Lleyn Peninsula/Gwynedd/Dolgellau.

The children study the weather as shown on the British Isles map and then draw symbols onto the two local area maps to create local 'forecasts'.

Suggestion(s) for extension
Children will enjoy working out whereabouts in the British Isles the local area maps are taken from. Children who are capable of doing so could draw their own local area maps for other parts of the country, possibly including their own region, and add weather symbols to fit in with the overall weather picture on the British Isles map.

Suggestion(s) for support
The important point for this activity is the children recognise that thematic weather maps at different scales assist meteorologists in their work. The part they are most likely to have difficulty with is locating the large scale maps on the British Isles map. To help the children with this, draw small boxes representing the edges of the two areas in the relevant places on the British Isles map.

Assessment opportunities
Examine the completed maps of targeted individuals and analyse whether they have correctly added the symbols to their maps. Look for evidence that the individual has correctly used and interpreted the given weather maps.

Opportunities for IT
Children could use a drawing package to create a larger scale map of the area for which they are making the forecast and add their own weather symbols to it.

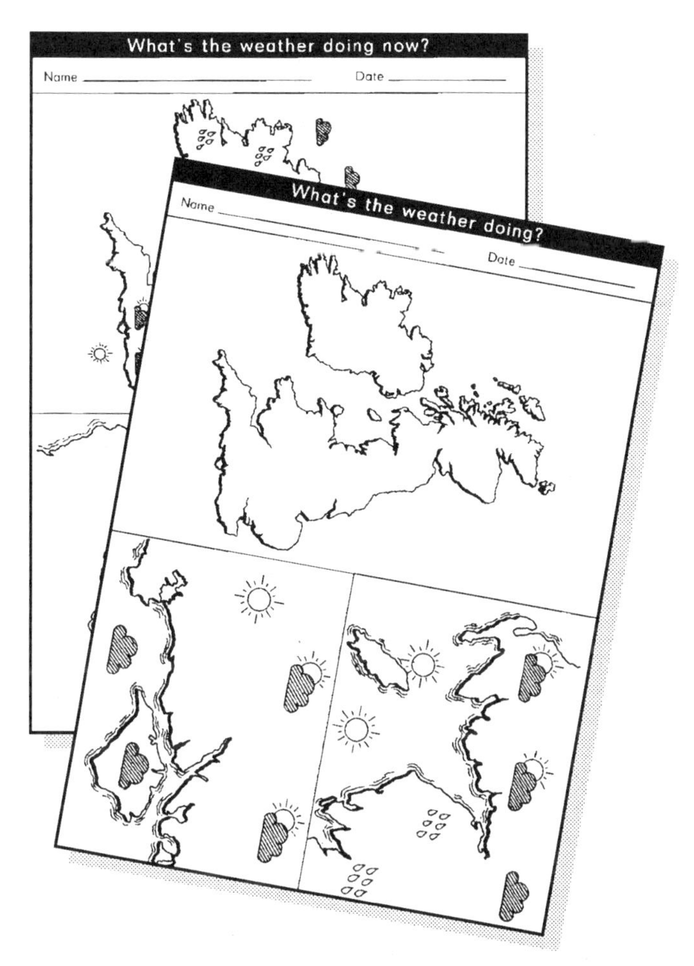

Schools with access to the Internet can download weather and satellite maps from different parts of the world for children to look at and use as the basis for a similar exercise. It might also be possible to use the data to make a forecast in a contrasting locality and then use e-mail to see how accurate it has been.

Display ideas

The children could display larger coloured versions of their maps as though on a television. Make the television set out of a large cardboard box. The children's completed British Isles and large scale region maps could be displayed on the wall behind the television together with an explanation.

Other aspects of the Geography PoS covered

1a, c, d; 3a, c; 8c.

Reference to photocopiable sheets

Photocopiable sheet 115 provides the child with weather charts of two regions of the British Isles. The children have to locate these places on the larger British Isles maps, transfer the weather information onto this map using symbols and then make up weather conditions for the rest of the country. Photocopiable sheet 116 provides the same type of activity in reverse. Children look at the weather chart for the British Isles and complete the large scale charts according to what the national chart shows but in greater detail.

MORE HOUSES NEEDED

To use and interpret a map of a town using co-ordinates.

Small groups.

5 minutes explanation; 10 minutes copying grid; 30 minutes design work; 10 minutes group/class comparison session.

Previous skills/knowledge needed

Children should be studying settlement as a theme.

Key background information

Co-ordinates are a very useful way of describing the position of something on a map. Simply by giving two readings, one along a horizontal scale and one along a vertical scale, another person can accurately locate a desired position by tracing where the two readings cross in two dimensional space.

There is an important convention if either letters only or numbers only are used for the scales. This is that the horizontal scale reading (known as the easting) is quoted and read before the vertical scale reading (known as the northing). The single number easting and single number northing system used in this activity is a very simple one and should be used with children before they eventually go on to use more complicated four-figure and then six-figure referencing systems.

Preparation

You will need four pieces of A3 paper with squares of $4cm^2$ containing a grid that is 7 squares × 10 squares and has a small amount of room down at least one of its long sides and one of its shorter sides. If you cannot obtain $4cm^2$ paper, then draw a grid yourself (the total measurements of the grid should be 28cm x 40cm which will fit on to an A3 photocopier) or enlarge a $2cm^2$ grid of the same format from A4 to A3. Collect together drawing and writing materials.

Resources needed

The four grids (as described in 'Preparation'), copies of photocopiable sheets 117 and 118 for each group, drawing and colouring materials.

What to do

Give each group a copy of photocopiable sheet 117 and one of the A3 4cm² grids. The sheet shows a map of a village with the existing roads and buildings marked on and labelled. The map has a grid superimposed over it and each individual square of the grid can be referenced using the numbers along the bottom edge and the left hand edge.

Explain to the children that this map shows a settlement which has not grown in terms of its roads or buildings for 100 years. Tell them that they are now going to be responsible for planning an expansion of the number of houses in the village as the population is growing. Explain that they will also need to site new shops, a new primary school, a new electricity sub-station and a new telephone box. Point out to the children that they need to decide on the type of shops they think the village needs.

Before they start, the children have to copy the existing buildings from their photoocpiable sheet into the correct locations on the larger grid and label the grid with the numbers along the bottom edge and the left-hand edge. It is important that they do this carefully. This first part of the activity will enable you to check that they understand how to locate features using the grid system.

Now provide each group with a copy of photocopiable sheet 118 which has the instructions as to what has to be added to the village. The children decide as a group where they are going to locate each building and road, and draw them onto their large grid maps accordingly. They record their decisions by filling in photocopiable sheet 118 and therefore recording the co-ordinate references of the new building they have planned.

Finish the activity off by gathering the groups together and comparing village designs. As you do this, get the children to refer to the positions of new buildings using the co-ordinate system. Groups will enjoy comparing co-ordinates to see whether they have buildings in the same squares.

Suggestion(s) for extension

Children can add yet more detail to their completed grid maps of the village. Then they can try out their ability at correctly using the co-ordinate referencing system by designing routes for each other around their new village using only co-ordinate references as the description of where to go.

Suggestion(s) for support

If you think that a group might struggle to complete the activity, give them a head start by drawing on the A3 4cm² grid the existing village buildings and roads from the photocopiable sheet.

Assessment opportunities

Choose one group to target for assessment reasons and observe whether individuals are correctly applying the co-ordinates principle in this context of thematic settlement mapping.

Opportunities for IT

The teacher could create the base map using a drawing or mapping package and save this to disk. The children could then retrieve this map and use it as the basis for their map work. The ability to move houses and buildings around using the copy and move facilities of the software will help them to edit and develop their maps as they work on it. The children

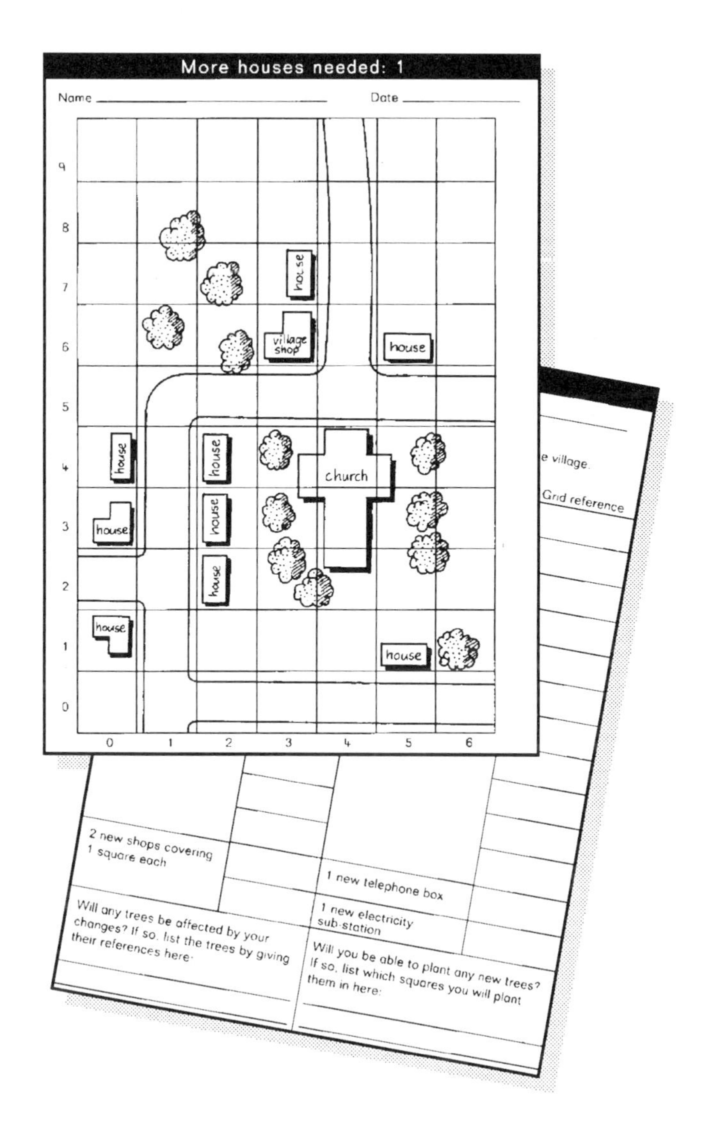

may need to be shown how to rotate buildings so that they can line them up along the roads. The final map can be printed out and the co-ordinates of the new building added.

Display ideas

You will have ended up with one complete A3 map from each group and they should all be different. Ask each group to make a simple small model of their village using either construction bricks (such as LEGO) or card box modelling. Place the models on a table top and the maps on the wall behind. Children from other classes can be invited to decide which model matches which map.

Other aspects of the Geography PoS covered

3a, c; 5a; 9b.

Reference to photocopiable sheets

Each group copies the map and grid on photocopiable sheet 117 on to their own 4cm² grid. They then decide where the additional buildings and roads listed on photocopiable sheet 118 are going to be positioned and prove their understanding of the co-ordinate system by completing the lower part of the sheet.

CITIES ON THE MAP

To use and interpret a thematic settlement map of the UK using four-figure grid references.

Individuals.

5 minutes introduction, 30 minutes photocopiable sheet activity.

Previous skills/knowledge needed

Children should have had some introduction to settlement in the UK and be aware of the difference between an inland town or city and a port. They need to have been introduced to simple co-ordinates and be ready to move on to the more complex four-figure grid referencing system. Children should be used to using symbolisation and filling in simple tables.

Key background information

Once a child is used to the idea of referring to a specific location in two-dimensional space by using a scale along the bottom of the map and a scale up the side of the map, and then seeing where readings from each scale intercept, he can move on to using the more complex four-figure grid referencing system.

This system uses the vertical and the horizontal grid lines themselves *not the spaces between them* and uses the eastings before northings convention whereby the horizontal reference (normally along the lower edge of the grid) is quoted before the vertical reference (normally along the left-hand side of the grid). Importantly, each of the two numbers which make up the unique reference are themselves made up of two numbers, so each square has a unique reference as in the examples below:

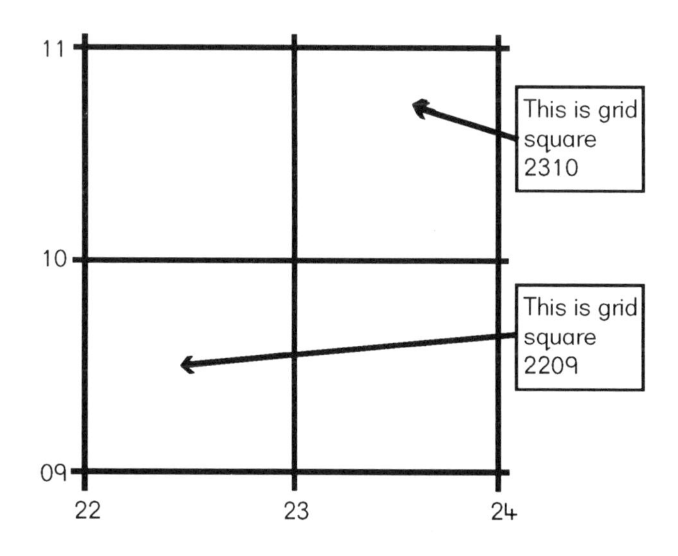

Anything which is in grid square 2209 can be given the unique grid reference 2209.

Preparation
Collect together any atlases or other reference books available which include information on British cities, sea ports and airports.

Resources needed
One copy of photocopiable sheet 119 for each child. Book or computer resources about British cities, sea ports and airports.

What to do
Give each child a copy of the photocopiable sheet 119. This provides a map of the UK which has had a co-ordinates grid superimposed over it. The grid has numeric reference scales up the left-hand edge and along the lower edge.

The children use the blank table on the right of the sheet to record which of the cities are inland cities, which are major tourist destinations, which are sea ports and which have airports. Most cities will in fact be combinations of these and a unique symbol is used for every city-type combination (one may simply be a port, another may be an inland city which is a major tourist destination and which has an airport, and so on). The children tick the relevant parts of the table to indicate what combination of qualities each of the cities has. The children also use the table to record the grid reference for each of the cities.

Suggestion(s) for extension
Children could use the reference books, atlases and any computer source material to help them locate further cities on the map and work out their grid-references. They could use the information provided by the map and any supporting book or computer resources to help them write about a selection of the cities.

Suggestion(s) for support
Pair the children so that a child who has mastered the process of reading the four-figure grid references is supporting a child who is less confident. One child can work out the reference and read it out to the other who then writes it down.

Assessment opportunities
The completed photocopiable sheets should provide you with evidence that individuals have managed to interpret the thematic map and correctly record the four-figure grid reference of each city.

Opportunities for IT
The children could set up a class database about the different cities they have researched. A range of information could be included and the fieldnames might include the following:

Name	Liverpool
Country	England
Area	North-west
Grid reference	depends on the maps used
Status	City
Facilities	Port
Distance from	a designated point, for example: the school, London

Once the database has been set up the children can answer questions such as:

▲ How many cities in the south-east?

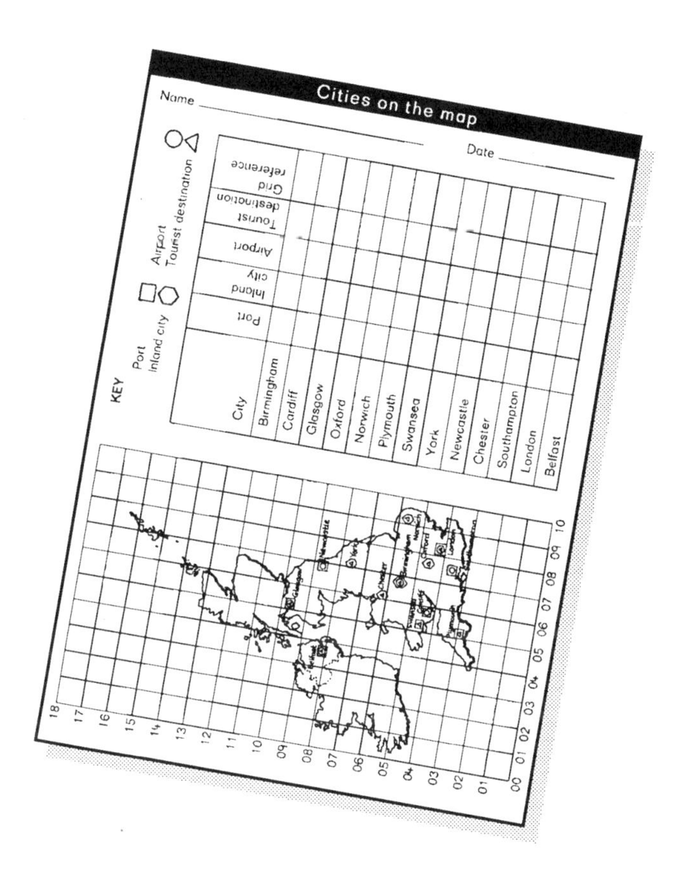

▲ How many places are within 100 miles of (school, London)?

▲ Which ports are cities?

▲ Which cities lie on the same northing grid reference?

Some databases such as Anglia's KEY series allow the grid references to be plotted onto a map so that the results of searches can be displayed on a map as well.

Display ideas

The children could make a large table top map of the British Isles and use three-dimensional symbols made of LEGO to mark where the different cities are. Different coloured blocks could refer to different characteristics of the city (whether it is a port, a tourist destination). A grid could be drawn over the map and children could physically play at siting the cities in the four-figure grid referenced squares according to instructions written by you and accompanying the display.

Other aspects of the Geography PoS covered

1a, d; 3e, (f); 9a.

Reference to photocopiable sheet

Photocopiable sheet 119 contains a map of the British Isles which has a four-figure grid referenced grid superimposed over it. The map has cities marked on it which may be sea ports, major tourist destinations, inland cities, contain airports or combinations of these. The children interpret the symbols and record what each city is and which grid square it is in by filling out the table on the right-hand side of the sheet.

RIVER NAVIGATION

To measure distance and direction using a linear scale and a compass rose on a thematic river map.

Individuals or pairs.

10 minutes introductory discussion; 25 minutes photocopiable sheet activity.

Previous skills/knowledge needed

Children should have been introduced to the correct use of a ruler for measuring in centimetres and should have an understanding of what a river system or drainage basin is. They must understand how to convert measurements using a simple scale.

Children should be able to measure distances in centimetres and metres, and direction using first the four and then the eight main points of the compass. They should be able to do this on the ground and on paper using a scale and a compass rose.

Key background information

Rivers start as small streams from springs in the hills. These streams join together to form bigger streams. Each joining stream is called a tributary and eventually a number of tributaries will add together to make a big river which has so much energy that as it leaves the hills and flows across flatter land, it twists and turns in what are called meanders. Eventually the river will flow out to sea or into a large lake at its mouth. The area in which rain falls, eventually to flow out to sea at a given river's mouth, is called that river's catchment area or its drainage basin.

Preparation

Collect together drawing and colouring materials. Obtain a range of picture resources which show different parts and features of a river (for example: waterfall, river cliff, babbling stream, a river boat, someone fishing).

Resources needed

One copy for each child of photocopiable sheets 120 and 121, drawing and colouring materials, picture resources (as above).

What to do

Gather the children together and discuss the different stages of a river using the resources you have gathered as a stimulus. Explain that they are going to follow directions to navigate their way upstream from the sea and that only if they follow the directions which are given in terms of distance and compass direction accurately, will they find the treasure which is hidden in the rainforest inland.

Give each child a copy of photocopiable sheet 120 and ask them to describe what the map shows (encourage the use of words like 'tributary', 'spring', 'meander' and 'mouth').

Next give the children their copies of photocopiable sheet 121 which has the directions to follow on the map. The directions given relate to the compass rose at the top of the map and the distances have to be converted using the scale at the bottom of the map which converts 10km to 1cm. The children follow the directions on photocopiable sheet 121 very precisely and record the letter which is at each end location in the recording grid provided. If they succeed in their navigation of the rivers, they will end up with a piece of treasure (in fact the word they are searching for is 'GOLDBAR').

Suggestion(s) for extension

Children capable of doing so could design their own river navigation games which they can then try out on friends of a similar ability. Make sure that the directions they design will involve the person trying to navigate their river system in measuring and using compass directions.

Suggestion(s) for support

Children can complete this activity very effectively in pairs. A more able child can support a less able one at measuring. Children who are a little less confident could take it in turns with a partner to 'crack' each clue.

Assessment opportunities

If children have completed the activity individually, their completed photocopiable sheets will provide evidence that they can measure with a ruler to depict a scaled down version of distances in kilometres, and they understand the main eight directions of the compass.

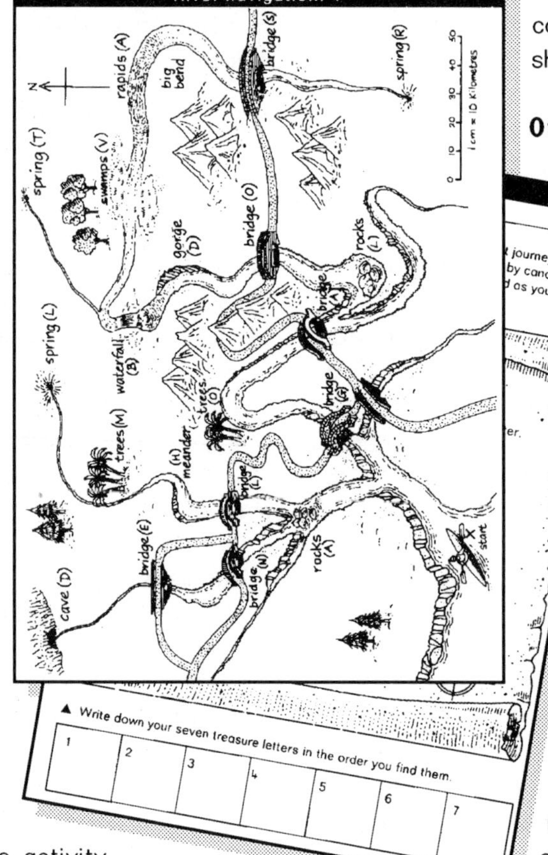

Display ideas

Make an explanatory wall display about measuring distance and direction. Key parts of the display could be a large compass rose and a selection of measuring equipment (a ruler, a metre rule, a tape measure). Get some of the children to colour their river navigation maps and display these along with one or two completed copies of the photocopiable sheet 121.

Other aspects of the Geography PoS covered

3a; 5a; 7a.

Reference to photocopiable sheets

Photocopiable sheets 120 has a map of a river system which children 'navigate' from the sea. They do this following the directions on photocopiable sheet 121. This involves them in measuring distances with a ruler which they have converted from distances given in kilometres using the scale on the map, and in using their knowledge of the eight points of the compass. As they work their way through the directions they will collect a 'treasure' of letters which, if recorded (in the grid on photocopiable sheet 121) in the correct order, will give them their final item of treasure. The word they are trying to find is 'GOLDBAR'.

ENVIRONMENTAL TRAIL

To make a thematic building materials map of the local area and then use it to follow a route.

Small groups (each group is 1/6th of the class).

15 minutes explanation; 40 minute walk – designing route; 30 minutes classroom work; 40 minutes walk – following route.

This activity is best done over an entire morning or afternoon.

Previous skills/knowledge needed

This activity is best carried out as a part of work on the materials which people use in their environment, where those materials originate and therefore on how people affect their environments by, for example, forestry and quarrying. Children will need to be able to work co-operatively in small groups and complete simple tables.

Key background information

It is important that children develop and improve their abilities at following routes. This is best done by involving children in designing routes for each other and then taking it in turn to follow them. A map is a very useful tool in setting a route for another person. If the base map is reasonably accurate, places to be visited on the route can be plotted and the route itself be drawn on.

Preparation

Collect a stock of blank A4 white paper which the children will be able to use to design a map. Arrange for at least five responsible adult helpers (six including yourself) for taking small groups of children out of school (in line with your school's/authority's policy for taking children out of school) and obtain any necessary parental permission. Collect writing and drawing materials, and clipboards (or suitable alternatives). Obtain at least one large scale map of the immediate area around the school and, using your knowledge of the local area, decide on five points within the vicinity of the school, each one approximately five minutes slow walk from the next.

Resources needed

A4 white paper, clipboards (or alternatives), adult support (see 'Preparation'), writing and drawing materials, a large scale local map, one copy of photocopiable sheet 122 for each child.

What to do

Each group is going to design a section of route which would take classmates five minutes to walk within the immediate vicinity of the school. Then each section is going to be put together for all the children in the class to follow. (The children will need to be accompanied by a responsible adult when designing their route and when following other children's routes.)

Gather the class together and show them the map of the local area with your five points marked on. Explain that the school itself and each of these points represent the starting and finishing points of different sections of a route which the class is going to design. There will be six sections of route altogether including the section from the school to the first point and the section from the last point back to the school. Discuss the different types of building material which the children might find in the local area and where these building materials might have originated. Divide the class into six groups and assign each group to an accompanying adult. Provide each group with a clipboard, some pieces of paper, drawing and writing materials.

In the first stage of the activity each adult takes her group to the starting point of their section of route. Each group then draws a map of their section and designs a route which connects their starting point and their finishing point. Along the route they have to mark four numbers (group 1 will use numbers 1–4, group 2 numbers 5–8, group 3 numbers 9–

12, and so on) which denote places where there is an interesting building material in use. For each of these places they note what the material is and where it is likely to have originated (for example: wood from trees and stone from a quarry). They then write a suitable question (for example what material is the step outside 'Jones the Butcher' made of?) Once all of the groups have prepared the route for their section, they return to class. Each group now makes a good copy of their section map and writes the questions on to the map linking them to each of the four numbered locations.

Environmental trail

Name ____________ Date ____________

▲ As you walk your classes trail write the answers to the questions about the building materials in this table.
The origin of a building material is the place where it originally came from (for example: wood – forest).

Place number	Building material	Origin of material	Place number	Building material	Origin of material
1			13		
2			14		
3			15		
4			16		
5			17		
6			18		
7			19		
8			20		
9			21		
10			22		
11			23		
12			24		

The second stage of the activity requires the groups to have their adult support again as they take turns to walk the whole route using the six section maps in order. This is best done with the groups having 'staggered starts'. Each child then takes a copy of photocopiable sheet 122 which they complete as they walk the route.

Suggestion(s) for extension

Able children might make their route a little more complex so long as the accompanying adult checks that the route will be capable of being followed when finished. They might like to make a similar route map of the route they follow from home to school.

Suggestion(s) for support

Children who are likely to find the route-making part of the activity difficult could be given the more straight-forward sections of route. Children are best in mixed ability groups for this activity.

Assessment opportunities

For your own records, compare notes with your adult helpers at the end of the second stage of the activity to find out which children were particularly adept at making and following the route map. The completed copies of sheet 122 will help provide evidence.

Opportunities for IT

School that have access to Ordnance Survey digital maps of their school area can use these to make suitable maps for the children to use for their route-plotting. With appropriate software such as *Aegis 2* the children can also plot the information about different building materials onto the maps.

The children could use a word processor to write instructions for their part of the route. These could be printed out and used as a part of the final display of the work.

Display ideas

Display your completed whole class route on a wall with the questions the children devised displayed around the maps and linked to the relevant locations by thread.

Other aspects of the Geography PoS covered

1b; 2a, b; 3a, b, c; 4; 5a; 10a.

Reference to photocopiable sheet

Photocopiable sheet 122 is used in the second stage of the activity for children to record the answers to the 24 questions which have been designed into their class's route around the local area. Children record what the building material at each location is and where they think it will have originated.

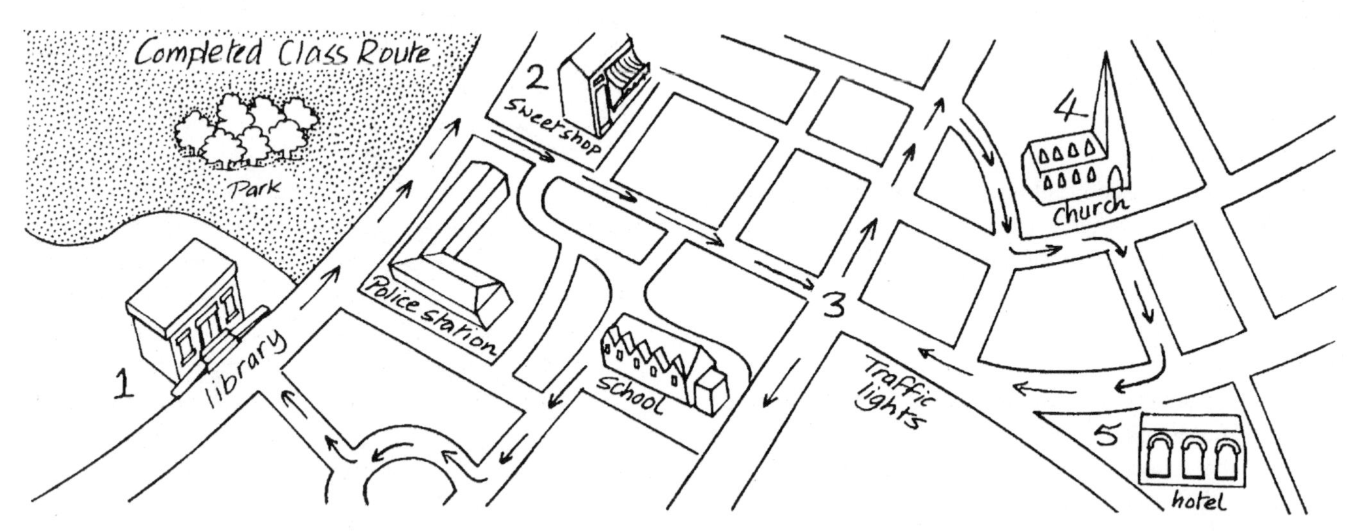

PLACES HIGH AND PLACES LOW

To use, interpret and add to a thematic map showing settlements in high and low places in the UK using atlas skills.

Group of 15 divided into five groups of three.

10 minutes introduction; 30 minutes map colouring; 20 minutes atlas research.

Previous skills/knowledge needed

Children need a basic knowledge of how to use an atlas. They should be aware of the differences between small settlements like villages and larger ones such as towns and cities.

Key background information

Children should become aware of the thematic maps which can often be found in world atlases. These maps are generally at the front of the atlas in the section covering the British Isles and typically might include maps on energy, agriculture, industry, historical events like battles and invasions, wildlife, seasonal weather conditions and land height. Many children's atlases as purchased by schools contain such maps. These maps can provide a useful overview of the country in the context of a theme being studied.

There are different ways of showing land height (altitude) on a map. It can be shown using spot heights (simply a dot with the height written as a number next to it), as contour lines (where every point on a line is at the same height) or as shading or colouring (where a band of shading or colouring represents land which is between two heights). In primary school atlases the latter approach is often adopted on thematic maps showing altitude in the UK.

Preparation

Gather together a selection of atlases with index and contents pages. Using a marker pen, draw an outline of the British Isles onto a large piece of white paper or card. Mark the borders between each of the constituent countries. (The map can be created by photocopying an A4 map of the British Isles [such as the one on photocopiable sheet 123] on to acetate and then using the overhead projector to project it on to the white paper which you can temporarily attach to the wall.)

Resources needed

A large piece of white paper (see 'Preparation') with the outline of the British Isles marked on it as large as possible. A selection of marker pens in different shades of the same colour (greens or browns are appropriate). Copies of photocopiable sheet 123 for support tasks and assessment purposes only. A selection of atlases.

What to do

Show the children the large outline map of the British Isles and discuss any high and low areas of Britain they may know of. Depending on where your school is located and the children's experiences some may have heard of The Lake District, The Pennines, The Fens or of famous valleys like the Severn Valley or the Thames Valley.

Explain that the children are going to colour the map, using the marker pens, showing where the areas of high land and low land are. For Britain it works best if you agree on the following categories of land height:

▲ Over 1000 metres
▲ Between 500 and 1000 metres
▲ Between 200 and 500 metres
▲ Under 200 metres

Decide which shade of your chosen colour will be for which category and then draw the key on to the corner of the map to help the children get the idea. It looks best if you use the darkest shade for the highest land and the lightest for the lowest. Give out the atlases and if they contain a thematic land use map draw the children's attention to it.

Divide them into five groups of three and allocate each group either the Republic of Ireland, England, Wales, Scotland or Northern Ireland. Explain that between them they have to colour in their part of the main base map using the agreed

colour key. Next tell the children that they have to use the index and contents pages of the atlas to help them to find three settlements in each of the land height categories in their country. Agree on symbols for city, town and village and mark these on the map's key along with the four land height categories. The children now mark these settlements on the map using the symbols in the key.

Rather than labelling each marker with the settlement's name, make a mixed up list of all of the final 60 settlements which will be marked (there are five countries, each with four land height categories, each containing three settlement markers). Display this list next to the completed map and invite viewers to choose a settlement from the list, look it up in an atlas (made available next to the display) and then decide which marker on the map is that settlement.

Suggestion(s) for extension

Children capable of doing so could name some of the highest and lowest parts of Britain and then make small labels with these places' names on, to stick on the map.

Suggestion(s) for support

You may have very simple atlases in school which contain land height maps that have been simplified. Consider making these available (perhaps by borrowing some from a Key Stage 1 colleague) to support children who have difficulty decoding all of the detail that is present on an atlas page. Photocopiable sheet 123 which has the contours already marked on, can be used to support children who are having difficulty with the large map activity.

Assessment opportunities

You can use copies of photocopiable sheet 123 with individual children to see if they can devise their own colour key for the four land height categories and then colour the map in accordingly, showing which parts of Britain are the highest and which are the lowest. Settlements could be located as in the main activity.

Opportunities for IT

The database could be extended in this work by adding the heights above sea level to the towns in the initial database. New towns could also be added with other appropriate information. This would give children another opportunity to practise the skills already taught.

An alternative approach would be to create a simple spreadsheet to record this information. The statistical facilities could be used to work out average heights, the range of heights, highest and lowest places. The graphical facilities could also be used to display additional information, for example, population, and then children plot scattergraphs to look for patterns between the two variables.

Display ideas

The activity generates a wall map for display. Place a selection of atlases on a table below the map. Display the completed list of settlements that the children have researched next to the large map and add instructions to viewers of the display, explaining that they use an atlas to look up any settlements they have not heard of and then decide which marker on the map represents it.

Other aspects of the Geography PoS covered

1a, d; 3c; 9a.

Reference to photocopiable sheet

Photocopiable sheet 123 can be used for assessment or support purposes. It provides a map of the UK with upland areas outlined. Children colour the map in, deciding on the colours to use for the four categories of land height: above 1000 metres, land between 500–1000 metres, land between 200–500 metres and land below 200 metres in height. They can then mark on the settlements for one or two of the countries.

Rivers

At Key Stage 2 children should be taught about rivers and their effects on the landscape. This teaching may take the form of a discrete unit of work (or topic) or it may be taught in conjunction with other themes (for example, weather), or as a part of your teaching about localities.

At Key Stage 2, children must learn:

▲ the parts of a river;

▲ that rivers have catchment areas (or drainage basins);

▲ where they eventually flow to;

▲ about the erosion, transportation and deposition of material, and the landscape features which result from these processes.

In this work they must learn about real streams and rivers in real places, including some local and first-hand work. Children must see the river as a system and should understand the journey from source to mouth with respect to physical, human and environmental geography.

The places studied should include your nearest river but the theme also provides an excellent opportunity for children to study nationally important rivers within a European context. It also provides opportunities for them to enquire into topical issues in real places.

The rivers theme provides one of the best opportunities within the 'thematic studies' section of the programme of study to do some physical geography and for the children to carry out some simple physical fieldwork. If you decide to visit a stream or river, consider the safety aspects and work within your school and/or LEA's safety policies.

WHERE'S THE WATER FROM?

To identify where river water comes from and how it gets into the river.

Whole class, then working in groups of approximately six pupils.

15 minutes introduction; 20 minutes practical; 20 minutes discussion.

Previous skills/knowledge needed

Children should have an understanding of the water cycle and an awareness that different materials have different properties. They should also have an ability to carry out simple experiments and an understanding of the notion of a fair test.

Key background information

The water cycle: rain falls to the ground to eventually flow via rivers to the sea, from where it then evaporates to move in the air over the land, eventually falling again as rain.

Water reaching rivers comes from a number of different sources. Ultimately, most comes from the sky in the form of rain or snow. Then it reaches the slopes which lead down to the river channel. Some of the water sinks into the ground (infiltration) to become groundwater (water which slowly moves through the pores and cracks of rock), some runs over the ground surface (overland flow) and some is evaporated back to the sky. Only a tiny amount of rain in the river channel is direct rainfall into the channel.

In rainy weather the river has water from underground groundwater, overland flow and from direct rainfall in the channel. In dry weather there is only water from groundwater in the river.

How the water gets from the slopes into the river will depend on the soils, rocks and land use of the slopes leading down to the river. If the slopes have impermeable soils and rocks, the water will flow quickly over the ground surface as overland flow to get to the river channel. If the soil and rocks are permeable the water will sink into the ground and flow slowly as groundwater to the river channel. If there is a town or city on the slopes, the water will run quickly over the concrete and tarmac either into drains and sewers or directly into the river. If there is a forest the trees will catch (intercept) the rain and it will either be evaporated back up to the sky, or it will reach the ground where it will sink and slowly move to the river channel as groundwater.

Preparation

This activity should be stimulated by a rain storm and the initial observations could then take place during the storm. However, the rest of the work takes place under dry conditions outside and inside the classroom. The activity consists of a number of different tasks, each undertaken by a different group, then shared at the end. Gather together a selection of different types of rock (see 'Resources needed'), and a washing-up bottle with the top cut off. You will need to make some 'infiltration rings'. This can be done by cutting 15cm sections of guttering fall pipe (see illustration). Choose the best site for each activity and have the relevant equipment at each site.

Resources needed

A potted plant, a hand watering spray, chalk, infiltration rings (see 'Preparation'), a ruler, a water container (2 litres), a hammer and wooden block, a stopwatch, two plastic funnels, two supports for the funnels, two measuring cylinders, pieces of chalk, sandstone, slate and granite rock, a water dropper, a plastic washing-up liquid container with its top removed, sand and clay or Plasticine, some water, photocopiable sheet 124 for each child.

What to do

Look out of the window preferably when it is raining and discuss what happens to the rain. Note that some stays on the plants having been intercepted, some remains on the ground surface as puddles, some runs down slopes and into drains, and some sinks into the ground. Talk about where the different things happen with particular attention to the nature of the ground surface. Note the difference between

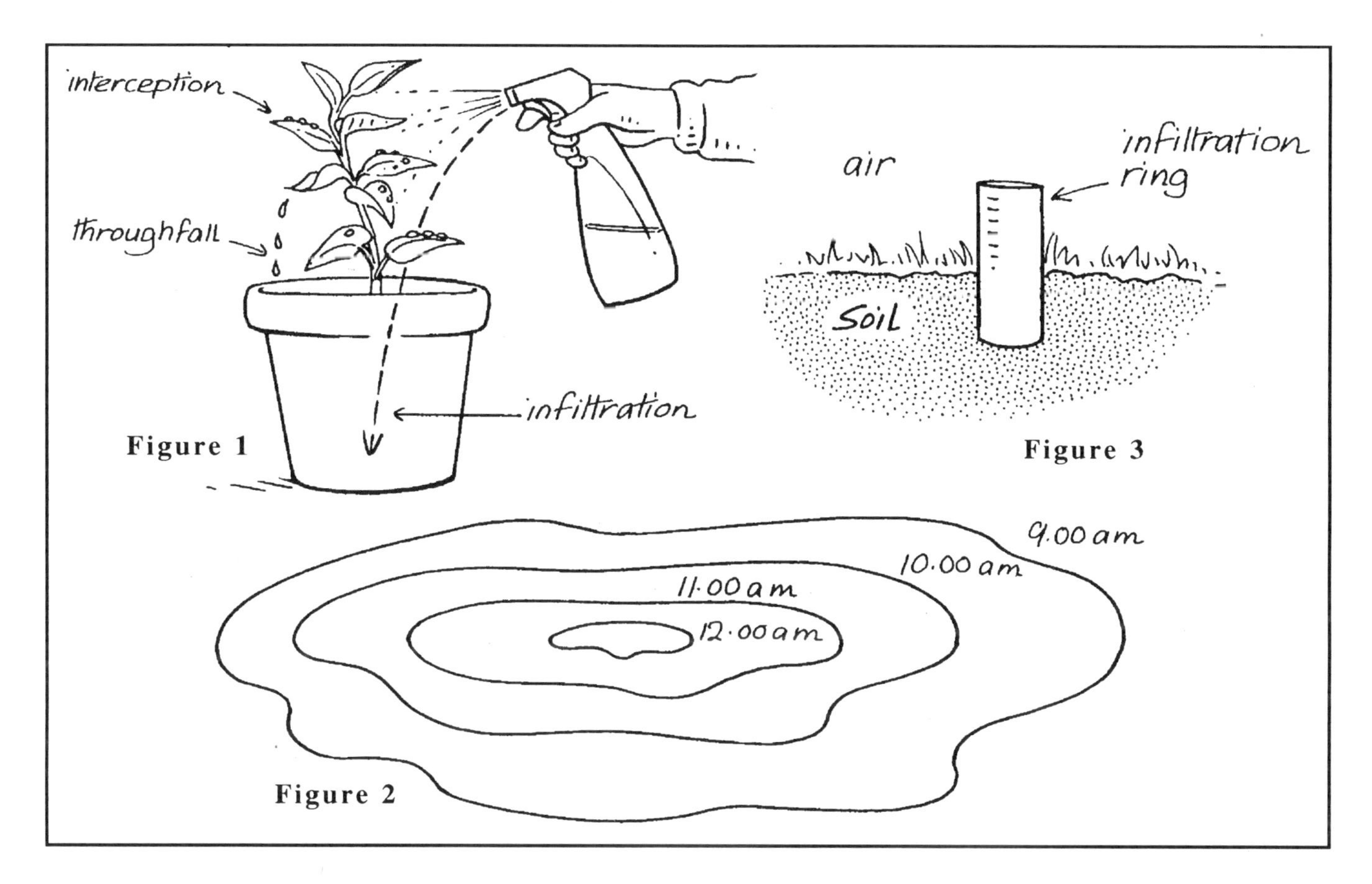

the areas of hard surface such as tarmac and concrete and the soft surfaces like soil and grass. However, be aware that areas such as footpaths across the grass and sports pitches may behave like hard surfaces. Also note the effect of gradient and slope in the playground.

After the rain give each group one of the following tasks.

▲ Take a potted plant outside or over a sink and simulate rainfall by spraying some artificial rain onto the plant. Note what happens to the water. Some will drip onto the soil beneath, and some will remain on the leaves as interception. Observe the plant over a period of time to see how long it takes for the water to disappear. At first some of the excess rain will drip off the plant leaves and sink into the soil. Some, however, will remain on the leaves as globules until the heat of the sun evaporates the water back into the sky.

This is exactly what happens on a large scale in a forest or woodland and gives children a good insight into part of the water cycle. It illustrates the key processes of *interception* (when the rain collects on the leaves like an umbrella), *throughfall* (when the rain drips off the leaves), *infiltration* (when the rain sinks into the soil) and *evaporation* (when the rain 'disappears' from the leaf surfaces). (See figure 1.)

▲ Outside, use or make a puddle in the playground and mark its perimeter in chalk at hourly intervals. During the course of the day the puddle will become smaller mainly as a result of the evaporation by the sun (even if the sun is not visible). It should be noted that another reason may be that the water sinks into the tarmac. This could lead on to a number of other experiments on evaporation and its relationship with wind speed, temperature and air humidity. (See figure 2.)

▲ Outside, use the hammer and wooden block to knock the infiltration rings approximately half way into a number of contrasting surfaces, such as the soil in a rose bed, the grass and somewhere where people walk across the grass. Fill the rings with water and measure how long it takes for the water to sink into the ground. This could be measured in terms of centimetres per minute.

This is the process of infiltration and it is important because it controls what happens to rain water. The effect of no infiltration can be problematic. The water either stays on the ground surface as puddles and can cause localised flooding, or it will run over the ground surface and may cause soil erosion if the soil is bare. Also if it runs quickly over the ground surface, it may reach the nearest river too fast and cause flooding to take place. Generally, therefore, it is crucial that the water infiltrates into the soil where it will not cause soil erosion and flooding.

The harder and more compact the soil the less likely it is to allow infiltration, so in the experiment you would expect the fastest infiltration to take place in the flower beds and the slowest where people's footsteps have compacted the soil. If the school has a grass football pitch this can be seen by comparing the waterlogged goal mouth where there is little infiltration because of the compaction caused by many footballers' feet with the dry conditions on the wing where only a few feet compact the soil. (See figure 3.)

▲ Inside or outside, set up two filter funnels, one of sand and the second of clay. Pour an equal amount of water into each and note how long it takes to begin to pass through, how much of the water actually passes through and how much is retained. This shows the *infiltration rate* (speed to pass through) and the *permeability* (how much stays in the soil and how much passes through) of each soil.

This information is important for farmers and gardeners because it shows how long it takes the soil to dry out again after a storm (and therefore how long it is before the farmer can begin to work the land), and how wet the soil remains after a storm (and therefore whether watering, also called irrigation, will be needed). At a more sophisticated level, the wetter the soil, the colder the soil and therefore the slower the growth of the crops.

In this experiment the sandy soil should allow water through most quickly but should retain the least amount of water. Therefore, a sandy soil is well drained but may need to be watered more frequently. (Look at figure 4.)

▲ Inside, take similar sized pieces of chalk, sandstone, slate and granite rock and place each one in a different saucer of water. Add drops of water to the surface of each and observe what happens. On some of the rocks (chalk and sandstone) the water should sink into the rock pores, on the others (slate and granite) the water will either stay on or run off the surface.

The property of rocks to absorb water is called *porosity* and it plays an important part in our lives. In the chalky and sandstone parts of the country where the rocks are porous, rainwater sinks into the ground where it becomes groundwater. In the nineteenth century many people got their water from wells and today, the underground water reserves which exist as a result of porous rock are crucial when drought problems arise. Where the rocks are non-porous, like in granite or slate areas, the water stays on the ground surface and most of the water runs into the rivers over the land surface. These areas can suffer in droughts as much of the water is evaporated and there is a lack of reserves.

▲ Take the washing-up liquid bottle with its top cut off to make a topless cylinder. Make small holes slightly offset at various heights up its side (see figure 5). Fill the bottom half of the cylinder with sand, then make an impermeable layer with clay or Plasticine and fill the top of the cylinder with sand. Place the cylinder in a water tray and gently pour water into it, noting where the water (a simulated spring) emerges. What is the effect of the impermeable layer?

As water rains onto the ground (is poured onto the sand of the cylinder) it infiltrates through the permeable soil until it meets an impermeable layer (the clay or Plasticine). Because it can infiltrate no further it is forced to flow sideways until it reaches the edge where it forms a spring. Notice that the spring appears initially just above the clay layer but if you continue to add water, the water table (water level) in the tube will continue to rise and successively higher springs (holes) start to run. If there were no springs the soil would simply become waterlogged at the surface.

In reality there are often layers of permeable and impermeable rocks. Springs tend to occur where a permeable rock like chalk is on top of an impermeable rock like clay.

When the exercises are completed, bring the groups together to share their results. Use these to discuss what happens to rainfall when it falls on a drainage basin (the area from which a river collects its water) and how the surface and subsurface of the drainage basin affects what happens. In conjunction with photocopiable sheet 124, which the children can now complete, talk about how human beings affect infiltration. When forests are cut down less rain is intercepted and evaporated by the branches and so more reaches the ground causing soil erosion and flooding. Also people make the soil more compact by walking up mountain paths or by grazing too many sheep and cattle on their fields. This has the effect of reduced infiltration and therefore localised flooding (more puddles), soil erosion and river flooding.

These two human orchestrated effects conversely cause less water to enter the ground so the plants may need watering and the wells and springs may dry up. The ultimate situation is where towns and cities cover the ground surface

Figure 4

Figure 5

with tiles, concrete and tarmac. The natural control of infiltration is lost so that one of two things occurs. Either less water reaches the soil and so the water level in the wells will be lower, or water runs down the roofs, gutters, roads and drains very rapidly so that the water reaches the river too quickly causing flooding. Localised flooding, in this situation, can be extremely problematic, especially if proper care is not taken to ensure drains are in the appropriate place and kept unblocked.

Suggestion(s) for extension

Give the children sand and clay and ask them to make a sand hill with an impermeable layer of clay rock. Add rain (water) carefully and note that the water sinks into the ground (the sand) and then re-appears just above the impermeable layer in a line of springs called a spring line. Relate this back to the tests done on rock porosity and permeability in the experiments above and ask them to suggest appropriate rocks to produce springs and spring lines in nature. Examples might include chalk or sandstone above granite or slate.

Suggestion(s) for support

Use the sand tray to show how water can sink into the ground. Do similar activities using a sponge. Show how plastic sheets can stop water sinking into the sand, do the same with clay or Plasticine. Some children will need a greater amount of introductory discussion using geographical terminology like 'evaporation' and 'infiltration'.

Assessment opportunities

Use sheet 124 to assess the children's understanding. Ask them to draw a diagram which shows what happens to rain when it reaches the tops of the trees in a forest. Do the same for rain when it hits the top of roofs in a city.

Opportunities for IT

The children could use a drawing or art package to create their own maps of a drainage basin. They could draw symbols or shade areas of different land uses such as forest, moorland, urban, sheep farming and arable farming. Labels could be added using the text facilities of the software. Similar work could be done using a mapping package such as *Aegis 2* or framework software such as *My World 2*.

Alternatively, the children could use a desktop publishing package to design a warning poster explaining how a village on low-lying land is at a risk of flooding. Encourage information about why the flood risk exists – perhaps it is because of clay ground at the bottom of a steep valley.

Display ideas

Set up the soil filter funnel experiment on a table and above it, graphically display the volume of water which passed through or was retained and the speed with which the water passed through the filter.

Other aspects of the Geography PoS covered

1b; 2a, b, c; 3a, b; 4.

Rivers

RIVER PARTS

To identify and learn appropriate vocabulary for the parts of rivers.

Groups of eight within class.

10 minutes introduction; 15 minutes practical; 20 minutes photocopiable sheet activity.

Previous skills/knowledge needed

The children should have the ability to observe carefully and interpret drawings. They should also have a simple understanding of the water cycle.

Key background information

All rivers have similar parts irrespective of size and location. All start at a source which may be a spring or a boggy area. The source may vary from winter to summer and from wet weather to dry weather. In winter and wet weather the river will rise higher up the valley (in dry weather the upper layers of the soil will be able to hold water more easily – rather like a sponge that is not yet saturated). A spring is a clearly marked place where water comes out of the ground. It is often in a hollow or sometimes at the foot of a cliff. Generally the water bubbles out of the ground under pressure. A boggy area is a place where the water comes out of the ground but the opening is not clear and so a wet and muddy area is left.

Rivers then flow downhill in channels. Channels join at confluences and carry on flowing down-slope. A small river joining a larger one is called a tributary. Where a river flows over hard rocks, a cliff with a steep gradient may be formed in the channel – this is called a waterfall. If the fall is less steep, a series of small steps called rapids may form. In other places (where the slope is gentler), the river may begin to meander. In this case the channel twists and turns with gentle bends which gradually become sharp ones.

Reference to photocopiable sheet

The photocopiable sheet shows the route (out of sequence) by which precipitation onto forest and urban areas reaches the river channel. The forest is an example of a natural sequence, the town is human-made. The aim of the exercise is for the children to sequence the very different processes and to show that the water which falls on a river catchment may follow different routes at different speeds before it reaches the river channel.

The forest sequence is as follows: rain/snow labelled as precipitation, interception on the leaves, drip, puddle, infiltration, spring.

The town sequence is as follows: precipitation, roof, gutter, drainpipe, pipe, sewage outlet.

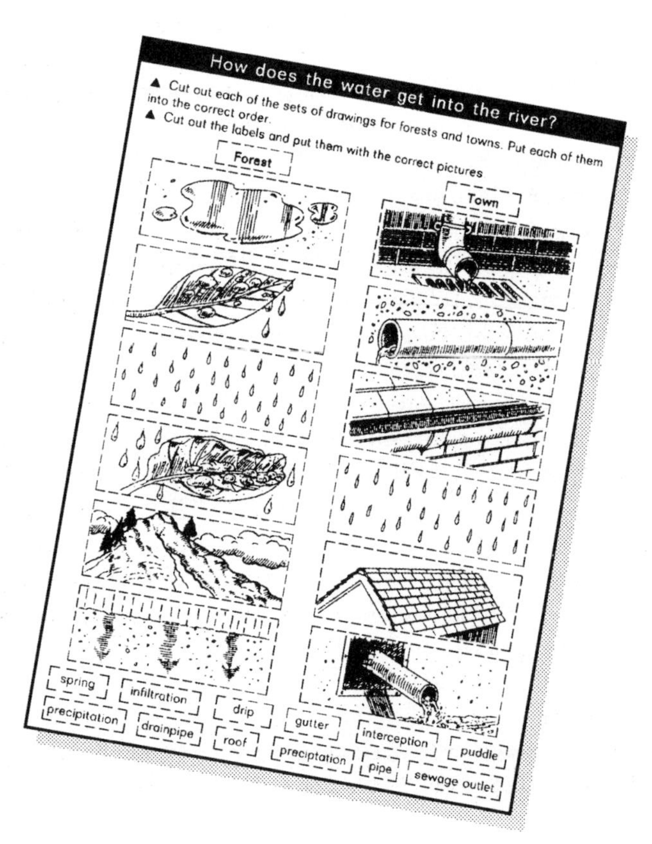

How does the water get into the river?

▲ Cut out each of the sets of drawings for forests and towns. Put each of them into the correct order.
▲ Cut out the labels and put them with the correct pictures.

Forest

Town

spring | infiltration | drip | gutter | interception | puddle
precipitation | drainpipe | roof | precipitation | pipe | sewage outlet

Eventually the river flows into a lake or sea via either a delta or an estuary. A delta is the place at the mouth of the river where the channel reaches the sea. The speed of flow of the river is reduced and all the soil and stones being carried by the river are deposited. As a result a triangular shaped deposit (like the Greek letter Δ) is formed and the river channel breaks up into lots of smaller channels. Not all rivers have deltas at their mouth. In these cases, if the mouth of the river is fairly wide and affected by tides, the area is called the estuary.

Preparation
Model the sand into the form of a mountain (a volcano-shaped mountain is easiest and best). You could place a resistant piece of material (such as slate, clay or Plasticine) across the place where the river will flow to encourage the development of rapids or a waterfall. (See figure 1).

Resources needed
A sand tray (with sand), a watering can filled with water, a sheet of clay or Plasticine or a piece of slate. Photocopiable sheet 125 for each child, glue, cocktail sticks, scissors, a small piece of card or plastic, satellite image of own region and atlas (for extension activity).

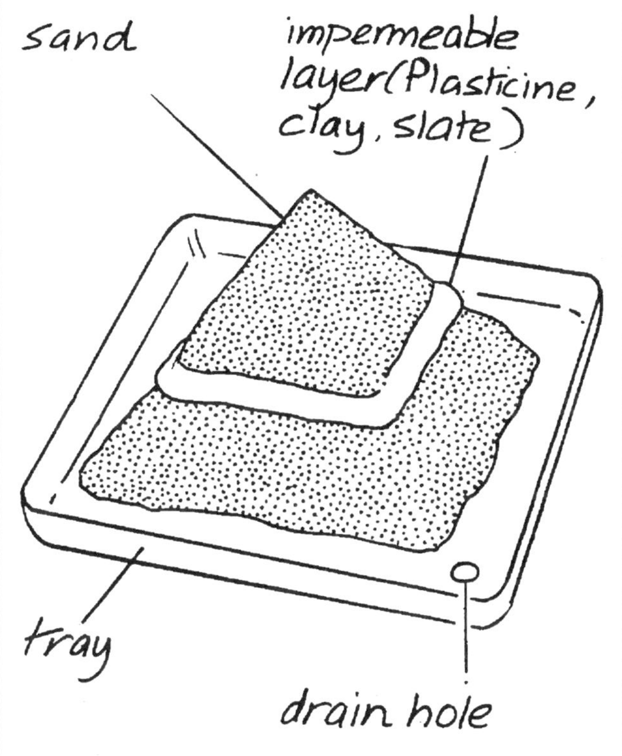

sand
impermeable layer (Plasticine, clay, slate)
tray
drain hole

Figure 1

What to do
As a whole class talk about the water cycle. Remind the children that all water comes from the sky in the form of rain or snow. Then discuss how the water can do one of four things:

▲ it can sink into the soil;
▲ it can stay on the ground surface as puddles and lakes;
▲ it can evaporate back into the sky;
▲ it can eventually run down-slope into a river.

It is vital that the children are aware that water can only flow downhill. Many children are under the erroneous impression that seas flow into estuaries and rivers. Show children the modelled sand and discuss the parts of the landscape identifying the mountain, slopes and sea or ocean. Draw their attention to the watering can and explain that they will use it to make rainfall.

Now work with the children in groups of eight. Ask a child to spray the rain onto the mountain from the watering can. (It can be better to spray the water onto a card or plastic surface to avoid erosion at the point of impact and to encourage runoff, although you would have to explain why you are doing this.) While the 'storm' occurs, draw attention to the flow of water and the features as they develop. At the end of the 'storm' ask the children to work individually to identify the main landforms shown on photocopiable sheet 125. They can then draw lines from the landforms to their likely position on the 'mountain' in the centre of the sheet.

As a whole class, when everyone has finished the photocopiable sheet activity, use the labels from one photocopiable master sheet 125 mounted on toothpicks or cocktail sticks to label the key features of the sand tray landscape. If some of the photocopiable sheet lables do not occur on your sand model, talk to the children about how you might be able to cause them to form. The children will enjoy altering and modifying the model.

Suggestion(s) for extensions
Use atlases and satellite images of large areas, such as the south east or north west, to identify the major rivers and their key parts. Relate the parts where possible to real places.

Suggestion(s) for support
If the children are needing support to see the landforms develop, model another pile of sand into the features it is hoped to simulate and label them. This can be done before the spraying activity so they can see the features more easily as they develop.

Assessment opportunities
Ask the children to draw a picture about the journey of a raindrop from the top of the mountain to the sea (via the river system) using the correct labelling in the correct sequence. Keep the account as a record noting the specificity of the vocabulary and the correct sequencing of features (where appropriate).

Opportunities for IT
The teacher could use a picture-based CD-ROM such as the Longman's LANDSCAPES series, to search for pictures

on a particular theme, such as deltas or meanders. They could be set up into a film sequence and children set questions to answer by closely observing the pictures.

The children could use a drawing package to draw out their own river system and label the parts of the river. This work could be extended to make a multimedia presentation using an authoring package where groups of children could research and present information on one part of the river system.

Display ideas

Using the sand tray as the focus, connect the features to a wall display of drawings, photographs and downloaded text describing the key features. You could position your model below the wall display. (Mixing cement with the sand before watering the model will have the effect of solidying your landscape features.)

Other aspects of the Geography PoS covered

2a; 3a; 5a; 7b.

Reference to photocopiable sheet

Photocopiable sheet 125 comprises a bare diagram of a 'mountain' surrounded in the side margins with pen pictures, and along the bottom with written labels of the key landforms which make up a river system. Following the practical rainfall modelling exercise the children are asked to link the landform drawings to the correct locations on the picture of the 'mountain'. At the end of the activity when all groups have completed their task, the word labels need to be cut out and attached to cocktail sticks. They can then be added to the sand tray model as a semi-permanent display of the landforms of a river system.

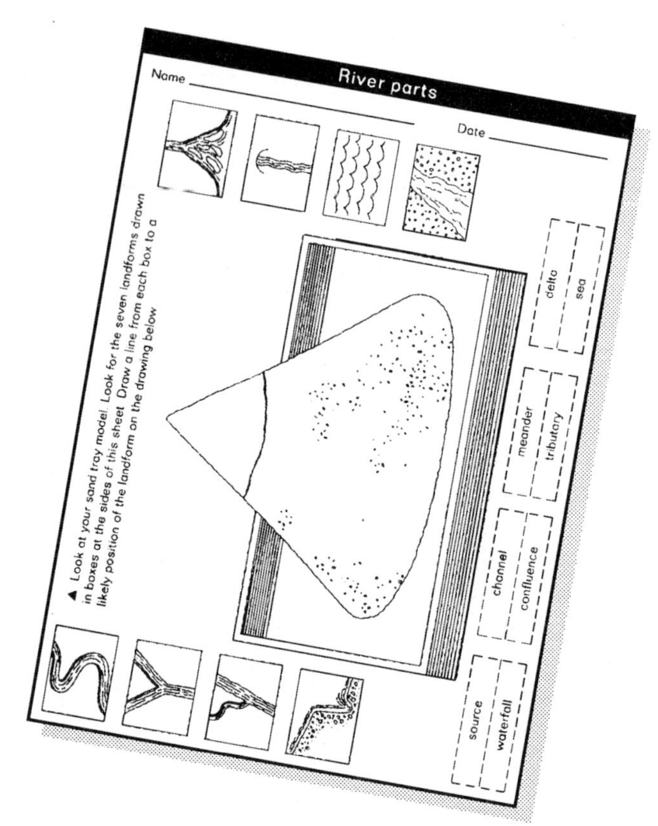

WHERE DO RIVERS GO?

To be aware that most rivers flow downhill to the lowest point which is a lake or the sea, and that most lakes have rivers flowing into and out of them.

Individual or pairs.

10 minutes introduction; 25 minutes class activity; 15 minutes photocopiable sheet activity.

Previous skills/knowledge needed

Children should be aware of the function of maps and atlases and have an ability to use them. They should also have an understanding of the water (hydrological) cycle.

Key background information

All rivers flow from areas of high land to areas of low land. Most rivers (94%) eventually flow into a lake and then the sea or ocean. However, some rivers, for example in the Sahara and Australia (6%), flow into lakes in the middle of the continents and evaporate out. They have no outflow.

Lakes are bodies of water lying in a hollow and surrounded by land. They exist at all scales from the local to the continental. Most are freshwater, but in desert areas where there is a lot of evaporation, they may be salt water. In most parts of the world rivers run into lakes and emerge again at another side, but in desert areas rivers often end in lakes. Lakes are temporary features of the landscape because they either gradually fill up with material carried and deposited by rivers or they form salt lakes which eventually dry up as a result of evaporation and form salt flats. Not all lakes are natural, some are made to store water and are called reservoirs. Many natural lakes are modified by dams to make them bigger.

Seventy one per cent of the earth's surface is a sheet of salt water which surrounds the continents. The continents divide this sheet into five oceans (in decreasing size – the Pacific, the Atlantic, the Indian, the Arctic and the Southern Oceans).

A sea is a large body of salt water which is smaller than but may form part of an ocean. Some are on the edge of continents like the North Sea and the China Sea. Others are landlocked except by a narrow channel or strait, such as the Mediterranean Sea. Large salt-water inland lakes are called seas, like the Dead Sea and the Caspian Sea.

Preparation

Before the start of this unit of work, you should write to the Environment Agency, the Regional Water Boards and the Regional Tourist Boards for information and posters on the three United Kingdom rivers (Rivers Severn, Trent and Thames) and four lakes (Lough Neagh, Loch Lomond, Lake Windermere and Llyn Tegid) to be studied. Also write to the local area boards for local information. Make a long-profile diagram of a local river (see photocopiable sheet 126 and the example of the River Nile) showing the river's starting point and height, its finishing point and height and other key points and their heights in between.

Resources needed

Large wall maps of the United Kingdom and the World, an atlas, paper and felt-tipped pens to prepare a wall display, modelling clay or Plasticine in brown and blue, computer with CD-ROM and Encyclopaedia discs (optional), a long-profile diagram of your nearest local river from source to mouth and showing the heights of key places, resources from the Environment Agency, Regional Water and Tourist Boards, photocopiable sheet 126 for each child.

What to do

Talk about any ponds, lakes and rivers that the children know about in the local area. Ask how they are used (for example, for fishing, swimming). Where does the water in them come from and where does it go to? Talk about the idea of a simple system with inputs (precipitation, groundwater and streams), stores (the pond/lake) and outputs (the outflowing river, water pipes, evaporation). Draw an analogy with water into and out of their own homes.

Take the three United Kingdom rivers specified in Map A of the National Curriculum – the Trent, Severn and Thames. Talk about the country in which they start and for the Severn and Thames the name of the upland where they rise (the Cambrian Mountains and Cotswolds respectively), which country they flow across, and which estuary and sea they flow into. Look at the atlas and discuss how the Cambrian mountains are shown on different maps. Are symbols of mountain peaks, different colours, contours or spot heights used? Let the more able pupils try to identify the more important tributaries, counties and towns passed en route.

Turn attention to the nearest large river to your school and attempt to trace its origins, lakes and other features en route as outlined above. Ask the children to find as many heights as possible from the source of the river to the point where it joins the sea. Plot these on the large long-profile diagram of the river drawn from source to mouth.

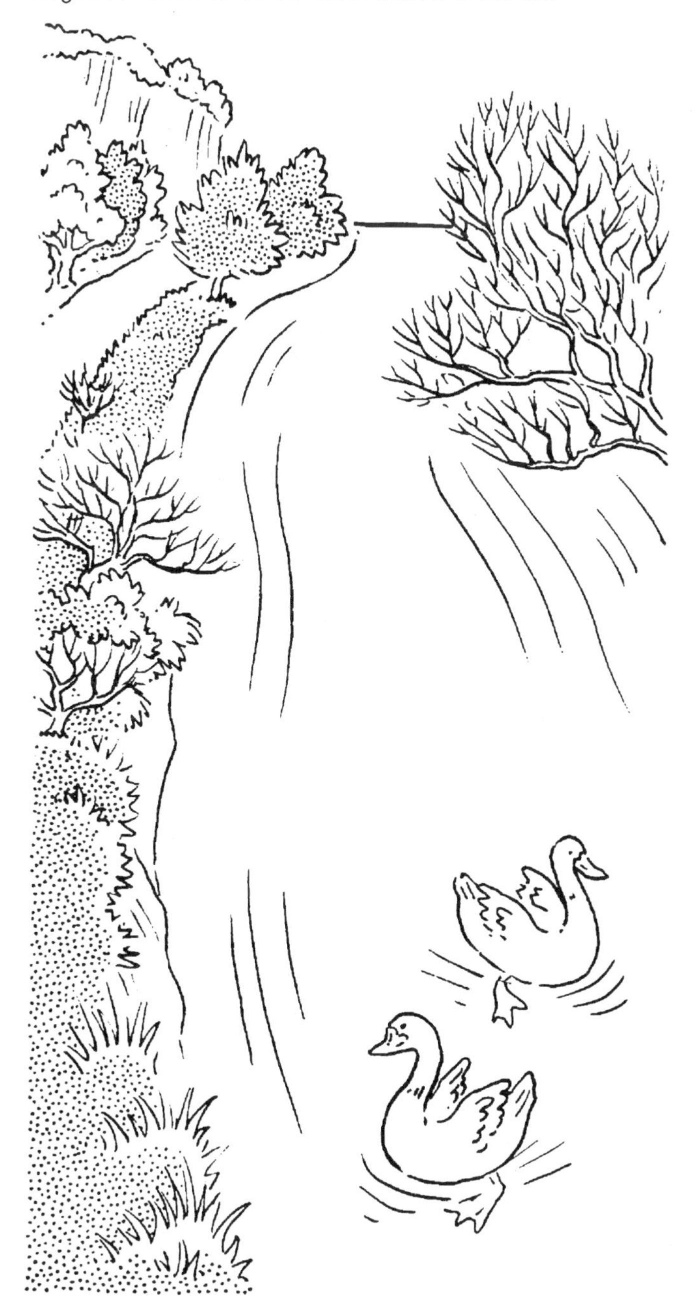

Next, the children take the largest natural lakes in the United Kingdom and systematically identify which river flows into and out of each, and to which sea each flows as follows:

▲ United Kingdom and Northern Ireland: Lough Neagh (River Bann, Atlantic Ocean);

▲ Great Britain and Scotland: Loch Tay (River Tay, North Sea);

▲ England: Lake Windermere (River Rothay flows in, River Leven flows out, Morecambe Bay [Irish Sea]);

▲ Wales: Bala Lake/Llyn Tegid (River Dee, Irish Sea).

Using a World wall map the children can locate some of the largest lakes in the world and, using their atlases, identify the main river flowing into and out of each one:

▲ Caspian Sea – former USSR (River Volga);

▲ The Great Lakes – Canada/USA (St Lawrence);

▲ Lake Victoria – Africa (River Nile [White]);

▲ Lake Kariba – Africa (River Zambezi);

▲ Aral Sea – former USSR (River Amu Darya and River Syr Darya);

▲ Lake Constance/Bodensee – Germany (River Rhine);

▲ Great Bear – Canada (River MacKenzie).

Give out photocopiable sheet 126 and ask the children to trace the source, route and mouth of the River Nile, the longest river in the world. They should pay particular attention to the two main lakes along its course.

Suggestion(s) for extension

Look at the atlas page of Australia and find Lake Eyre. First draw a map of the lake and its tributaries, then use an encyclopaedia to find out about its history. Repeat for Lake Chad in North Africa. Discuss reasons why these lakes have no outlets. The main reason is to do with the arid climates of each area which is largely to do with their location in the middle of their respective continents, and hence distance from the nearest oceanic water from which water vapour comes to eventually provide rainfall.

Suggestion(s) for support

Using modelling clay or Plasticine, make a model of a mountain with a river leading to a lake and then a river leading out of the lake. Use brown Plasticine for the mountain and blue for the river and lake. Label the features.

Assessment opportunities

From these activities it is possible to assess the children's awareness of physical features such as ponds, lakes and rivers, more advanced children will be aware of patterns in the distribution (sequence) of features such as mountain and upland sources, rivers with natural and artificial lakes along their courses and mouths, deltas and estuaries at their end. The more able may succeed in comparing the features and patterns for different climatic areas particularly with reference to inland seas and lakes, and use an understanding of physical processes to explain these differences. The children should gain experience of using resources through searching, discovering and abstracting information from maps, atlases and CD-ROMs. This will lead them to an awareness of how resources are essential to research. Throughout the activities an increasing awareness of scale from the local rivers and ponds to the national and global picture should emerge.

Opportunities for IT

The children could use a CD-ROM encyclopaedia to research additional information on each of the world lakes. The information could be printed out so that it can be used as a part of the display. Alternatively, the children could save the information in ASCII or plain text so that it can be loaded into a word processor where it can be re-drafted to remove unnecessary information or precised. It may also be possible for children to use pictures from this or picture-based CD-ROMs.

Display ideas

Draw a large scale wall map of the United Kingdom and superimpose on it the three rivers (Severn, Thames, Trent) and the four lakes (Lomond, Neagh, Tegid, Windermere) examined above. Use the information collected, plus the materials from the Environment Agency, Regional Water and Tourist Boards, to produce a display.

Other aspects of the Geography PoS covered

1a, d; 3a, d, e, (f); 5a.

Reference to photocopiable sheet

The photocopiable sheet 126 shows the River Nile from source to mouth. It aims to illustrate the movement of water from upland mountains and plateaux, down via lakes (natural and human-made) to the sea. The children will need access to an atlas and associated skills to complete the exercise.

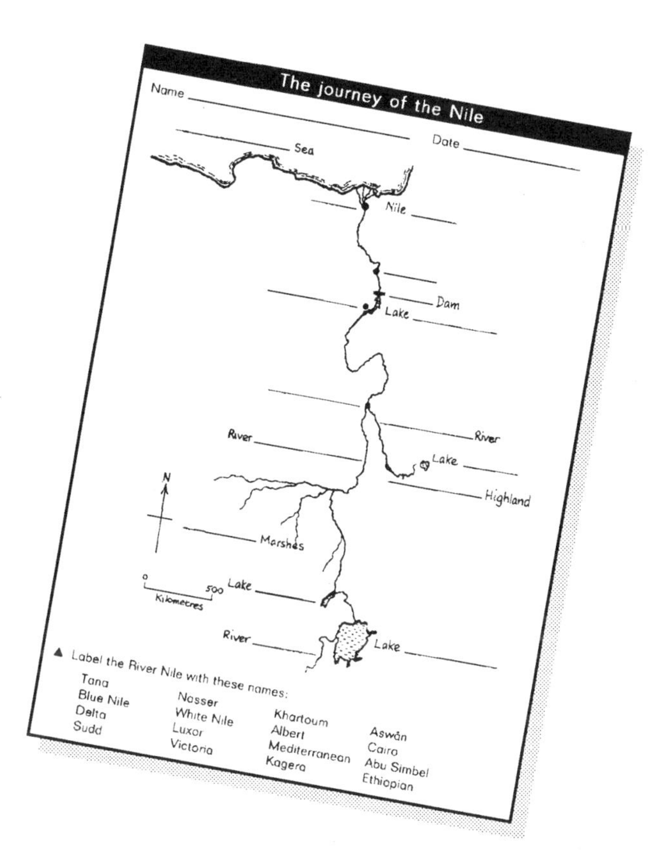

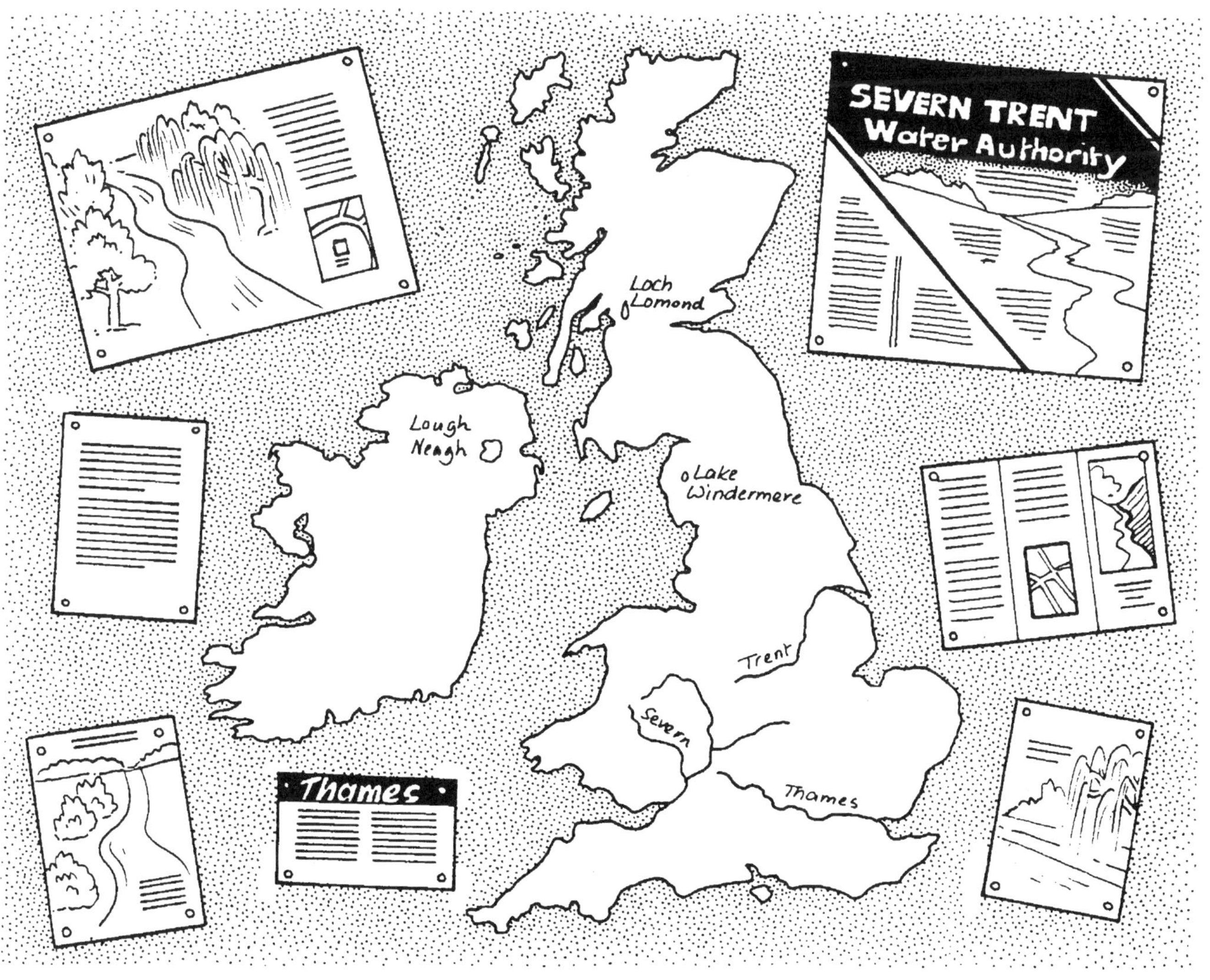

RIVERS WORKING

To understand that rivers erode, transport and deposit materials.

Whole class, then four to eight pupils.

15 minutes introduction/demonstration; 20 minutes observation/experimentation; 15 minutes completion of photocopiable sheet; 10 minutes follow-up discussion.

Previous skills/knowledge needed

Children should understand the concept of a fair test and have the ability to measure time and small stones.

Key background information

The work of a river can be likened to a human being having to carry a rucksack. Both involve carrying a load and to do that energy is required. When both run out of energy the load is dropped. All rivers carry out three processes (jobs): they erode (pick up), transport (carry) and deposit (drop) material from their banks and beds. Material moved is called the river's *load*. That which rolls and slides along the bed of the river is called *bedload* and material which bounces along or is carried suspended in the water is called *suspended load*. Material may vary in size from clay and silt, through sand, gravel, pebbles to boulders.

Generally, the larger the material, the heavier it is and the faster the river has to flow to erode and transport it. However, other factors, like the shape of stones and their density, are important. Fast flowing rivers and fast flowing parts of rivers tend to have large boulders and slower rivers have smaller material on their beds.

The availability of a river's energy (normally its velocity) determines whether material can be picked up, transported or deposited. Generally big rivers have more energy than small ones and the same river will have more energy during storms and floods than during low-flow conditions. As material is moved down rivers from source to mouth the bedload tends to become smaller and rounder as a result of breakage and smoothing.

Preparation

Acquire a rucksack, a length of guttering and a number of stones. Sort the stones into three size categories (small: 5mm long, medium: 15mm long, large: 25mm long). Paint each category of stone with a different-coloured waterproof paint and allow to dry. Place the stones in the rucksack. Collect the following: for experiment one a length of guttering, tape or rule, three different-sized wedges, rubber piping, a tap, a bucket and matches; for experiment two a length of guttering, a metre rule or tape, rubber piping, a tap, a bucket and matches; for experiment three a length of guttering, a metre rule or tape, rubber piping, a tap, a bucket, and three different sets of different-sized stones (five for each set); for experiment four (support activity) a length of guttering, a tap, a rubber tube, bucket, medium-sized stone and wedge.

Resources needed

See equipment needed for the four experiments in 'Preparation' above. A jar and soil, copies of photocopiable sheet 127 for each child.

What to do

Introduce the lesson by discussing humans carrying a rucksack using words like pick up, transport and drop. Talk about the need for energy and strength to do this. Talk about rivers and their strength and from where they get their energy. This is gained from the speed of flow, which in turn is the result of the steepness of the river course and the smoothness of the bed of the river (that is, gradient and friction).

Ask: how do rivers use their energy? Just like human beings they carry a load in the form of boulders and pebbles. The analogy with a rucksack could be continued by opening the rucksack and emptying out the pebbles which are to be used later in the lesson. Introduce the words erosion (for pick up), transport (for carrying) and deposit (for dropping) when talking about the work of a river.

Introduce the children to the idea of the length of plastic guttering being a river and the stones being the materials in the river. Show the children how to measure the velocity of the water in the guttering. Use a small piece of wood as a 'Pooh stick' and see how many centimetres it will travel in three seconds. The velocity can then be expressed in centimetres per second by dividing the number of centimetres travelled by three seconds.

Divide the class into groups of approximately six to eight pupils. Each group will carry out one activity. At the end they will share their results and experiences. Results of the group activity can be recorded on photocopiable page 127 and the results of other activities added at the end of the session.

Each group will attempt to answer questions by carrying out the following enquiries and completing the appropriate tables and graphs.

▲ Does a steep river flow faster than a gentle river? Here the children are expected to use the three different-sized wedges to produce different slopes for the channel. The larger the wedge the steeper the gradient and the faster the velocity. The results should be recorded on photocopiable sheet 127 experiment one and both the table and the scattergraph completed. (See figure 1.)

▲ What is the effect of the amount of water in the river on the velocity of the river? Here the children are expected to hold the gradient of the gutter constant but carry out three tests to measure the velocity of a low, medium and high volume of water running through the gutter. The volume of water can be controlled either by varying the control on the tap (low, medium or high) or by fixing a clip to the rubber piping. Again the results should be recorded on sheet 127 experiment two and both the table and scattergraph completed. The larger the volume of water the faster it should flow because a lower proportion of the water is in contact with the friction of the bed and banks of the guttering. The conclusion is that rivers in flood erode and transport more material than a river in normal flow. (See figure 2.)

▲ What is the relationship between river velocity and erosion and transportation? Here the children are expected to select the three different sizes of distinctly coloured stones (large, medium and small). Five of each sized stones should be placed close to each other in the guttering. Then the pebbles should be exposed to the three different velocities (slow, medium, fast) in turn to see which of the stones are moved and which are not moved by the different velocities. Is there a relationship between velocity and erosion? All the stones should be moved by the fast flowing water, only the medium and small stones by the medium velocity water and only the smallest by the slowest moving water – therefore, the greater the velocity the higher the erosion. The children record their results on photocopiable sheet 127 experiment three. (See figure 3.)

After the experiments have been completed the teacher should hold a discussion to clarify the processes of erosion, transportation and deposition and the factors which affect these processes, most notably, the speed of flow of the water, the gradient of the stream, the volume of the water and the size of the material on the bed of the river.

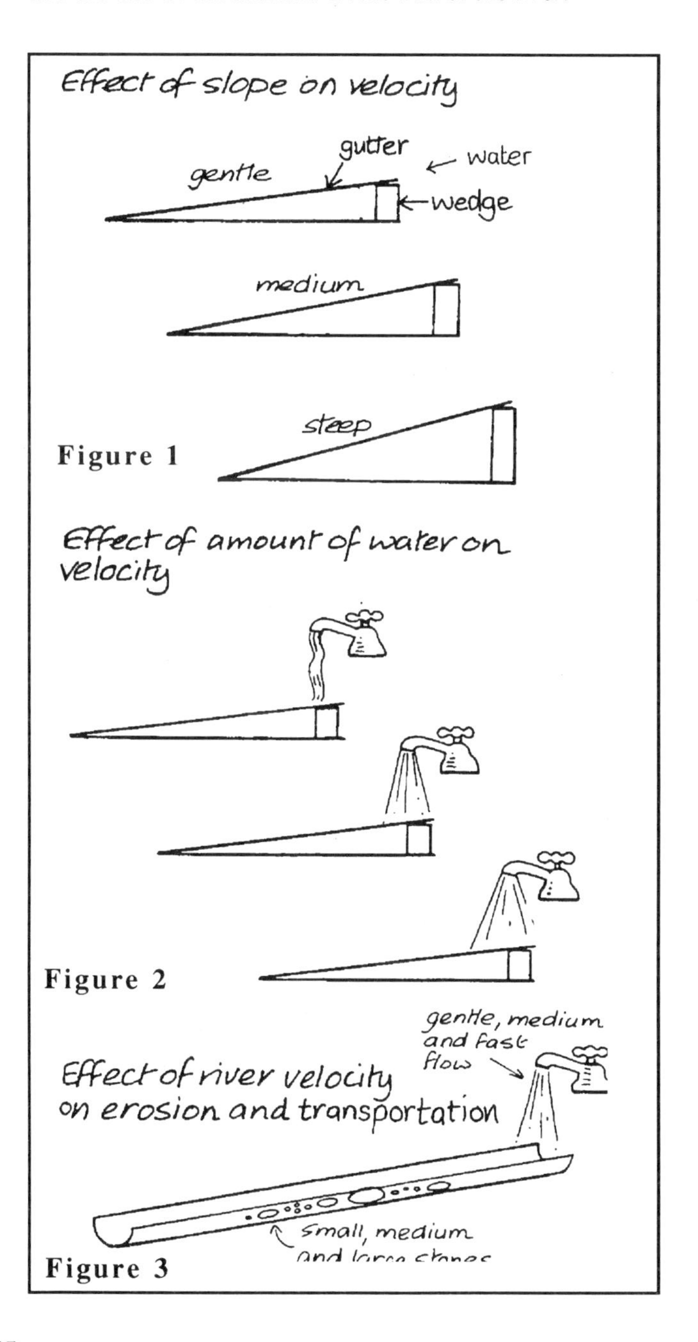

Figure 1
Figure 2
Figure 3

Suggestion(s) for extension

Carry out further experiments to see the effect of pebble shape on transport using flat and spherical stones. Which are most easily moved? Additionally, identify dense and less dense pebbles of the same size and shape and examine the effect of density on erosion and transportation.

Suggestion(s) for support

Use the following experiment to help those children who need support. What happens to a stone during a flood? Here the children are expected to place one medium-sized stone near the head of the guttering with the slope constant. The passage of a storm is simulated by gradually increasing the discharge of the river by turning up the tap, then gradually turning the tap down as the storm passes. Observe what happens to the stone before, during and after the storm. The stone should be still (deposited) before the storm, moved (eroded) and carried (transported) during the storm, and dropped (deposited) after the storm.

Help the children to understand the concepts of erosion, transportation and deposition by taking a jar of water, adding some soil and stirring. Observe the different-sized material in suspension and note its deposition as the effects of the stir diminish. Show how the coarse material is deposited first. Relate this to river flow.

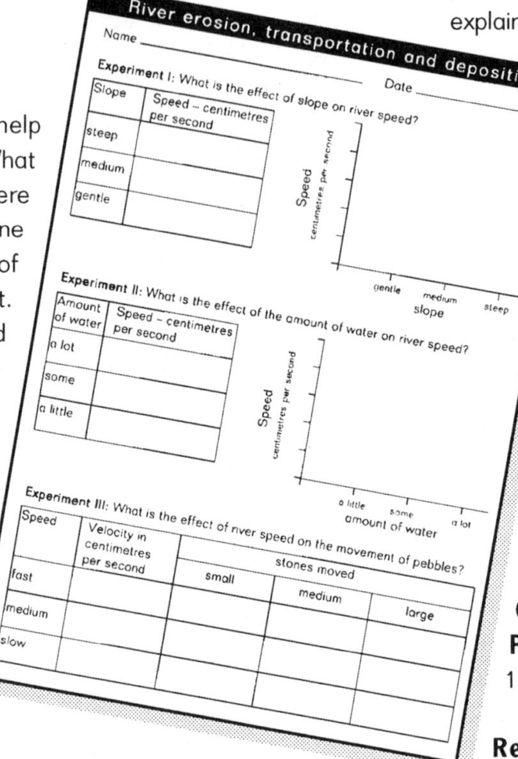

River erosion, transportation and deposition

Name ____________________ Date ____________

Experiment I: What is the effect of slope on river speed?

Slope	Speed – centimetres per second
steep	
medium	
gentle	

Experiment II: What is the effect of the amount of water on river speed?

Amount of water	Speed – centimetres per second
a lot	
some	
a little	

Experiment III: What is the effect of river speed on the movement of pebbles?

Speed	Velocity in centimetres per second	stones moved: small	medium	large
fast				
medium				
slow				

Assessment opportunities

Asking the children to devise and implement a fair test is a useful form of assessment. In addition, the attempts to explain the results on the photocopiable sheet and any discussion with particular reference to those results that do not correspond to what is expected, will differentiate the pupils.

Display ideas

Make a display of different types of stones classified in terms of size, shape and density. Then make an adjacent display distinguishing between those that are easily moved and those that are not. Incorporate the guttering pipe and other equipment used for the experiments.

Other aspects of the Geography PoS covered

1b, c; 2a, b, c; 3a; 7a.

Reference to photocopiable sheet

Photocopiable sheet 127 aims to formalise the children's observations of the processes of erosion, transportation and deposition and to give pupils the opportunity to tabulate and graph their results.

RIVER LANDFORMS

To be able to recognise river landforms, the materials they are made of, the processes which cause them and that they change through time.

Individuals within whole class.

20 minutes introduction and classification; 20 minutes photocopiable sheet activity; 10 minutes discussion.

Previous skills/knowledge needed

Children should have a knowledge of the parts of a river system and understand the processes of erosion, transportation and deposition. They should be able to observe photographs carefully.

Key background information

All landforms are recognisable because of their shape (form). Landforms may be made either of solid bedrock (like a waterfall) or of sediments which are fragments of broken rock such as silt, sand and pebbles (like a delta). Some landforms are produced by erosion (like a valley and a waterfall) and others by deposition (like a flood plain and a delta). Generally, erosion takes place in the upper parts of rivers and deposition in the lower parts.

Erosion is the result of the force (or energy) of a river acting against the resistance (or strength) of the rocks and sediments. Where a river has surplus energy it will erode material and transport it away downstream. When it loses energy it will *deposit* material, the biggest first and the smallest and lightest later.

The main influence on the energy of a river is its gradient which influences its speed of flow. The faster the flow of a river the more energy it has and the more erosion and transportation takes place. When a river loses its energy it is no longer able to carry its load and so the material is deposited. This happens whenever the slope decreases, such as at the foot of the mountains, and where a river enters a lake or sea.

Generally bedrock like granite and limestone is harder than sediments like sand and gravel and difficult to erode. Some rocks like shale are very soft and easy to erode while some sediments like clay are very cohesive (sticky) and are quite difficult to erode despite being soft.

A *waterfall* forms where a river falls over the edge of a cliff. The highest waterfall in the world is the Angel Falls in Venezuela which falls 979 metres. The rock at the top of a waterfall is usually hard and is called the *cap rock*. The rock beneath the cap is often softer and more easily eroded. At the foot of the waterfall where the full force of the falling water is felt, a *plunge pool* is formed. Through time the edge of a waterfall retreats as the cap rock is eroded and undermined by the erosion of the softer rocks beneath. As it retreats it leaves a gorge behind.

A *gorge* forms when a river cuts into its bed and erodes downward into the rock. The Grand Canyon on the Colorado River in Arizona, USA is the largest in the world. If the river erodes rapidly or the rock is very hard the gorge develops very steep sides. If it happens slowly or the rock is soft a gentle *valley* will be formed rather than a gorge.

A *flood plain* is a flat piece of land either side of the river channel. It is called a flood plain because it is flat (a plain) and it is often flooded (a flood plain). The biggest flood plains in the world are that of the Mississippi and the Ganges Rivers which are tens of kilometres wide. A flood plain is made of fine sediment like silt and clay and these are deposited whenever the river floods out of its channel onto the valley bottom beside it. The water slows down and so the sediment it was carrying is deposited onto the flood plain building it up layer by layer.

A *delta* is shaped like the Greek letter Δ. It is found wherever a river carrying a lot of sediment enters a still body of water like a lake or a sea. At this point the river loses its energy and drops its sediment forming a delta and making the river channel split into smaller distributaries. The

Mississippi and Nile deltas are the most famous but the largest is the Ganges delta which is 75 000 square kilometres in area.

Preparation

Collect photographs and other resources of basic river landforms including: valleys, gorges, river cliffs, meanders, ox-box lakes, flood plains, terraces, deltas, waterfalls, rapids, potholes, gullies, braided streams and estuaries. Find an encyclopaedia with a gazetteer or a CD-ROM containing the landforms of the world.

Resources needed

A set of photographs of basic river landforms, one copy of photocopiable sheet 128 for each child, paper, a map of the world and CD-ROM or encyclopaedia for the extension exercise, a sheet of card for the support exercise.

What to do

Show the children pictures of the river landforms. Discuss the processes of erosion and deposition and attempt to classify the landforms accordingly. Then discuss what each landform is made of, distinguishing between bedrock and sediment. Ask the children to classify the landforms into four sets, those that are erosional and made of bedrock, those that are erosional and made of sediment, those that are depositional and made of bedrock and those that are depositional and made of sediment. The diagram below may help you:

Give each child a copy of photocopiable sheet 128 and ask them to look at and discuss the pictures and the key which show how river landforms develop through time. Note the following:

▲ the gorge erodes deeper with time;
▲ the waterfall is both eroding downwards and backwards leaving a gorge in front of it and a deep pool at the base of the waterfall (called a plunge pool);
▲ the flood plain is being formed by the deposition of layers of material each time the river floods over its banks;
▲ the delta is formed by the deposition of material transported downstream from the mountains when the moving river meets the relatively still water of the sea.

The children now finish the tasks on the photocopiable sheet by describing what has happened and answering the questions on a separate sheet of paper.

Finally discuss with the whole class the ways in which processes of erosion and deposition produce landforms which are constantly changing (over very long time periods), and the similarities and differences between each of the landforms.

landform	erosional	depositional	bedrock	sediment
valleys	*		*	*
gorges	*		*	
river cliffs	*			*
meanders	*			*
ox-bow lakes		*		*
flood plains		*		*
terraces		*		*
deltas		*		*
waterfalls	*		*	
rapids	*		*	
potholes	*		*	
gullies	*			*
braided streams		*		*
estuaries		*		*

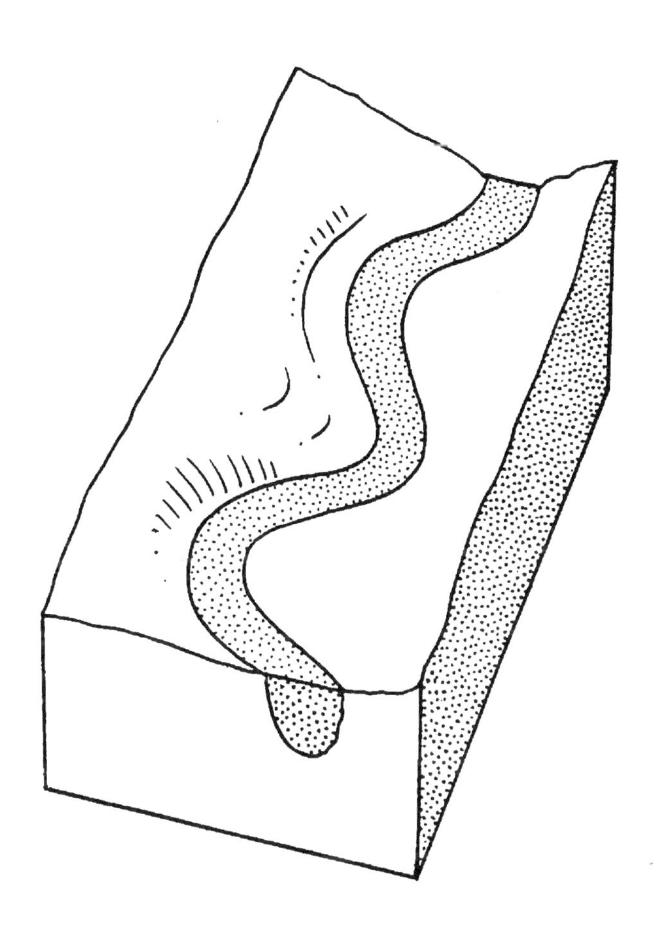

Opportunities for IT

The children could draw up a list of the worlds 20 or 30 longest rivers and use a CD-ROM to research information about them to make a database. The fieldnames could include:

River:	Nile
Continent.	Africa
River rises in:	Lake Victoria
Estuary in:	Egypt
Empties into:	Mediterranean
Length:	??
Waterfalls:	??
Lakes:	??
Gorges:	??

Display ideas

Make a class display of the photographs of the landforms with annotated comments identifying the erosional and depositional features and the materials of which the landforms are made. Try to cut up the changing landforms from photocopiable sheet 128 so that the features are shown in a developmental sequence.

Other aspects of the Geography PoS covered

3a, e; 5a; 7a.

Reference to photocopiable sheet

Photocopiable sheet 128 shows profile or plan views of river landforms through time. Children are required to understand the key to trace the evolution of the features. They then have to describe how and why these landforms change on a separate sheet of paper.

Suggestion(s) for extension

Use either a CD-ROM or encyclopaedia to find the names of the largest or deepest gorges, waterfalls and deltas in the world. Locate them on a map of the world and write brief notes on the different features, in bubble diagrams connected to the maps.

Suggestion(s) for support

Children could make a three-dimensional cardboard model of a valley, flood plain and river channel and use it to identify the landforms and processes on the slopes, valley bottom and river channel.

Assessment opportunities

Photocopiable sheet 128 will allow discussion and recording of the changing form of the landforms and then an attempt at explanation of the changes. This should provide opportunities to differentiate between those children who are simply describing, those who are comparing features, those who are recognising and understanding processes and those who are explaining and looking for similarities and differences at different places.

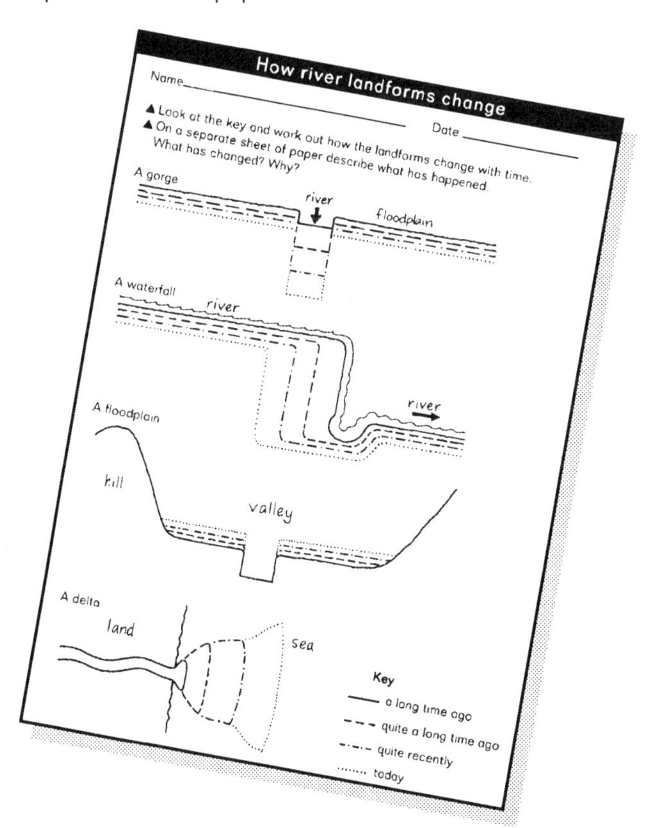

How river landforms change

Name ______ Date ______

▲ Look at the key and work out how the landforms change with time.
▲ On a separate sheet of paper describe what has happened. What has changed? Why?

A gorge

A waterfall

A floodplain

A delta

Key
—— a long time ago
- - - quite a long time ago
-·-·- quite recently
······ today

KEEP SAFE BY RIVERS

To develop awareness of the potential dangers associated with rivers. To understand how to act in a safe and sensible manner when working with rivers.

Groups of four within whole class.

20 minutes discussion; 20 minutes photocopiable sheet activity.

Previous skills/knowledge needed

Children should have an awareness of the concept of safety and danger, perhaps in the context of home or road safety. They should also have the abilities to read and interpret a drawing, and to work effectively in a group.

Key background information

It is important, if at all possible, that children have opportunities to study rivers first-hand during Key Stage 2. Teachers may feel reluctant to involve their children in fieldwork in and around rivers, yet they are also aware that children love water and are fascinated by rivers. There are many potential dangers some of which are to do with the physical nature of rivers, others are to do with the behaviour of children in and around them.

In a river the current is always a danger. The force of the water on young bodies even at a relatively low speed can cause them to fall over. Many stony rivers are very slippery while muddy bedded rivers are sticky; both types of river can cause children to lose their footing. The stones on the beds of rivers are sometimes wobbly and this can cause problems especially if trying to cross a channel. Abrupt changes in the depth of rivers can also cause potential dangers. The temperature of water can be much colder than the surrounding air and even warm water can cause the body to lose heat especially on windy days. In polluted water there are risks if the children allow water and microbes to get into cuts or their mouths. The banks of the rivers are also potentially dangerous especially on the outside of meanders where the bank overhangs the river and there is a danger of the bank collapsing into it. Rivers with cliffs above are also potentially dangerous due to falling rocks.

Children's behaviour may also be a problem. Skimming stones across a river may be fun but can be dangerous, hanging or swinging from overhanging trees is also problematic, while running or sliding down steep slopes or banks above the river can be lethal. Attempting to swim or boat in a river is also potentially dangerous particularly above rapids or waterfalls or in stretches of water where the river runs fast. Wading across to islands can be great fun but there is a need to be aware of fast-rising rivers particularly below dams. Also ensure that the children never have bare feet. It is better to have wet trainers than feet cut on sharp rocks or broken glass.

Preparation

It is important to be well prepared for river work. Almost inevitably someone will get wet and so a good stock of alternative clothing and footwear is vital. Cuts should be anticipated and first aid kits ready. A hot drink is also useful as is a supply of high energy food. It is useful if a pair of wellington boots is available.

Resources needed

Photocopiable sheet 129, one for each child, paper.

What to do

It is assumed that this exercise will precede a field visit to a river (or pond). Start by talking with the whole class about television reconstructions of accidents and rescues that they remember. Stress both the cause and the response to the accident. Then move on to accidents and danger in the home or on the roads. If the school has received a visit from the Road Safety Officer refer back to it.

Discuss the concept of danger and accidents and what is meant by the term 'accident prone'. Without becoming too morbid talk about accidents the children have been involved in and whose fault it was and whether anything could have been done to prevent it. Move on to the potential for accidents in the classroom and school. Try to identify the most dangerous places and the most dangerous activities and, in effect, carry out a risk assessment of the classroom or school. Discuss how accidents can be avoided and if an accident occurs what should be done.

Finally talk about the proposed visit to the river and refer to the accident potential, especially for those who cannot swim and then divide the whole class into groups of four. Distribute the photocopiable sheet 129 one for each child, and ask them to discuss and complete it in their groups.

Suggestion(s) for extension

Tell the children that are going to produce a Class Code of Practice or information poster for their river visit. To do this they will need to carry out a questionnaire survey of other children in the school to find out their opinions. Ask the children to devise the questionnaire raising issues discussed in 'Key background information' and using the 'causes, effects and responses to accidents' framework. Examples could include 'Have you ever heard of an accident in or by a river?', 'Have you ever been involved in an accident in or by a river?', 'Give me a list of three dangerous things about rivers', 'If you were taking infants to a river what would be your most important rule?'

Suggestion(s) for support

Ask the group to compose, write and send a letter to the Environment Agency, the local water company or the Royal Society for the Prevention of Accidents asking for materials on safety in rivers or arranging a visit for a speaker to talk to them about the dangers of rivers and canals. If such a visit occurred this group could be responsible for the hospitality during the visit.

Assessment opportunities

Record the responses of the children to the photocopiable sheet and observe their behaviour while on fieldwork.

Rivers

Opportunities for IT

The children could use a drawing or art package to create a poster about river safety. They could use pictures drawn from collections of clip art or retrieved from CD-ROMs to make their posters more interesting. Children may need to be shown how to use the text facilities on such software, so that they can make their message stand out clearly. Children could also use a word processor to draw up a list of river safety points.

Display ideas

Use a blown-up version of the photocopiable sheet as a centrepiece. Choose the selected dos and don'ts, and Codes of Conduct and mount these appropriately around the river diagram. In addition cut and mount the safety ideas from the Environment Agency and the Royal Society for the Prevention of Accidents. Finally attach safety labels to each of the points on the blown-up diagram.

Other aspects of the Geography PoS covered

3a, b, e; 7a, b.

Reference to photocopiable sheet

This is a drawing of a river scene which illustrates a number of potential dangers that could be encountered.

Dangers by rivers

Name ______ Date ______

All the children could be in danger of an accident.

▲ On a separate sheet of paper list the activity they are doing, why it is dangerous and what they can do to prevent these dangers.

The children have to list, on a separate sheet of paper, the activities, work out what the dangers are, and then suggest how to prevent these dangers.

The drawing comprises a river with a waterfall. Upstream the river is relatively shallow, downstream it is deeper. The far side of the river has a steep rock cliff and the near side is flat with a meadow. (3) On the cliff there is an obvious risk of rockfall. (6) There is also a large tree with branches overhanging the river and from which a child is swinging. (7) In the foreground there is an overhanging bank with a child effectively standing over the river with no support. (8) Also in the foreground the river becomes abruptly deeper just beyond where a child is wading with nothing on his feet and is entangled in weeds. (5) In the middle of the river a child is swimming in a fast current. (4) Just above the waterfall is an island on which a child is sitting having a picnic. (2) Also nearby is another child in an inflatable dingy and (1) another skimming stones from one bank to the other. (10) Upstream there is a sewage outfall pipe. (9) At another location a child is fishing with a bamboo net while another child watches intently with his eyes perilously close to the end of the bamboo pole.

Weather

During Key Stage 2 children should be taught about the weather and how it varies from place to place and with the passage of time. Work may be in the form of a discrete unit of work (or topic) or it may be taught in conjunction with other themes (for example, environmental change) or as a part of your teaching about localities.

During the Key Stage, children must learn about:

▲ how site conditions (the features of a place) can influence the weather at a local level;

▲ seasonal variations in the weather;

▲ the variations in weather conditions which exist around the world.

Study of the weather should have its root in fieldwork around the school grounds and in meaningful study of other real places (perhaps as a part of contrasting locality studies). Information technology and other sources of topical and up-to-date information about the weather should be used. Study should start with observation and recording of conditions in the school grounds and move to study through time with that of the seasons, and study across space with that of the weather in other places.

The weather is one of the most easily studied characteristics when contrasting your locality with other localities and, as a theme in itself, it is important that you provide children with opportunities to study it at a range of scales and in a range of contexts which might, for example, include learning about places in Europe.

MEASURING OUR WEATHER

To measure and record the weather at one site.

Whole class, then small groups to take measurements.

40 minutes explanation/demonstration of instruments; 10 minutes per day for one small group during survey period.

Previous skills/knowledge needed

Children should already have a basic weather vocabulary and should recognise the importance of accuracy in taking measurements and recording data.

Key background information

Temperature should be read on the Celsius scale (°C) using a large, easy to read, portable *thermometer*. Safe and good quality examples can be purchased from educational suppliers. Children will need to be taught that a thermometer must be left for a period before the temperature is read, that it should be positioned in the shade and that it should be read by positioning eye level with fluid level.

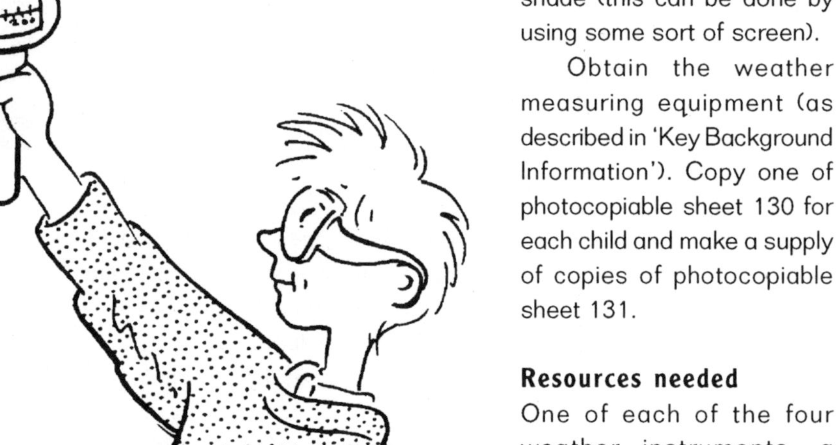

Wind speed is measured using an *anemometer*. These are usually either the rotating cup or the 'hanging flap' varieties and can be hand-held or permanently located somewhere. Inexpensive plastic anemometers are available from educational suppliers. Make sure that you understand how the recording scale works before you explain it to the children.

Plastic *wind direction indicators* (wind vanes) are also available from educational suppliers. Normally they operate using a swivel mechanism whereby a heavier large 'sail' is blown by the wind to turn a lighter pointer so that it points in the direction the wind is coming from. A southerly wind is therefore a wind coming from the south, not the other way round. A wind direction indicator must be lined up using a compass so that its compass points are aligned correctly.

A *rain gauge* is essentially a simple round container which is positioned on (or slightly buried into) the ground. It has a funnel which catches the rainfall and then channels the water to drip into a collecting vessel inside. For a serious meteorologist the circumference of the funnel is important because it determines how many raindrops actually fall into this rain guage. However, for primary children the most important factor is that it is always the same gauge which is used. A rain gauge has to be left for exactly 24 hours and then examined, emptied and reset for the next 24 hours.

Preparation

Consider your school site and think of a location which will be safe for a small group of children to visit at the same time each day to take weather measurements. This place should be away from any buildings and the ground should be as flat as possible (so as to allow accurate wind and rainfall measurements). There should be somewhere in the shade nearby or some way of producing a small amount of shade (this can be done by using some sort of screen).

Obtain the weather measuring equipment (as described in 'Key Background Information'). Copy one of photocopiable sheet 130 for each child and make a supply of copies of photocopiable sheet 131.

Resources needed

One of each of the four weather instruments, a compass for use with the wind vane, a beaker or ruler for use with the rain gauge, copies of photocopiable sheets 130 and 131 as instructed in 'Preparation' above.

What to do

Show the class the four weather measuring instruments and ask them if they know what each is and how it works. Teach the children the exact way to obtain accurate readings from each instrument emphasising the need for precision when obtaining scientific data.

Take the class out to the site you have identified as a good position for taking the measurements and explain why you have chosen it. As a group have a go at taking measurements with each instrument, giving individuals who want to a chance at trying out each one.

Back in class show the children the data recording sheet (photocopiable sheet 131) and explain how recordings can be made over a period of four weeks at a time with each sheet.

Give each child a copy of photocopiable sheet 130. The children should complete this sheet by filling in the missing words in the text, using those provided at the bottom of the sheet. The sheet can be used to assess their understanding of what each instrument is and how to use it.

The class can now be organised into a rota with groups of two, three or four taking the measurements each day and filling in the data recording sheet in use at that time. Point out that the sheet allows for measurements to be taken on Tuesdays, Wednesdays, Thursdays and Fridays, allowing the rain gauge to be set up on the Monday to give a reading on the Tuesday. Explain to the children that readings should always be taken at exactly the same time each day and the rain gauge then emptied and dried.

Once data has been collected for a period of time, the children could draw graphs to show the variations throughout the period. If the recordings are maintained throughout the school year, average readings for each half term could be compared and graphed to emphasise seasonal variation.

Suggestion(s) for extension

The children could build a simple weather station so that the thermometer, the anemometer, the wind vane and the rain gauge can be permanently left outside. A good design consists of two stakes driven into the ground with a crossbar fastened between them. The anemometer and the wind vane can be attached to the crossbar with the wind vane's direction labels aligned using a compass. The thermometer could be fastened to whichever side of one of the stakes is in the shade at the time of day that the measurements are taken.

Suggestion(s) for support

Group the children so that less confident ones are with those more able at using instruments. It may be that children could learn about one of the instruments at a time. Drawing each instrument as it is introduced can help them get used to the idea of it.

Assessment opportunities

Photocopiable sheet 130 can be used as evidence that individuals understand what each instrument is and how it is used. It is particularly useful in assessing statement 3b of the programme of study.

Opportunities for IT

The children could be given an opportunity to use a digital thermometer. They might compare the results to that of the traditional thermometer. It is possible to purchase thermometers which have the temperature sensor at the end of a wire so that it can be located outside of the classroom and left running throughout the day, and temperatures taken at regular intervals. Another approach is to use a data-logging device such as LOG IT, which will record temperature over time. This can usually be connected to the computer and the results plotted on a graph as they occur. These data-loggers can now be attached to handled computers such as the PSION so that graphs can be plotted out in the field away from any source of electricity.

A more ambitious approach is to set up an electronic weather station which will automatically record temperatures,

wind speed, rainfall, barometric pressure and humidity over time. Once the children have collected their results they can be entered into a spreadsheet or database for further work. Children could also use dedicated weather software, such as WEATHERMAPPER, to record and analyse their readings over time.

Display ideas

Make a display of the weather instruments and, when you have measurement data for a period of time, make a large version of your data collection sheet and any graphs created.

Other aspects of the Geography PoS covered

1c; 2a, b, c; 3a, b; 4; 8b.

Reference to photocopiable sheets

Photocopiable sheet 130 is used for the children to demonstrate their understanding of each type of weather instrument. Photocopiable sheet 131 is a weather data recording sheet for use over a long period of time and to allow the generation of data which can be graphed and compared across time.

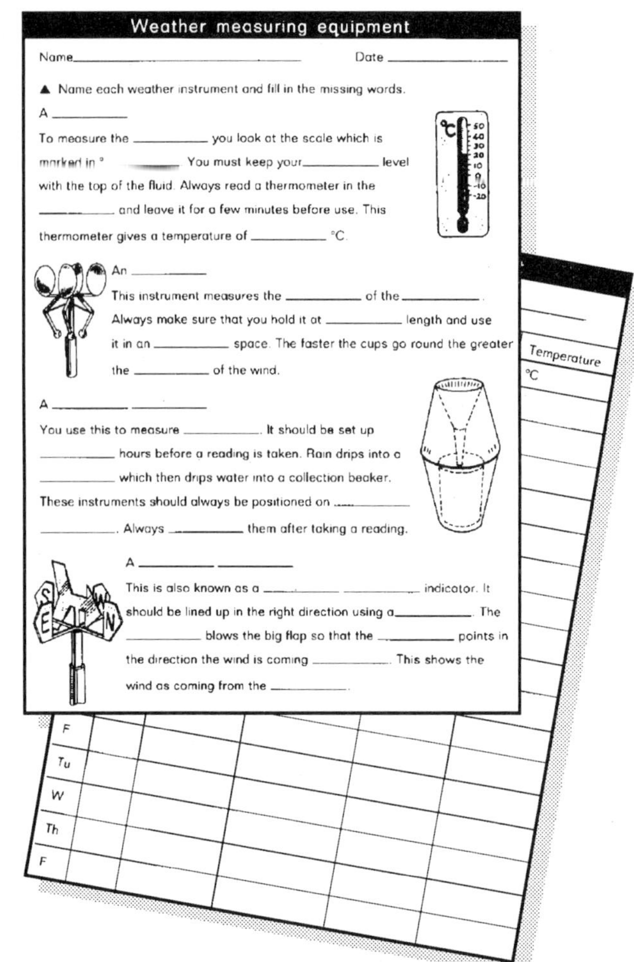

Weather measuring equipment

Name__________ Date __________

▲ Name each weather instrument and fill in the missing words.

A __________

To measure the __________ you look at the scale which is marked in ° __________. You must keep your __________ level with the top of the fluid. Always read a thermometer in the __________ and leave it for a few minutes before use. This thermometer gives a temperature of __________ °C.

An __________

This instrument measures the __________ of the __________. Always make sure that you hold it at __________ length and use it in an __________ space. The faster the cups go round the greater the __________ of the wind.

A __________ __________

You use this to measure __________. It should be set up __________ hours before a reading is taken. Rain drips into a __________ which then drips water into a collection beaker. These instruments should always be positioned on __________ __________. Always __________ them after taking a reading.

A __________ __________

This is also known as a __________ __________ indicator. It should be lined up in the right direction using a __________. The __________ blows the big flap so that the __________ points in the direction the wind is coming __________. This shows the wind as coming from the __________.

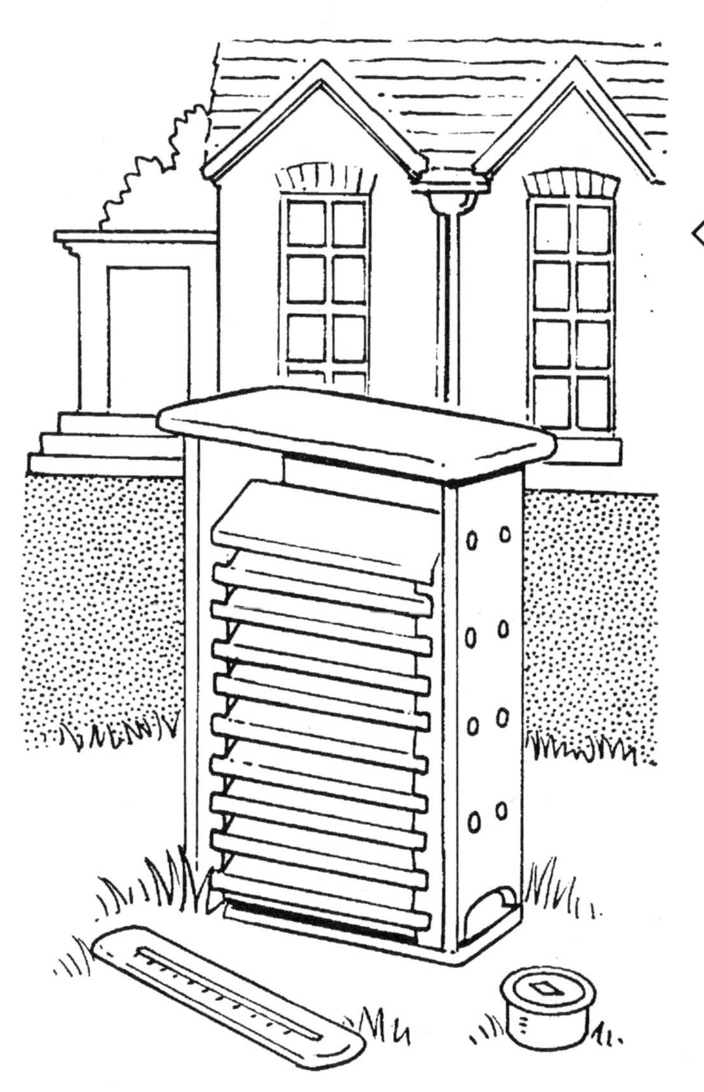

OUR LOCAL WEATHER

To understand that different places within a small area can experience variations in weather conditions.

Whole class divided into eight groups.

30 minutes introduction; 20 minutes photocopiable sheet activity; 10 minutes recording at the same time of the day over a period of two weeks; 20 minutes photocopiable sheet completion.

Previous skills/knowledge needed

Children should be capable of using a thermometer, a wind speed gauge (anemometer), a wind direction indicator (wind vane), a rain gauge, and they will need to be able to use a simple light meter such as used by a photographer (most 'through the lens [TTL]' cameras have a simple display version of one of these when you look through the viewfinder). These skills can be taught or improved as a part of this activity.

They will need to read where south is using a magnetic compass and will need simple map-reading skills.

Key background information

The five most easily taught, understood and useful weather variables in the primary school are those of temperature, wind speed (or strength), wind direction, rainfall and level of light. For information on the first four of these see 'Key background information' in the activity 'Measuring our weather' (on page 64).

Meteorologists like to measure cloud cover, sunshine readings and light levels to help them build up a picture of the weather and how it changes over time. An easy way for primary children to measure these sorts of variables is to point a light gauge due south at the same place at exactly the same time each day and to take recordings accordingly. Photographic light meters can be used for this, or a 'through the lens' camera always set to the same aperture (f number), pointed directly south, set on a platform (like a window ledge) and the shutter speed read from the scale seen inside the view finder.

Preparation

Gather the five items of weather recording equipment listed above. Ideally you will need two of each, but you must have at least two rain gauges. Obtain or make a large scale plan of your school and its grounds.

Resources needed

The weather instruments (see 'Previous skills/knowledge needed'), a large scale map of the school, a magnetic compass, a clipboard, graph paper, copies of photocopiable sheet 132 for each child and at least eight copies of photocopiable sheet 133.

What to do

Show the children the large scale map of the school and its grounds and discuss places where weather conditions might vary at the same time. Look for places which contrast.

- ▲ windy places/places sheltered from the prevailing (usual direction of the) wind;
- ▲ sun traps/places normally sheltered from the sun.

Introduce the children to the weather recording instruments and take some time to explain each one and to demonstrate how to use them. The amount of time needed for this will depend on the children's previous experiences.

Explain that the class is going to record the temperature, wind speed, wind direction, rainfall and light level in two different locations around your school grounds. Discuss with the children which locations would be good ones and get them to explain why. It might be that you would like to take the children on a short walk around the school grounds to select your two locations. One important selection criterion is that both locations must be capable of accommodating a rain gauge overnight. Explain to the children that they will measure the weather on Tuesday, Wednesday, Thursday and Friday of the same week. This is because the rain gauge needs emptying and drying 24 hours before any measurements are taken (and thus will need to be reset on Monday ready for Tuesday's reading). Agree on the exact time each day that the measurements will be taken (morning playtime is often a good time).

Once the locations have been selected, distribute copies of photocopiable sheet 132 and ask the children to complete the first section saying how they think each weather category will differ between the two locations and why.

Put the children into eight groups and designate each group the job of measuring the five weather criteria in one of the locations on one of the survey days. When it is a group's turn, they complete the relevant section of photocopiable sheet 133. The other groups copy details after each reading has been taken until, by the end of the Friday, each group's sheet is completed.

To finish the activity each child completes the second section of photocopiable sheet 132 saying whether their predictions were correct and explaining the final results.

Suggestion(s) for extension

Children could consider how people in and around the school adapt their actions because of variations in site conditions. Ask them to write a list of examples of this, for example:

- ▲ places suitable for a summer afternoon outdoor story;
- ▲ good places to dry the netball team's wet games kit;
- ▲ a good place for the milk to be left in the morning.

Suggestion(s) for support

Mix your eight groups by ability. Make sure that you are present for the first two recording times to ensure that the children have understood how to use the instruments, and then delegate a child or children who have understood well to act as peer tutors for the other groups. Be prepared to provide particular support when less able children are writing their explanations of differences in their readings.

Assessment opportunities

Photocopiable sheet 132 should provide you with evidence that the children have understood how site conditions can influence the weather.

Opportunities for IT

The children could use any of the equipment discussed in the previous the activity on page 64 for this work. Additionally, where they are using data-logging equipment, a light sensor can be set up to record light levels.

Two spreadsheets could be set up displaying the readings at each site and comparing them.

Display ideas

Display all of the instruments with explanations by the children as to how they are used. Display the children's result of their weather recording with the instruments and an explanation of the differences found in the two locations.

Other aspects of the Geography PoS covered

1b, c; 2a, b, c; 3a, b; 4.

Reference to photocopiable sheets

Photocopiable sheet 132 is used by the children to make predictions of the outcome of their comparison of five weather criteria in two different locations. They complete the second part of the sheet after they have finished their observations saying whether their predictions were correct and explaining any discrepancies.

Photocopiable sheet 133 is used to record the weather conditions in the two locations over a period of four days.

Two places

Name ______ Date ______

Sampling locations

1 ______ 2 ______

Before you have taken all your readings

Which location will have:

highest temperature ______ lowest temperature ______

highest wind speed ______ lowest wind speed ______

highest rainfall ______ lowest rainfall ______

brightest light levels ______ dullest light levels ______

In which direction do you think the wind will be blowing:

in location A ______: in location B ______?

Say why you expect these findings:

After you have taken all your readings

Were your findings correct? ______

What differences were there to your findings? ______

temperature ______

wind speed ______

rainfall ______

light levels ______

wind direction ______

Explain any differences:

Friday	temperature		
	wind speed		
	wind direction		
	rainfall		
	light level		

SEASONAL WEATHER GRAPHS

To recognise patterns in how the weather varies over the course of a year.

Pairs.

20 minutes introduction; 40 minutes graphing activity; 20 minutes drawing activity.

Previous skills/knowledge needed

Children should have knowledge of the main types of weather prevalent in Britain (mild, damp weather and cold or warm, dry weather).

Key background information

Pattern is very important to the geographer and is particularly so in the context of weather study. It is the fact that the weather behaves according to patterns that makes forecasting it possible. The *weather* is what the atmospheric conditions are in a place at a moment in time. That place's *climate* is its long-term prevailing weather conditions and is a result of several factors including latitude, altitude, proximity to large bodies of water, and aspect (which direction a slope faces).

The *seasons* are a complex result of the fact that the earth's axis is tilted (meaning that when the northern hemisphere is near to the sun, the southern hemisphere is further away and that when one position on the Earth has a summer, its antipodes – point on the opposite side of the planet – has a winter) and the fact that the Earth's orbit is eliptical.

It is important that children recognise the seasonal patterns which exist in the weather.

Preparation

Obtain precipitation (rainfall), sunshine and temperature figures for your region for the period of one year. These can be obtained from your local 'Weather Centre', by asking for information from the Meteorological Office, by contacting a local Meteorological Association, your local secondary school's or university's geography department, or by searching local records or the Internet. Present this information in a way that the children will be able to interpret and make copies of it.

Resources needed

Copies of data on precipitation, sunshine and temperature for your region (see 'Preparation'), drawing materials, copies of photocopiable sheet 134 for each pair, paper.

What to do

Discuss the difference between the terms 'weather', 'climate' and 'seasons', and ask children to describe the seasons in the area that you live.

Show the children the data you have obtained on precipitation, sunshine and temperature for your region and explain that they are going to design three time lines to demonstrate the seasonal variations in weather conditions. Explain that they are also going to draw a time-line picture montage to show the changing weather for a year in their region.

Give each pair a copy of photocopiable sheet 134 and a copy of the weather data. Help the children to decide on a number system for the three vertical scales which is appropriate to the data you have. Each pair of children now completes the three graphs using the data and then draws a line connecting each of the marks they have put on to the graphs. The children should now draw (on a separate sheet of paper) pictures to show a 'good' day and a 'bad' day for each of the seasons. Each of these pictures will illustrate typical weather conditions at that time of year.

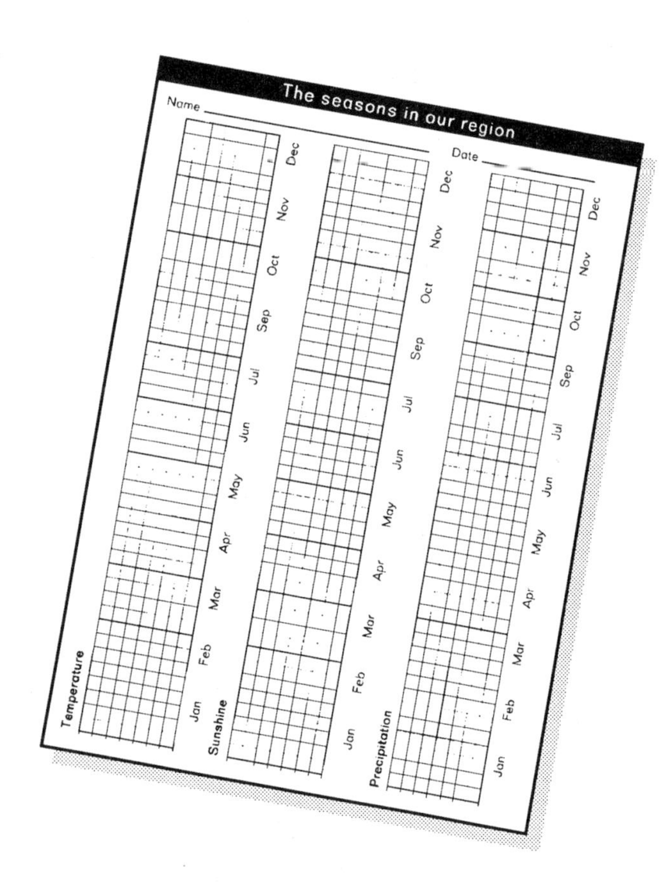
The seasons in our region

Name

Date

Temperature: Jan Feb Mar Apr May Jun Jul Sep Oct Nov Dec

Sunshine: Jan Feb Mar Apr May Jun Jul Sep Oct Nov Dec

Precipitation: Jan Feb Mar Apr May Jun Jul Sep Oct Nov Dec

Suggestion(s) for extension

In your search for weather data, you might have obtained additional information. This might include wind speed, wind direction, air pressure or humidity data. Children capable of doing so could graph this data in a similar way to that used in the main activity. They should then be able to compare this data with the rest of the data already graphed. They might find, for example, that high wind speeds and wind from the south west correspond to occasions when there is wet weather.

Suggestion(s) for support

If individuals are having problems with transferring your data on to the graphs, either pair the children so at least one child will be capable of doing this, or work with pairs in difficulty yourself, perhaps doing the precipitation graph as a group before the pairs, then attempt to graph the other two data sets.

Assessment opportunities

Ask targeted individuals to talk you through their completed photocopiable sheet and to explain the drawings they have done on their separate sheet of paper. They should be able to demonstrate understanding of the seasonal weather patterns in your region.

Opportunities for IT

The tabular format of a spreadsheet makes this an ideal tool for entering and analysing this kind of information. The children could work in groups to record the information on a spreadsheet over the year. They will need to know how to move around the spreadsheet, scrolling the screen and correcting mistakes they may make. Older children can be shown how to enter formulae to calculate averages, totals and the range of readings for any periods of time.

The graphical facilities of the spreadsheet can also be used to plot the graphs. If daily data is available the spreadsheet could show these readings in one column with monthly totals, averages and ranges in adjacent columns.

Display ideas

Discuss the completed picture lines that the children have drawn. Share the different ideas that children have used in their drawing and ask the class to choose the most successful images for each of the seasons. Now ask groups of children to create large paintings, drawings or collages of these pictures. Each one could be on A3 or even A2 paper. Display these drawings in order as a wall display and add a large version of the three graphs with an explanation.

Other aspects of the Geography PoS covered

1c; 2c; 3a, e; 4.

Reference to photocopiable sheet

Photocopiable sheet 134 is used by the children to transfer local weather data provided by you on to graphs. The class will have to decide on the scale intervals for the vertical scale.

SEASONS AROUND THE WORLD

To recognise that seasonal weather patterns vary around the world.

Whole class divided into 10 small groups for research part of activity.

20 minutes demonstration and discussion; 40–60 minutes research activity; 10 minutes concluding discussion.

Previous skills/knowledge needed
Children should be used to carrying out research using non-fiction books, computer software or the Internet. They should be practised in using atlases.

Key background information
Children find it hard to fully understand how it can be summer in New Zealand while it is winter in Great Britain. This is a result of the tilt of the Earth's axis (23.5°) and the Earth's elliptical orbit around the sun, and how more sunlight hits one part of the Earth at a given point in time than at a point on the opposite side of the planet.

Children also need some help to understand that seasonal variation combines with factors like latitude, altitude and the physical shape of the land, proximity to large masses of water and the behaviour of air masses in ensuring that different parts of the world have their own climates. A place's climate is its characteristic weather over long periods of time.

Preparation
Collect a supply of books and other materials about places around the world, their climates and weather. Obtain a globe which can be rotated on a stand and a supply of atlases.

Resources needed
The selection of resource material on other places around the world, a globe, atlases, copies of photocopiable sheet 135 for each group and 136 for each child.

What to do
Place the children into groups. Discuss how the seasons are different around the world at any point in time. Distribute copies of photocopiable sheet 135 and use the small diagram and the globe to explain how the tilt of the Earth means that when it is summer in Europe it is winter in Oceania.

Discuss the world map on the same sheet. This map shows the five main climatic zones of the world (although experts divide these down into at least 12 zones normally). The zones are:

▲ Tropical (can be sub-divided into Equatorial rain forest, Monsoon and Tropical rain savannah);
▲ Dry (can be sub-divided into Desert and Steppe);
▲ Warm temperate (can be sub-divided into Dry summer, Dry winter and Rain in all seasons);
▲ Cool temperate (can be sub-divided into Dry winter and Rain in all seasons);
▲ Cold (can be sub-divided into Highland and Polar).

Now explain that each group has to work as a team to complete photocopiable sheet 136 which asks them to find out about the weather in at least two places within each of the five zones on the map. For each of the five zones they have to decide on two places which are within that zone, name them, and then write a brief account of what the weather is like in the summer and the winter in each place. The children could work in ten small groups of two, three or four children with two groups researching each of the climate zones. (Therefore, four places for each zone will have been studied.)

Once all of the groups have completed the research on

the two places in their zone ask the children to move around the classroom pairing up with those who have done other zones and 'swapping' information until they have filled in all of their sheet. Conclude the activity with a brief class discussion and emphasise the fact that the climate is very variable in some parts of the world (for example, in Britain's warm, temperate zone), less variable in others (such as desert areas) and how the weather varies from season to season around the world.

Suggestion(s) for extension

The children could research why the climate differs in the areas they have chosen (because of maritime influences/high altitude/proximity to a pole and so on). They could write this information up to accompany their completed copy of photocopiable sheet 136.

Suggestion(s) for support

Finding places in the books and other source materials may be difficult for some children. If this is likely to be the case spend some time in preparation looking through the resources yourself and identifying places around the world which satisfy the activity requirements. You could write the names of these places on the board leaving the children to assign each to the correct zone and then complete the rest of the activity.

Climate map of the world

▲ Colour the key and then the map to show the five climatic zones.

Key: 1 Pink – Tropical; 2 Orange – Dry; 3 Green – Warm temperate; 4 Blue – Cool temperate; 5 Purple – Cold

How the angled axis of the Earth causes the seasons to be different in the northern and southern hemispheres

Assessment opportunities

Sit with any child (or a group of children) you wish to assess and talk about the results of the activity. Ask the child to explain what the seasons are like in each of the five places studied and note any verbal evidence that the child understands how seasonal weather patterns vary between places. The photocopiable sheet could be used again to assist in your assessment of the children's understanding.

Opportunities for IT

The children could use encyclopaedia CD-ROMs or specific CD-ROMs about the weather, or the Internet to research information about different climatic regions. The information could be processed and presented using a word processor. Alternatively children could combine their information to make a class book about the weather using a desktop publishing package, or a multimedia presentation using authoring software.

If the school has access to an Internet link the children can use e-mail to swap weather information with schools around the world.

Display ideas

Position two globes either side of an orange, yellow or red ball which represents the sun. Angle the Earth's axis the same way on both of the globes so that the first has the south pole nearer the sun and the second has the north pole nearer. Make four large, movable labels saying 'winter in Britain', 'summer in New Zealand', 'winter in New Zealand' and 'summer in Britain' and then write instructions asking the viewer to place the two correct labels next to the relevant globes. (The first two labels should be with the first [left] of the globes).

The children's completed work and a world map could be displayed on the wall behind the table display.

Other aspects of the Geography PoS covered

1a, b, c, d; 3a, d, e; 8c.

Reference to photocopiable sheets

Photocopiable sheet 135 provides a diagrammatic explanation of how the seasons are different in different parts of the world at the same point in time. It also contains a map showing the world's five main climatic zones which the children colour in. They use resource materials together with this map to help them complete photocopiable sheet 136 with information about the weather in summer and in winter, in two world locations in each of these five climatic zones.

OUR WEATHER CORRESPONDENT

To recognise that weather conditions vary around the world and that they can be extreme in nature.

Whole class divided into eight small groups.

10 minutes introduction; 30 minutes group research; 20 minutes group presentation planning; 5 minutes presentation and discussion time per group.

Previous skills/knowledge needed

Children should be used to working co-operatively in small groups. They need to have interrogated source materials such as reference books, atlases, computer sources such as CD-ROM and ideally the worldwide web on the Internet. They should be used to creating and making role-play presentations.

Key background information

Climate varies enormously around the world and depends upon, among other factors, a locality's seasonality, latitude, altitude and the physical shape of the land, proximity to large masses of water and the behaviour of air masses in its region.

Some parts of the world experience what, by our terms, can be extreme conditions in the weather. A hurricane is an extreme version of a tropical storm. It is a spiralling vortex centred on a system of low atmospheric pressure and its winds can massively exceed 120km/hour (approx. 75mph). Hurricanes start over areas of tropical ocean and move inland, eventually losing their power but causing terrible damage as they travel.

Monsoon rain is the rain that falls in a monsoon region. These are regions where there are very distinct wet and dry seasons as a result of the movement of the inter-tropical convergence zone (an area of low pressure over the equator). This movement causes warm, moist air to be drawn in from the oceans, rise and then fall as precipitation during one part of the year, and then very dry air to move in the opposite direction during the other part of the year.

Hot desert weather, such as that experienced in areas of low latitude like the Sahara, is very dry and very hot. The heat is a result of a large area of land being close to the equator and this causes low rainfall by attracting very large high pressure weather systems.

Heavy snowfall is experienced mainly in high latitudes and high altitudes as a result of low temperatures. Snow is solid precipitation which has formed at temperatures below freezing point.

Preparation

Collect source materials on extremes in weather around the world and (ideally) open computer software about the world's weather or log your computer on to a search engine on the worldwide web. Obtain a large world wall map.

Resources needed

Source materials on world weather (which may include computer software or the Internet), a large world wall map, one copy of photocopiable sheet 137 for each child.

What to do

Discuss the extremes which can exist in the world's weather and, using the world map, identify parts of the world where such extremes might be found.

Divide the class into eight small groups and assign each group one of the following types of extreme weather condition:

▲ hurricane
▲ monsoon rainfall
▲ hot, dry desert weather
▲ heavy snow

Each weather type will be assigned to two groups.

Now ask each group to complete photocopiable sheet 137 to help them in preparing a three minute documentary about their weather type. The sheet encourages each group to base their documentary on real places around the world and, if possible, on real examples of occasions when hazardous weather has affected a locality.

The children will need some support in finding their information and may find certain computer software, especially CD-ROM programs, as helpful. If the children have access to a computer connected to the Internet they will find large quantities of information using an educational search engine (see 'Preparation').

Once groups have completed their research they spend some time planning the documentary-style television presentation on their subject. You may need to discuss documentary programmes the children have seen to help them understand what is required. They decide who is presenting which parts of their 'programme' and they make any necessary visual aids.

Each group then presents their documentary. Actually filming the finished results using a video camera can greatly help in focusing the children's efforts and produce an interesting (and entertaining) result.

It is often worth following each presentation with a short question and answer session as this will give other members of the class a chance to talk about each weather condition.

Weather documentary planning sheet

Name
Date
Programme planning team:
Weather type* – Hurricane/Monsoon rainfall/Hot, dry desert/Heavy snow
*ring the subject of this programme
World locations where this weather is found.
Explanation of the weather type.
Real examples of this type of weather being hazardous.
1
2

Suggestion(s) for extension

Some children enjoy and are capable of careful and extensive research, and they should be encouraged. Ask such children to produce a 'programme guide' or accompanying booklet about the weather condition.

Suggestion(s) for support

It is easy for less confident children to get 'lost' in a group research situation. If this is likely it is a good idea for you to intervene and designate such children specific lines of research and a specific role in the completed programme.

Assessment opportunities

Have a role in a question-and-answer session at the end of each presentation to monitor whether targeted children have fully understood the way that certain regions of the world are prone to extreme weather conditions.

Opportunities for IT

The children could use a word processor to help them present their information about a particular weather type. They could also use it to write the script or handout for their presentation, and then overhead transparencies could be produced using either a word processor or desktop publishing package. The presentation could include pages saved from the Internet or film clips from suitable CD-ROMs displayed on the computer monitor. An electronic presentation could be made using an authoring package. This would include text, pictures, moving images, and even sounds.

Children could use a word processor to write their own weather forecasts in the genre of a weather report. They may need to listen to some radio broadcasts or read some newspaper forecasts to get a feel for the style and language that should be used.

Display ideas

Each group can make a wall and/or table top display using any visual aids they have used and incorporate books which cover the weather type they have studied. The large world wall map could be a focus for this display. If the completed presentations were filmed, you could incorporate a video player and a television monitor with an instruction card on how to play and then rewind the tape.

Other aspects of the Geography PoS covered

1a, d; 2a, b, c; 3a, e, f; 8.

Reference to photocopiable sheet

Photocopiable sheet 137 is used by children in each group to focus their research about an extreme weather condition. It also takes the form of a 'weather documentary planning sheet' to help the children plan a documentary-style television presentation about their group's weather type.

Settlements

During Key Stage 2 children should come to understand how settlements vary and how they change through time. Settlements may be studied through a discrete unit of work (or topic), they may be studied in conjunction with other themes (for example, environmental change), or as a part of your teaching about localities. Children must learn:

▲ how settlements vary in size;

▲ that economic activities in settlements affect their location and what they are like;

▲ that land in settlements is used in different ways;

▲ about a real issue resulting from how land is used in one or more settlements.

Teaching about settlements provides the teacher with an excellent opportunity to concentrate on human geography and to involve the children in learning about their own settlement using first-hand experience and developing their fieldwork skills. The children should learn about other settlements in the UK and the rest of Europe.

Learning can be greatly enhanced if the children address real topical issues within their own or other localities and the National Curriculum stipulates that they should examine a real land-use issue. The temptation with settlement study is to rely almost exclusively on teaching about your own. It is hoped that while this chapter may assist in doing this, it also encourages teaching which refers to a range of contrasting settlements. Teaching about your own settlement should involve the children in developing a broader geographical awareness.

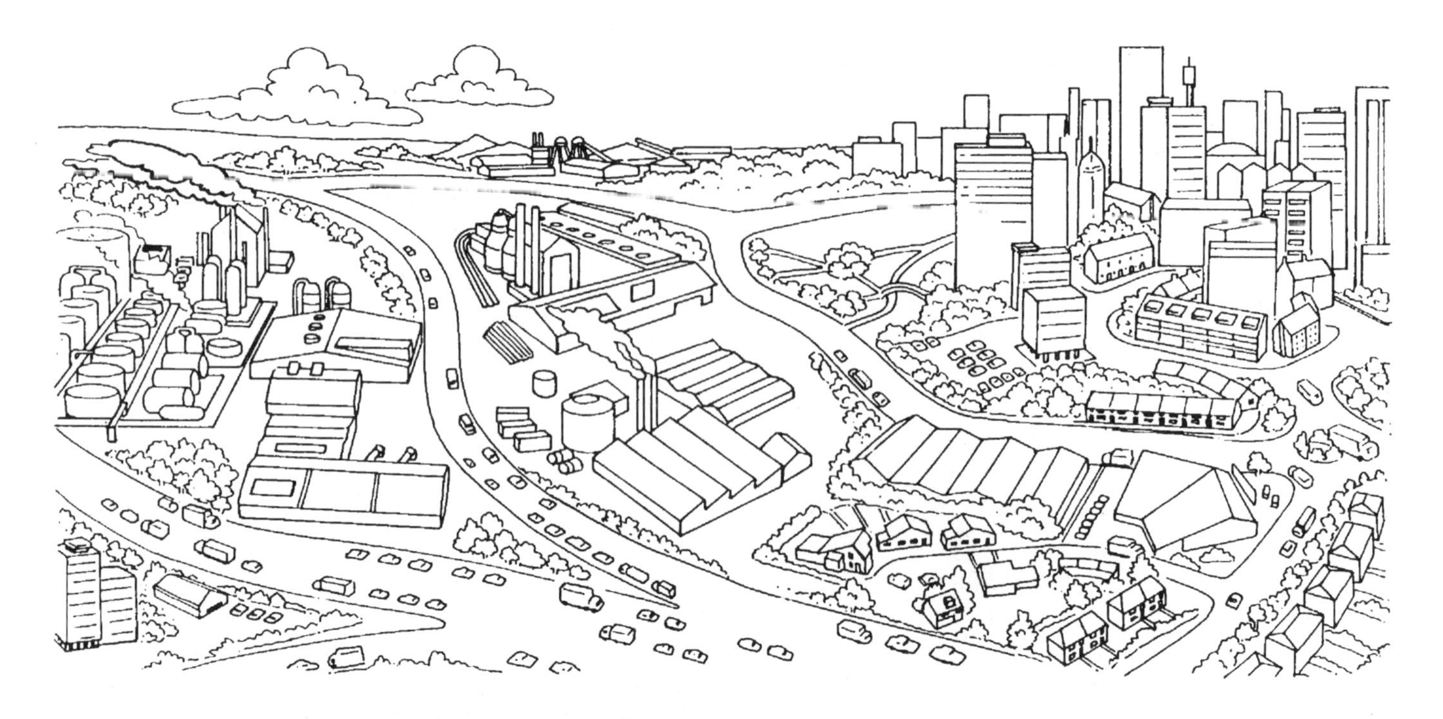

VILLAGE, TOWN OR CITY

To recognise that settlements vary in size.

Pairs.

15 minutes discussion; 25 minutes paired road atlas activity.

Previous skills/knowledge needed

Children should have been introduced to work on area in their mathematics work. They will need to know how to transfer a positive version of a traced image to another piece of paper by using pencil to copy the image on to the other side of the tracing paper, and then shading hard on the first side to push the pencil on to the paper.

Key background information

Settlements vary in size from the single rural house or cottage through to the world's largest urban conurbations (large areas of cities which have joined together). Children need to learn that people live in groups for all sorts of reasons and there are both advantages and disadvantages to communal living. Learning about settlements is made much easier if there is an agreed vocabulary referring to types of settlement. Generally, most people understand that between the single house and the conurbation there are hamlets, villages, towns and cities. Children must come to fully understand what these common terms mean (although there is much disagreement about strict definitions, such as 'a city needing a Cathedral').

Loosely speaking, a *hamlet* is a small collection of buildings, often centred around one farm with maybe three or four additional houses or cottages. A village is identifiably larger than this and has service functions to it such as a public house, a church, a village hall and a shop. A *town* has multiple versions of these service functions and in itself has a reason for being, in addition to simply being a grouping of houses for agricultural, forestry, fishing or mining workers, for example. It may be an agricultural market town or be (or have been) the centre for an industry. A *city* is a complex and noticeably larger settlement which combines numerous industrial, commercial and other reasons for existing and has a complex set of services to support it.

Preparation

Collect a selection of maps of different parts of Britain which are all at the same scale and preferably from the same survey. The easiest way of doing this is to gather together a selection of road atlases with scales of approximately 1:200 000 (often referred to on the cover as 3 miles to 1 inch). Ideally aim to provide one road atlas per pair of children. Collect together a supply of A4 tracing paper.

Resources needed

A selection of road atlases, a supply of A4 tracing paper, drawing and writing materials, copies of photocopiable sheets 138 and 139 for each child.

What to do

Show the children the atlases they are going to be using. Ask one of the children, using a page at random, if she can point to an area which is obviously built-up and then to an area which is not built-up. Use this as a starting point for a discussion about different types of settlement and ask the children what settlement types they know of. Hopefully they will volunteer words like 'village', 'town' and 'city'. Now go on to discuss the difficulties in deciding where a settlement finishes and the surrounding countryside begins – made particularly difficult by the spread of the suburbs and by what is often referred to as urban 'sprawl'.

Tell the children that despite these problems they are going to have to identify the limits of different settlements and draw a boundary line for their edges. The children will need to discuss how they decide on the bounds of their chosen settlements. It can prove useful to stop and have a group discussion at this time. Share out the atlases and explain that they can work with any settlements so long as the scale is kept the same for each of the four settlements they are going to trace. Now challenge each child to identify one city, one town, one village and one hamlet.

Distribute tracing paper and ask the children to place it over the settlement they are going to trace first and then to draw a line around what to them seems like the most obvious 'edge' to the settlement. The children do this for all four sizes of settlement and then turn over what will now be their pencil line 'circuits', and draw over their pencil marks on the other side of the paper. Next, they place their pencil drawn circuit (the correct way up) of one hamlet and one city onto photocopiable sheet 138 and the pencil drawn circuit (the correct way up) of one village and one town onto photocopiable sheet 139. Once they have positioned each 'circuit', they shade hard over the pencil lines to transfer the pencil from the other side of the sheet to the surface of the photocopiable sheet.

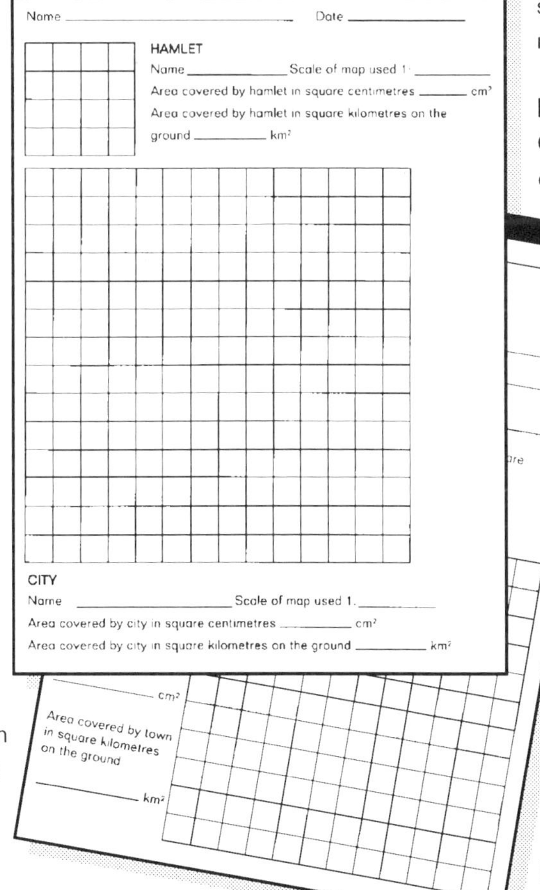

Hamlet and city

Name ____________ Date ____________

HAMLET

Name ____________ Scale of map used 1: ____________

Area covered by hamlet in square centimetres ______ cm²

Area covered by hamlet in square kilometres on the ground ______ km²

CITY

Name ____________ Scale of map used 1: ____________

Area covered by city in square centimetres ______ cm²

Area covered by city in square kilometres on the ground ______ km²

______ cm²

Area covered by town in square kilometres on the ground

______ km²

They complete the rest of the sheets by filling in the name of each settlement and the number of 1cm² squares it covers (adding together pairs of half squares to make whole ones), which will give the area in square centimetres on the map that each settlement covers.

Using the information in the atlas that each child has worked from you can then help them to work out the real area covered by the settlement on the ground. An example for an atlas mapped at 1:200 000 is: 1cm on the map will be 2km on the ground; or 1cm² on the map will be 4km² on the ground.

Suggestion(s) for extension

Children could go further than simply measuring the area of the ground which different settlements cover and go some way to describe the characteristics of the settlements. They could draw onto their outline maps of the four settlements the location of any roads, major buildings and other landmarks which are shown on the original map they were working from. This would help develop their understanding of the differences between settlements of different sizes.

Suggestion(s) for support

Put the children into mixed ability pairs so that a more able child can support a less able one with the technical business of tracing the different settlements and transferring the pencil marks from one surface to the other.

Assessment opportunities

Ask the children to carry out the activity as individuals and then use the completed photocopiable sheets as evidence that they can select settlements from a map according to whether they are hamlets, villages, towns or cities.

Opportunities for IT

The children could use a word processor to create labels for the class display of the work. Extra information about the places could be added to the labels, such as population, grid reference, special features about the place. The children can experiment with appropriate fonts and sizes to make sure that the labels can be read from a distance.

Display ideas

Children could trace their settlement outlines onto coloured paper (say yellow for hamlets, green for villages, blue for towns and red for cities) and then cut them out. An effective display can be made by sticking the same coloured outlines in groups under the headings 'hamlets', 'villages', towns' and 'cities' on a wall display and then printing out each settlement's name on the computer. These name labels can be linked to their corresponding outline by threads, or simply placed directly beneath them.

Other aspects of the Geography PoS covered

1a, c, d; 3a, d, e.

Reference to photocopiable sheets

Photocopiable sheets 138 and 139 have 1cm² grids on them and spaces for the children to trace outlines of a hamlet and a city (sheet 138) and a village and a town (sheet 139). Once the outlines of the settlements have been traced, the children calculate the area that the settlement covers on paper and then the area that it actually covers on the ground.

TYPES OF SETTLEMENT

To understand that the characteristics and locations of settlements reflect the types of economic activity present.

Individuals (best worked in table groups).

15 minutes discussion and examination of maps; 30–40 minutes map and photocopiable sheet activity.

Previous skills/knowledge needed

Children will need to understand the meaning of the terms 'town' and 'city' and they should be used to working with the 1:50 000 Ordnance Survey 'Landranger' series of maps.

Key background information

Towns and cities exist where they do and have the character that they have for a range of historical reasons. The economic activities that take place in a settlement are often very largely responsible for the location of that settlement in the first place and the way it has grown. The following are some of the most easily identifiable reasons for settlements having grown in the UK.

▲ Communication-oriented settlement: on an historic cross-roads or the lowest bridging point of a river.
▲ Market settlement: a market focus for a dairy region or a cereal crop region.
▲ Ancient defensive settlement: on the highest point of an area or at a point protected by a bend in the river.
▲ A port: a fishing harbour, a minor coastal port or an international terminal.
▲ A mining settlement: a coalfield pit-head settlement or the focus of a mineral region.
▲ A manufacturing settlement: a settlement which has developed an expertise in making certain products.
▲ A resort: a seaside resort, a settlement in a national park or a ski resort.

Some settlements have other origin factors (for example, monastic settlements, garrison towns). Any one village, town or city may have several of these factors at the root of its growth, but many settlements will exhibit one factor as centrally important in their development.

Preparation

Collect as many copies of local sheets of the 1:50 000 'Landranger' Ordnance Survey series of maps as possible. Ideally, the maps will include your local area and other surrounding areas. You should make sure that you include maps which cover urban, rural, inland and coastal areas.

Resources needed

Several different Ordnance Survey 1:50 000 'Landranger' map sheets (see 'Preparation'), a copy of photocopiable sheet 140 for each child, writing materials.

What to do

Share out the map sheets and give the children a little time to look at them, to discover which part of the country or area the sheet they have been given covers, and to discover anything interesting or unusual which exists in the area they are looking at. Tell the children that the map they are looking at (so long as it is a complete 'Landranger' sheet) covers an area which is 40km x 40km or 1600km^2 and, therefore, it will include a lot of settlements of different sizes.

Give each child a copy of the photocopiable sheet and talk through the different types of settlement which are shown in each of the maps. Ask them to talk through the different shapes of each of the settlement types shown on the sheet. Ask individuals if they can explain why each of the settlement types developed and if they know of anywhere which is like any of the places on the sheet.

Now ask the children to look at their Ordnance Survey maps again and to try to identify settlements of each of the types on the photocopiable sheet as instructed. The children will benefit from sharing the collection of Ordnance Survey map sheets around so that, for instance, they all see a sheet with a seaside resort on it.

Settlements

Suggestion(s) for extension

Encourage the children to realise that most settlements have, in fact, a complex mix of factors leading to their existence. A port may also be an old defensive settlement (for example, Dover), or a manufacturing settlement may also be a communication-oriented one (for example, Widnes). Ask them to choose two or three of the settlements they have identified from the map, to draw a simplified map of each one (using the style on the photocopiable sheet) and then to write an explanation of the factors which have contributed to that town's location and characteristics.

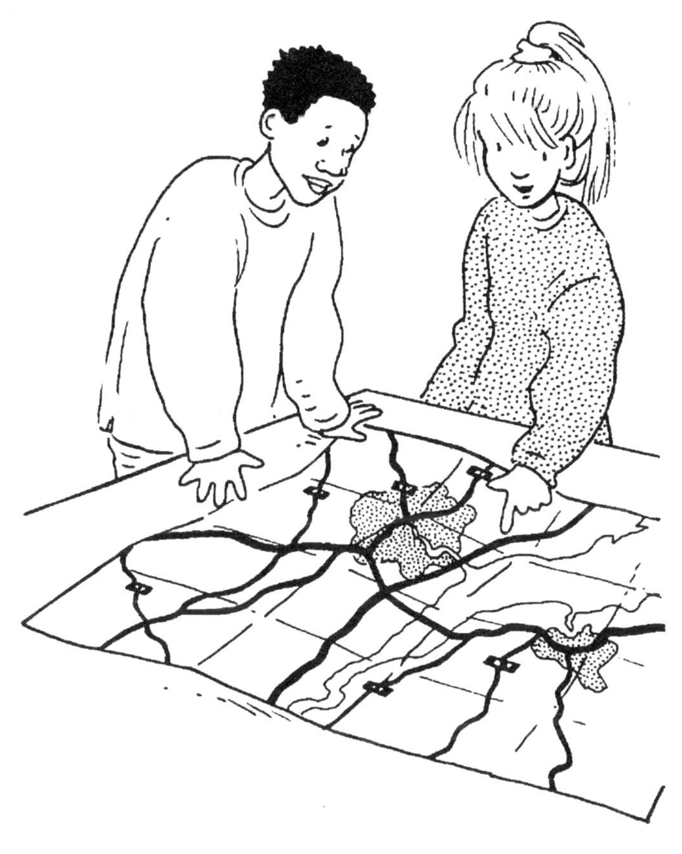

Suggestion(s) for support

You could identify on the map sheets, one good example of each of the seven types of settlement on the photocopiable sheet (ideally, one settlement on each of seven different map sheets) and circle them with a pencil. The children then only have to decide which settlement type on the photocopiable sheet is which of the settlements you have ringed on the maps.

Assessment opportunities

Use the completed sheets as evidence that individuals recognise that the characteristics and locations of settlements reflect the types of economic activity in them.

Opportunities for IT

The children could set up a simple database to record the class work on settlement types. The database could simply contain the following fields:

Name	Dover
Location	Inland/Coast
Communication	yes
Market	no
Defensive	yes
Port	yes
Mining	no
Manufacturing	no
Resort	no

An alternative would be to use a database with tokenised fields so that all of these settlement options could be available and the children select those that apply: For example:

Name	Dover
Location	Coast
Type	Port/Defensive

The children could then search for towns which have a particular category, for example, those on the coast which are not ports. The children can then use the database's graphical facilities to present their information.

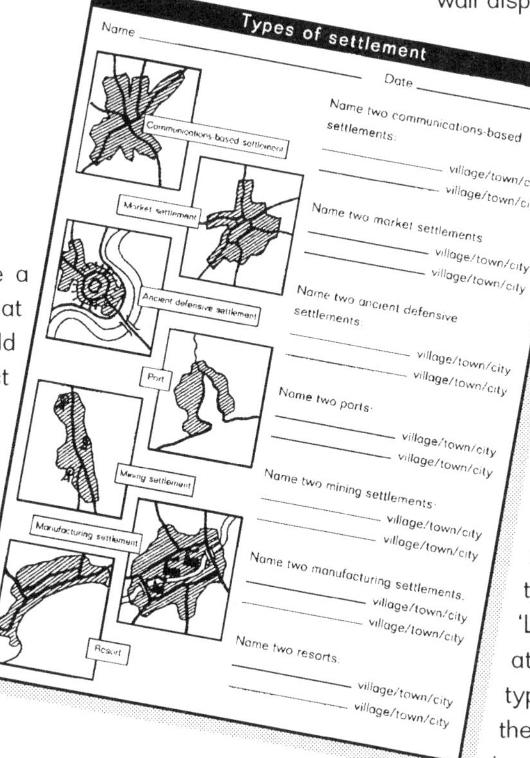

Types of settlement

Name ______________________ Date ______________

Communications based settlement

Market settlement

Ancient defensive settlement

Port

Mining settlement

Manufacturing settlement

Resort

Name two communications-based settlements:
______________ village/town/city
______________ village/town/city

Name two market settlements
______________ village/town/city
______________ village/town/city

Name two ancient defensive settlements
______________ village/town/city
______________ village/town/city

Name two ports:
______________ village/town/city
______________ village/town/city

Name two mining settlements:
______________ village/town/city
______________ village/town/city

Name two manufacturing settlements.
______________ village/town/city
______________ village/town/city

Name two resorts:
______________ village/town/city
______________ village/town/city

Display ideas

Choose two or three settlements in your area which exhibit some of the factors demonstrated on photocopiable sheet 140 and ask the children to help you make large simplified wall display maps of them. Make large labels with each settlement's name and each of the reasons for its location and shape. Write instructions for the viewer of the display telling them to decide which labels go with which settlement map.

Other aspects of the Geography PoS covered

1a–d; 2a, c; 3a, d; 4; 5a, c; 9b.

Reference to photocopiable sheet

Photocopiable sheet 140 has small maps of seven different settlement types. Children use Ordnance Survey 'Landranger' maps to find examples of at least two each of the settlement types, and they record the names of these settlements and whether each one is a village, a town or a city.

MAPPING LAND USES

To recognise that land in settlements is used in different ways.

Groups working within a class.

20 minutes discussion and filling in of colour keys; 60 minutes fieldwork activity in local area; 20 minutes creating 'best copy' of field map; 20 minutes compiling land-use category percentages.

Previous skills/knowledge needed

Children should be aware of vocabulary which describes the ways that land is used such as 'farming', 'residential', 'leisure' and 'manufacturing'. They should be acquainted with expectations as to their behaviour when outside the school gates. They should understand what a map key is.

Key background information

Land-use surveying is a very important geographical technique that often produces surprising results. It enables the geographer to gain an objective view of how land in a place is used and to study how land use changes through time (for example, agricultural land and countryside being developed for housing). Land-use surveying is also useful to the planner because it provides a picture of how the land is being used which can then be compared to past surveys, therefore allowing planners to identify changes in land use.

In the summer of 1996 thousands of children across the whole of the United Kingdom helped survey well over 1000 1km squares of the country using a very similar technique to that used in this survey activity. The children helped to create a national picture of how land is used in Britain to compare with the results of similar surveys in the past. The survey was co-ordinated by the Geographical Association.

Compiling land-use categories is always problematic. The 14 categories used in this activity are meant to be comprehensive but are very broad. Surveyors will find that sites have more than one category in them, for example a hospital may well have an office block in it. The surveyor always goes for the predominant use – it is a hospital with an office in it, not an office with a hospital in it! It is also important to record the ground floor use only; to do more than this starts to become very complicated.

Preparation

Organise responsible adult assistance in line with your school or LEA policy for taking children out of school and obtain written parental permission for the activity.

You need to provide each child with a square map of your locality which measures 15cm x 15cm (and will fit neatly on to an A4 sheet of paper). If you use your local 1:10 000 Ordnance Survey map, centred on your school, you could enlarge a 1km grid square by 150% (make sure that your school or your LEA has the required Ordnance Survey copyright permission licence). Make one large copy of this map square for class use which includes the routes that each group will follow. Identify on the maps a number of different routes which groups of accompanied children could take in order, as a team, to eventually survey the whole area. Make copies of photocopiable sheet 141 for each child and write the 14 land-use categories on to a large land-use category display key for use in introducing the activity. Make copies of photocopiable sheet 142 on to acetate for each child. Collect sets of at least 14 different colours of pencil crayons and if possible at least one similar marker pen in each colour. Gather clipboards for each child (or alternative) and waterproof protection for the clipboards if rain is likely.

Resources needed

The 15cm x 15cm map sheets of your local area for each child, one larger copy of this map for class use, the copies of photocopiable sheet 141 for each child and the acetate copies of photocopiable sheet 142. Clipboards, waterproof coverings for the clipboards, sets of pencil crayons with at least 14 different colours, marker pens in the same colours (if possible).

What to do

Tell the children that they will be doing a survey outside the school. Introduce the class to the idea of recording how land is used across space and that a map is ideal for recording such information. Using the pre-prepared land-use category display key (see 'Preparation'), show the children the land-use categories they will use and take some time to discuss what each category might include. It will be important to stress that only open land and the ground floor use of buildings should be recorded. The children can help designate colours to the land-use category display key which you or a volunteer from the class then colour accordingly using large marker pens.

Once you are confident that the children understand the land-use categories and once they have copied down the colour key on to their copies of photocopiable sheet 141, distribute the A4 copies of the square area of your local large scale map. Use the enlarged copy of this to show the routes that the groups will take and ask them to copy the routes down on to their own map copies. Hand out the clipboards.

Assign each group to an accompanying adult and make sure that the adult and the group understand which route they are surveying and that the children fully understand how to behave. The children may need considerable support in the field to identify features and to orientate their map, and they should be careful to record the predominant ground floor land use only as they walk their route. The children use at least one copy of photocopiable sheet 141 to provide them with the necessary colour key for their surveying. Where the children are unsure about what the land use is, then the adult may be able to help. Any uncertainties can be noted down in rough and then discussed back in class.

Once each group has completed their bit of the survey, the field maps should be copied by one member of each group on to the large version of the map in the classroom. Each child then makes a 'best copy' of the whole survey area by copying from the class map.

Distribute acetate copies of photocopiable sheet 142 (see 'Preparation') and explain that the square on this acetate should be positioned over their completed 'best copy' of the map. Explain that there are 100 squares in the acetate square and that they have to decide on the predominant land-use category in each one of these small squares. They go along line after line of the ten lines of the square and keep a tally record of how many times each land use category comes up using column one of the chart on photocopiable sheet 141. They add up the number of tally ticks for each category and then write what is now a percentage figure in the second column of the chart.

It is important to discuss the finished results of each child and group because there will inevitably be large anomalies. Try to explain these anomalies with a class discussion.

Suggestion(s) for extension

Children could identify places in their study area where there is evidence of change in land use either in the past, or of imminent change in the future. Ask them to write about these changes and to explain their ideas to the rest of the class.

Suggestion(s) for support

Group the children so that those who might find categorising the land uses difficult are mixed with more able children, or consider grouping these in a separate, smaller group which surveys a smaller, less complicated part of the area.

Assessment opportunities

Combine an examination of individuals' completed copies of photocopiable sheet 141 with any discussion you have with such targeted children to determine whether they have understood how land is used in your area.

Opportunities for IT

The children could use a simple spreadsheet to record and analyse the data collected from the land surveys.

The spreadsheet could be set up with the titles across the top matching the categories of the survey. The children

can then analyse the results including averages and totals, and plot the results in pie charts or other graphs.

If children have access to a fax machine or e-mail through the Internet they could swap information about land use with a school in a contrasting locality.

Display ideas

A group of children can produce a large version of the completed, coloured version of the map. It could have the 10 x 10 square superimposed over it either by using threads or by drawing the lines, and the final data set could be displayed.

Other aspects of the Geography PoS covered

1a, b; 2a, b, c; 3a–d; 4; 5a.

Reference to photocopiable sheets

Photocopiable sheet 141 provides the land-use categories for the survey. The children need to assign a different colour to each category. It also provides the places where the children record their tally and percentage results on returning to the classroom. Photocopiable sheet 142 is to be used as an overlay square and is divided up into 100 smaller squares. This is best photocopied onto acetate so that it is transparent. If this is not possible, it could be traced instead.

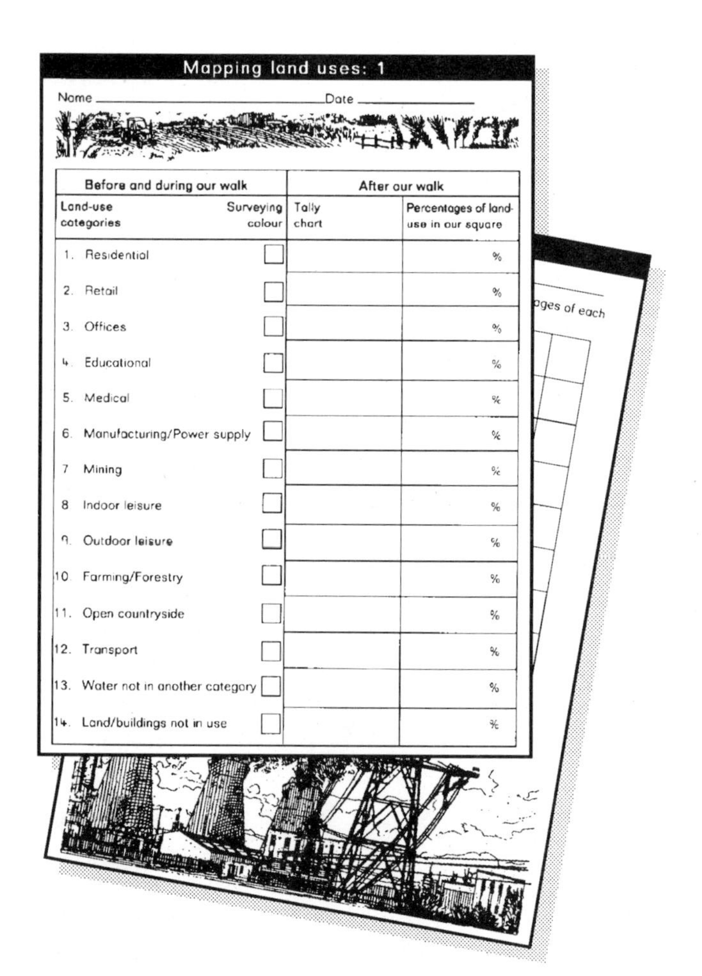

Mapping land uses: 1

Name ______________________ Date ____________

Before and during our walk		After our walk	
Land-use categories	Surveying colour	Tally chart	Percentages of land-use in our square
1. Residential			%
2. Retail			%
3. Offices			%
4. Educational			%
5. Medical			%
6. Manufacturing/Power supply			%
7. Mining			%
8. Indoor leisure			%
9. Outdoor leisure			%
10. Farming/Forestry			%
11. Open countryside			%
12. Transport			%
13. Water not in another category			%
14. Land/buildings not in use			%

CHANGING LAND USES

To consider how changing land use affects people and some of the issues that arise out of the change.

Class divided into one group of five children and four other equally-sized groups.

10 minutes role-play introduction; 15 minutes group preparation of presentation; 40 minutes role-play.

Previous skills/knowledge needed

Children will benefit from having had some experience of role-play and drama. They should have had some experience of studying land use in their and/or other localities.

Key background information

Our human environment – the buildings, roads, fields and other features which are part of the world affected by humans – is forever changing. Sometimes whole parts of this world remain largely unchanged for many years. There can be periods of very rapid change that can be on a small or a large scale. It is important for children to realise that what may seem like quite insignificant changes to some people can be very important to others. Where at least two people have different views of a change, that change becomes an issue. Issues over changing land use which the children might be aware of could include:

- ▲ farmland being redeveloped for housing;
- ▲ old industrial premises being redeveloped for housing;
- ▲ school playing fields being redeveloped for a supermarket.

Preparation

Arrange the classroom so that there are four separate sets of seating, each one set formally facing inwards and in a horseshoe, and a fifth set of five seats set in between the two points of the horseshoe (see illustration on page 83).

Position a table in front of each group and make a formal table label for each one with the following written on:

▲ Local residents	*Lower Pleasant Residents Association*
▲ Local councillors	*Pleasantford Town Council*
▲ Conservationists	*The 'Keep-It-Green' Trust*
▲ Developers	*Quick–Build UK plc*

Resources needed

One copy of photocopiable sheet 143 for each child and one copy of photocopiable sheet 144, preferably copied onto card and enlarged if necessary.

What to do

Introduce the role-play to the children. Explain that they are going in to role as another person and that the role-play will only work if they forget about what they themselves think about the issue.

Distribute the copies of photocopiable sheet 143 and explain that the first map shows a small area of a town and that the second map shows development plans for the same area. A small urban park is at risk from development as an additional area of housing.

It is worth taking some time to discuss some of the issues through before the children assume their roles. Make sure that they fully understand what is meant by the terms 'resident', 'developer', 'conservationist' and 'councillor'.

Assign the children, in more or less equal numbers, to the four role-play groups but, at this stage, keep five children back with you. (Grouping the children can be done by giving the children some choice but often works better if you decide for them.) Once the children are sitting at their group tables, ask them to study their copies of sheet 143 carefully so as to acquaint themselves fully with the plans, and designate a leader to each group. Then give out each group's 'role card' (from sheet 144) and ask the leader to read it out and lead a 15-minutes discussion in which their group lists their main arguments for or against the building of the houses.

While the four groups are doing this you explain to the five children remaining that they are going to be a special committee of 'judges' who will listen to each group's arguments in turn, and then decide on whether and how the development should go ahead. This group could spend a few minutes considering what issues are likely to come up.

Each group now takes it in turn to list their views to the meeting with the committee of judges making notes of the main arguments being put forward. The children will realise quite quickly that there are two groups in favour of the development and two against it. Try to give each child a turn to speak, possibly by asking each group's leader to nominate each member to make one of the points, with the leader then summing up the group's feelings.

The committee of five now 'retire' to discuss their feelings about the presentations and to vote on an outcome (the fact that there are five will ensure an outcome if no abstaining is allowed). The findings of the judges are then delivered to the meeting by one (brave) judge.

Suggestion(s) for extension

Children will hopefully realise that development outcomes in real life are often a result of compromise. In extension, children could copy down the basic outline of the development area (perhaps by tracing it from sheet 143) and design a compromise solution which allows for more houses but still retains some green space.

Suggestion(s) for support

You will have to maintain flexibility as to how much you become involved. If some children are finding it hard to follow their role you could have an arrangement (best explained at the outset) whereby you stop the role-play to allow you to discuss an issue through with the whole class.

Assessment opportunities

Ask the children to demonstrate their understanding of the issue by writing a list of the main arguments in favour of and against the development, listing who held each of the views in the role-play. The children could then write a few sentences explaining their own views as to what the outcome should have been and saying why.

Opportunities for IT

Information Technology offers opportunities to present information in a stylish way. Presentation software like *Powerpoint* could be used for the groups to prepare their talk. Clip art and graphics packages can be used to design

MORE PUPILS – MORE SPACE

To study a possible real land-use issue within the school grounds.

Groups of four working within a class activity.

10 minutes introduction; 20 minutes walk around school; 30 minutes mapping and photocopiable sheet activity.

Previous skills/knowledge needed

The children should have carried out land-use activities in their school grounds or in other localities. They should have a knowledge of their school grounds, be aware of its boundaries and where they are allowed and not allowed to go. Children should be aware of real issues existing in their locality and the importance of individuals having opinions and making their opinions known about such issues.

Key background information

This activity will help children learn how to explore a changing land-use issue. Pupil numbers are constantly fluctuating in schools. Primary schools are particularly sensitive to changing school rolls which can affect the size of classes and the number of teachers working in a school. The building of a new housing estate near to a school can increase school numbers whereas the building of another primary school in the vicinity can reduce them. The most efficient response to increasing numbers will be to bring redundant classrooms into use, bring in portable buildings or build new rooms.

posters and leaflets for or against the proposals. Word-processing and data presentation packages offer children the opportunity to present their findings and views associated with local geographical issues in an appealing way.

Display ideas

Have a follow up model-making lesson in which the children in each group make a model of the site (to an agreed scale – possibly built on an enlarged version of the photocopiable sheet 143 map) as they would like to see it. The completed models could be very effectively displayed on a table top with the 'role-play cards', any writing and copies of the map mounted on a wall behind.

Other aspects of the Geography PoS covered

1b; 2a, b, c; 3a, d, e; 9b.

Reference to photocopiable sheets

Photocopiable sheet 143 shows a map of an urban residential area including a small park and the same map with a developer's plans for a housing development on the park. This sheet is used as stimulus for the role-play activity. Photocopiable sheet 144 is designed to be copied (preferably) onto card and then used as 'role-play cards' explaining the point of view of each of the groups. The sheet is cut into four cards.

Settlements

Preparation

Obtain or draw a simple large scale map of your entire school and its grounds. Ensure that this is as accurate as possible. It should include all exterior doors and might include the location of interior corridors. It is very important that it includes outdoor features like steps, trees, play areas and seats.

Resources needed

A copy of your large scale map of the school and of photocopiable sheet 145 for each child, paper.

What to do

Discuss the existing school site with the children. Talk about which classes are in which rooms, where children go to get a library book, eat their school meal or change for PE. Discuss any spare space that there may be around the school for extra teaching.

Describe a scenario to the children where school numbers are suddenly going to rise by about 30 children. Explain that the headteacher and the governors have decided to build a new classroom but that there is a lot of disagreement about where it should be located. Provide each child with a copy of your large scale map of the school and its grounds and put the children into groups of four. Explain to the groups that they have to walk around the school grounds making sure that they understand the map. As they do this they have to look for places where an extra classroom could be placed and, importantly, they have to consider where any extra connecting corridors might have to be built and where additional cloakroom areas and toilets might be located.

On return to the classroom the group sits together and decides on four different solutions to the problem. They then decide which of them is to draw the map of which solution (each one taking a different one) and draw them onto their individual copy of the large scale map.

Having done this they use photocopiable sheet 145 to draw a picture of how the new classroom will look and to answer some key questions about their design on a separate sheet. Conclude the activity with a brief class session where each group of children explains their ideas to the rest of the class and answers questions about them.

Suggestion(s) for extension

Ask the children to draw a new plan of the school as it would look with their suggested extra classroom, or to adapt your original plan and then to decide which age groups of children or classes they would locate in which classroom (for example: infant classes may be best located together).

Suggestion(s) for support

If the activity is likely to be too demanding on individuals, ask each group of four to decide on one solution only and then to work as a team to answer the sheet's questions. The group could draw a larger picture of the completed classroom.

Assessment opportunities

Observe targeted children during their work but then specifically as they report their ideas back to the rest of the class. Make notes on their ability to justify their decision about locating their classroom and then look at their map and answers to the questions on the photoocpiable sheet, and completed large scale maps to support your considerations.

Opportunities for IT

The children could use a drawing or simple Computer Aided Design (CAD) package to help them plan their new classroom. To speed up the activity the teacher could use the software to prepare a plan of the school in advance and save it to disk so that children can retrieve it and then add their extension to it.

The children could also plan the inside of the classroom using framework software such as *My World 2* with the Room Planner file, or SPEX.

Display ideas

Each group of four could decide on their favourite design out of the four they have generated. They could either make a model of their design or make an 'architect's drawing' of their idea. These could then be displayed in a combined table-top and wall display.

More pupils – more space

Name ______________ Date ______________

▲ Draw an accurate picture of what your design will look like

▲ Answer the following questions on a separate sheet of paper.

1. What will your design look like from the outside?
2. What other learning areas will be affected by your design once it is finished.
3. Where will children using the classroom hang their coats?
4. Which toilets will children in the new classroom use?
5. How will children using the new classroom escape in the event of fire?

▲ Justify why you think your design is best.

Other aspects of the Geography PoS covered

1b; 3b, c, d; 5d; 9b.

Reference to photocopiable sheet

Photocopiable sheet 145 is used to support the activity in which children design and locate a new classroom for their school. The sheet asks them to answer some key questions about their design, to make a written justification of it and to draw a picture of what they think their classroom design will look like.

SETTLEMENTS IN OUR REGION

To recognise the main settlements in the region, and their size and location.

Four groups within a class.

10 minutes introduction; 30 minutes group researching, drawing and sticking activity; 15 minutes photocopiable sheet activity; 10 minutes follow up activity (optional).

Previous skills/knowledge needed

Children should understand that there are different types and sizes of settlement, and that we label settlements according to their size (for example: village, town) and other characteristics such as their location or important economic activities within them (for example: port, mill town).

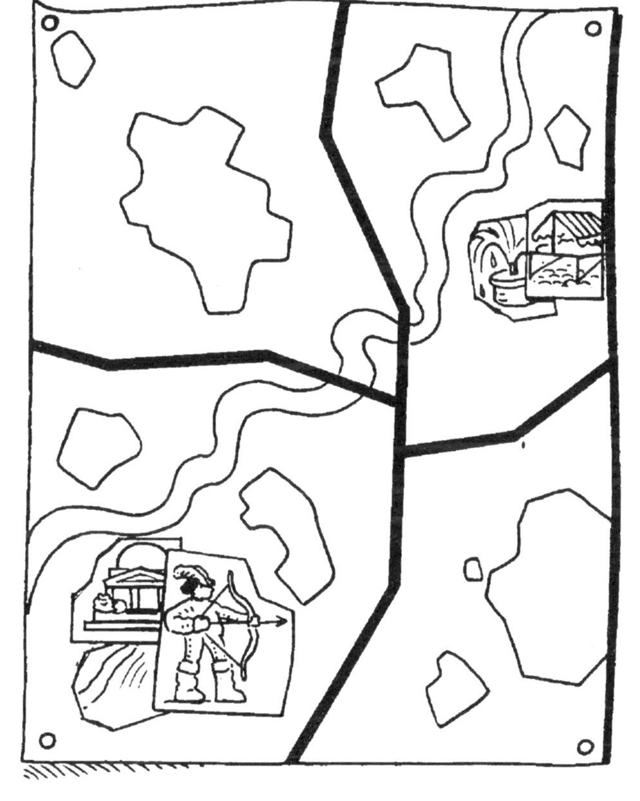

Key background information

It is important that children learn that settlements exist in different sizes, that they exist for a complicated range of reasons, that they perform a wide range of functions (for example: residential, industrial, commercial) and that they are always undergoing the processes of change. It is also important that children's 'mental map' (the maps we carry in our heads) of the area that they might regularly travel within (their own region) develops as they themselves develop. It is generally extremely useful to have a simple basic mental map of your own region, to know whether a place mentioned when someone is giving you directions is generally to the north or to the west of where you are, and to know how big it is and how far away it is.

Preparation

Draw a very simple outline map of the area centred around your school which encompasses places that people living around the school might visit on day trips. It should include places where locals might go to shop, to make day visits to relatives or to visit places of interest for enjoyment. The map should be a simple, background one and cover a large wall display. Settlement outlines should be marked but not named. Divide the map into four sub-regions by drawing lines. The lines need not be straight and their course should be determined by making sure that each of the four segments which result have about the same proportions of settlement areas in them. As far as possible ensure that the lines pass between settlements and not through them.

Make a collection of maps of any type and scale covering places in this region. These maps might include:

▲ road atlases;
▲ Ordnance Survey maps;
▲ 'A–Z' style atlases and maps;
▲ thematic maps of town or city centres.

Resources needed

A large scale simplified regional map (see 'Preparation'), a collection of maps of the region and a wide selection of any pamphlets, information books, booklets, computer information sources or other resources about places in your region. Drawing and writing materials, scissors, glue, a supply of blank A4 white drawing paper, a copy of photocopiable sheet 146 for each child.

What to do

Explain to the class that they are going to create what is known as a 'pictorial' map of the region in which they live and go to school. Show them the large outline map you have made and discuss the outlines of the settlements that you have marked on. Children might recognise some of the shapes of settlements on the map. If your region has a coastline within it this may be even easier.

Assign each of the four groups one of the four map segments and show them the reference books you have collected. Explain that, using their own knowledge of the region and the reference materials available, they have to fill the settlement outlines on the map with photomontage drawings of real places, features and activities in, or associated with, that settlement. The children now work in their groups to develop these drawings and then to arrange and stick them onto the base map.

As the children are working ask members of each group to produce name labels for each of their group's settlements, made to an equivalent size to that of the settlement's. Each

Settlements

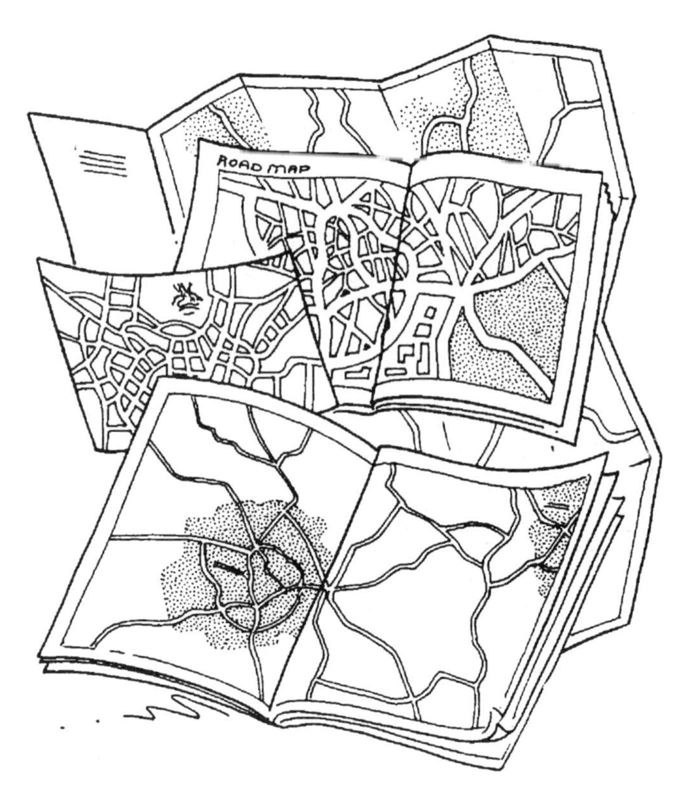

individual should now be given a copy of photocopiable sheet 146 and asked to have a go at drawing the map of the region in the box provided, using the class map to work from. They then write in the answers to the questions about places that they and their families visit in the region.

Now cover over the class map and ask the children to try drawing the map with each of the settlements in their correct relative positions.

Suggestion(s) for extension

The children will realise that the relative position of settlements to each other is easier to remember if the lines (communication routes) which connect the settlements are included on the map. Roads, railway lines, canals, rivers and motorways can be marked on the children's own drawn versions of the maps and marked on the large version by members of the class.

Suggestion(s) for support

To support the child who finds the last, 'blank paper test' difficult, you could draw a simple outline of the region yourself including outlines of the larger settlements. Individuals could then add other smaller settlements in the correct places and label all of the settlements.

Assessment opportunities

The 'blank paper' map drawing activity suggested as a follow up will provide you with excellent summative evidence of the children's knowledge of the major settlements in their immediate region, their relative position to each other and their relative size.

Opportunities for IT

Extra pictures of the settlements in the area could be provided in the form of a Kodak CD-ROM. This can be made by the school by simply taking a range of photographs and taking the films to a chemists who can create a CD-ROM. These pictures can be viewed on screen, printed out on a colour printer or included within children's word-processed or graphics work.

An alternative approach would be to make a multi-media presentation of the settlements in the area using authoring software. Groups of children could research information about a particular settlement. They could find information from CD-ROMs, tourist guides and other reference materials.

Display ideas

The large scale regional photomontage map will, in itself, provide an attractive display. Arrange a display of the source materials on a table below the completed map, and display examples of the children's completed photocopiable sheets and 'blind' attempts at the map around the larger, colourful photomontage.

Other aspects of the Geography PoS covered

1a, d; 3c, d, e; 4; 5a.

Reference to photocopiable sheet

Photocopiable sheet 146 is for the children to draw their own smaller version of the map of their region. They draw the map in the box and then answer the questions at the bottom of the sheet which ask about where they travel to for shopping of different sorts and any trips out.

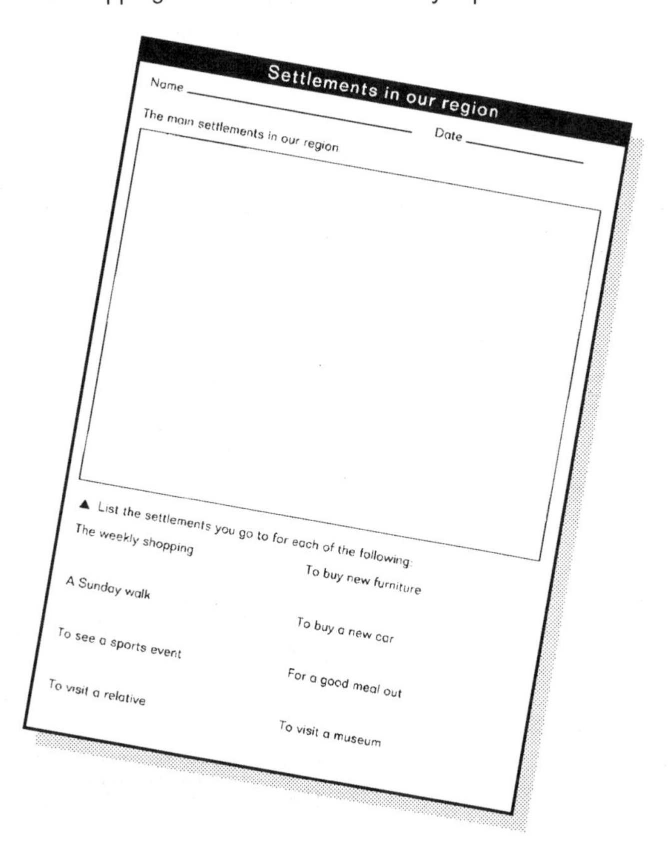

Settlements in our region

Name ______ Date ______

The main settlements in our region

▲ List the settlements you go to for each of the following:

The weekly shopping

To buy new furniture

A Sunday walk

To buy a new car

To see a sports event

For a good meal out

To visit a relative

To visit a museum

Environmental changes

At Key Stage 2 children should be helped to investigate how environments change. An environment might be a fairly small area (such as a part of the school grounds) or it might be the general, wider environment. Work on environmental change may form its own unit of work (or topic), or it may be taught in conjunction with other themes (for example, settlement), or as a part of your teaching about localities.

During Key Stage 2, children should study cases which illustrate:

▲ how people affect the environment;

▲ how and why people seek to manage and sustain environments.

Children should study environments at a range of scales from the immediate to the global and they should study issues in real places which might include other localities in the UK and the European Union. It is important that children come to understand that real people are affected by the decisions of others and that they learn to develop educated and informed opinions about issues connected with environments.

Study of their own school and other local environments will help children see that there is almost always more than one side to any argument, and might also provide a forum for the children not only developing their awareness and expressing their opinions, but also for them taking direct action to maintain or even change a situation. The study of real issues in real environments can provide a very meaningful slant to the localities studied under the 'places' section of the programme of study.

NOISE NEAR OUR SCHOOL

To understand that people affect their environment.

Groups of four or five within class.

15 minutes introduction; 30 minutes fieldwork; 15 minutes follow-up.

Previous skills/knowledge needed

Children should have the ability to work safely in groups out of the classroom. They should understand the concept of a fair test and be able to observe, identify, classify and use a tally system.

Key background information

There are many forms of noise some of which may be considered a form of pollution. In both urban and rural areas traffic is a source of much noise. The amount of traffic noise depends on the type (lorries/cars), number (many/few), condition (old/new; neglected/serviced), speed (fast/slow), driving style (maniacal/careful), and driving stage (revving/accelerating/idling) of the vehicle, as well as the road surface (cobbled/concrete/tarmac), and the surroundings (walls/grassland). Noise can be measured with noise meters using the decibel scale but many primary schools are unlikely to possess such expensive and specialised equipment. An alternative approach utilises the sound produced by normal conversation or by another source of noise such as a cassette player. This noise source is established in the area to be surveyed and the amount of environmental noise is proportional to the distance it is necessary to move away from the conversation or cassette before it becomes inaudible. The longer the distance it is necessary to move from the noise source, the quieter the environment. In busy towns it may only be a few metres, in quiet countryside it could be up to 20 or 30 metres.

Preparation

Identify four sites of contrasting roads within a short distance of the school. Ideally these should form the block around the school and should comprise a main road and a range of less busy roads. Obtain a large scale base map of this area. One sound source (such as a cassette player and cassette or transistor radio) should be obtained for each group. Arrange adult support in line with school policy for taking children out of school.

Resources needed

Per group: a base map of the study area, a source of sound, clipboard, waterproof board covers, pencil and copy of photocopiable sheet 147.

What to do

To introduce the concept of noise to the class, ask them to sit in silence for one minute and to listen very carefully. Afterwards make a list of the noises heard. Classify the noises in different ways, such as human, natural or machine-made, or 'good' and 'bad'. Rank the noises from the quietest to the noisiest. Discuss the noisiest and quietest parts of

the school and also the noisiest and quietest times of the school day. By doing this you are introducing the idea of place to place and time to time variations in noise.

Now move onto a discussion of how noise can be measured. Can the children think of ways of measuring noise? One way would be to use a sequence of simple descriptive words such as silent, very quiet, quiet, normal, noisy, deafening. Another approach would be to make comparisons between places, such as common classroom sounds with the sounds experienced in other familiar places like an empty church, a library, a shopping street, a football match or a disco. A more 'scientific' approach might be to use the noise sources or a noise meter described above under 'Key background information'.

Noise near our school

Name ______________________ Date ______________

Road information	Our Class Noise Survey 1	2	3	4	others
Type of road					
'A' road					
'B' road					
'C' road					
side road					
Road surface					
tarmac					
concrete					
cobbles					
other					
Roadside features					
walls/buildings both sides					
walls/buildings one side					
hedges/bushes/trees both sides					
hedges/bushes/trees one side					
open grass/flat land both sides					
open grass/flat land one side					
Other features					
bus stop in section					
traffic lights					
steep road					
other noise					
Traffic information					
Vehicles					
Number of vehicles in one minute					
bikes					
motor bikes					
cars					
vans					
lorries					
buses					
total number of vehicles					
Pollution information					
** Noise level*					

* To record noise you can use words (like quiet or noisy), numbers (1–5), the distance you have to walk away from a cassette player before you cannot hear it, or the actual noise in decibels

The discussion should next turn to traffic noise in the local area including the different types of traffic and roads. The discussion should include a consideration of what causes the noise (engines and road surface), and the influence of the many factors described above (see 'Key background information') such as type of vehicle, type of driving and driver, and the surrounding environment (trees and bushes as compared with brick walls and concrete).

Divide the class into groups of four or five children and explain that in their groups they are going to survey traffic noise at each of the four sites. Allocate each group to an adult helper and remind them of safety rules outside the school. Give each group its photocopiable sheet and other equipment and take them outside. Take each group to each of the four sites in turn (not necessarily the same sites at the same time and in the same sequence). Spend the same period of time at each site (the precise amount of time depends on individual circumstances and conditions but five minutes should be adequate). At each site the group should use the photocopiable sheet to record the required information about road type and features, traffic type and volume, and noise level.

On returning to class, discuss the noisiest and quietest roads and see if this can be related to any of the factors measured. The enquiry can be completed by asking the children how they could reduce the amount of traffic noise in the area.

Suggestion(s) for extension

Children could be asked to devise a way of measuring the effect of different vehicle types or the effect of the same vehicles being driven at different speeds. To do this they will have to be clear about the notion of a fair test. In the case of the different vehicle types the children might be expected to identify three or four contrasting vehicles (bicycle, car, lorry and motorbike) and then measure a sample of these being driven on the same road and at the same speed for each vehicle type. Questions as to the number of each vehicle type measured (and whether the same number for each type of vehicle should be counted) will arise.

Suggestion(s) for support

Play the children tape recordings of different types of vehicles and see if they can identify them. Play with model cars on different surfaces (carpet, lino, wood) to show how these can influence the noise produced. Take the children into the school car park and tell them to listen to the different noise levels associated with, for example, an idling and an accelerating engine, or a small and large engine.

Assessment opportunities

Use the completed charts from sheet 147 as evidence of how accurate the tallying process is. Listen to the group discussion and note the different contributions of targeted children.

Display ideas

Use a large scale map of the roads as a base map on which photographs and sketches of each road can be superimposed. Add the noise levels graphically and use pictographs to show the volume of traffic.

Other aspects of the Geography PoS covered

2a, b, c; 3a, b, d; 4; 5d.

Reference to photocopiable sheet

The photocopiable sheet is to be used in the field. It is a tick (tally) chart which will help the children to record the required information in a systematic way. The 'others' column is for an additional road location if required. The row for noise level is for recording the sound level measured at each site. The actual information recorded will depend on the unit of measurement used by each group. This could be words such as quiet or noisy, numbers on a 1–5 scale of noise levels, or it could record a number which represents the distance (in metres) the children had to move away from a cassette player before it became inaudible.

AT THE SHOPS

To recognise that environments change through time and that sometimes careful observation is needed to understand changes.

Pairs within whole class.

20 minutes introduction; 50 minutes fieldwork; 15 minutes follow-up.

Previous skills/knowledge needed

Children should be able to work safely in pairs and use their powers of observation. They should also be able to record information in the form of words and drawings. They will need the confidence to talk to adults and the ability to read and orientate a simple map.

Key background information

The notion of continuity and change is important in geography as well as in history. Small local shopping parades provide familiar yet stimulating places to look at environmental change. Some changes take place slowly while others take place literally overnight. Some evidence is obvious to the eye, other evidence requires talking to local people or comparing the present with the past using old maps, photographs, census records and street directories.

Evidence of slow change includes a gradual deterioration in the environment with graffiti, damage and increased dog fouling. It also includes the gradual replacement of shops selling goods (food, newspapers) with shops selling services (building societies, video exchanges). Rapid change might include that of a butcher's shop to a newsagents which is often done by shopfitters literally overnight, or the replacement of traditional red telephone boxes with modern ones. Shops may change in terms of function, ownership, or both.

To discover change it is vital that the children learn to observe very carefully. In this exercise the emphasis is on the use of the eyes while looking at shops, shopping parades and a base map. The base map with the ordered sequence of places to visit, will give useful map-reading experience. Additionally, the map is a historic document and can be used to identify change if so required. Careful use of the eyes alone may be sufficient to yield evidence of change to some children, for others more directed questions may be needed to focus observations. Examples of evidence of change include a GR pillar box, a shop with its old telephone number still showing (for example, CHI 6473 instead of the present 722 6473), footscrapes outside a shop, a shop with its original name in ceramic tiles and its new name elsewhere in plastic.

Preparation

Select a small shopping parade in close proximity to the school. Locate a relatively large out-of-date scale Ordnance Survey map of the area (scale 1: 10 000; 1: 2500; 1: 1250) and mark on a route involving places with obvious changes, in a numerical sequence corresponding with the order in which they are to be visited. Visit the field study area and attempt to identify as many changes as possible. Look for recent additions, attempts at modernisation or conservation.

Carry out a safety assessment. Since each shopkeeper will be interviewed by pairs of children it would be advisable to visit each one to request their permission and agreement to participate. Leave them a copy of the questions the children are likely to ask. Recruit extra adult help to assist in the supervision of the field trip.

Resources needed

A large photograph of a modernised house, preferably with a photograph of or next to a house in its original state, one copy of photocopiable sheet 148 for each child, a base map showing the shopping parade to be visited for each pair of children, paper, a clipboard, pencil and waterproof cover per pair to record the information.

What to do

At the start of the lesson introduce the concept of change by talking, for example, about name changes due to marriage, the ageing process, and old and new houses. Ask the children what has changed most in their lives and what has changed least. Show the children a large photograph of a house with obvious evidence of modernisation such as modern windows, a TV aerial or a satellite dish, an extension and a garage. Ideally, if this were juxtapositioned with a house that has not been modernised the comparison would be more obvious.

Move the conversation on to changes in shops and shopping parades. Talk about types of shops which did not exist 50 years ago such as video stores, Internet cafés and pizza parlours. Introduce the idea of continuity and change. Discuss changes within individual shops as well as within the shopping parade in its entirety.

Divide the class into pairs and distribute the photocopiable sheets to the children. As a preparation for the fieldwork ask the children to identify the changes in the shopping parade portrayed in the photocopiable sheet.

Next ask the children to devise a short questionnaire so that they can interview shopkeepers and shoppers. The questions should provide them with the opportunity to gain knowledge of how the shopping parade has changed or stayed the same. Alternatively you could provide those who need support with questions on a sheet, similar to the following:

▲ Are you a shopper or a shopkeeper?
▲ What changes have you seen in this shop in the last few years?
▲ Do you think each of these changes has been for the better or worse?
▲ What changes have you seen in the shopping parade in the last few years?
▲ Do you think each of these changes has been for the better or worse?
▲ What changes would you like to see here?

Next take the children to the shopping parade. Ask each pair to follow the prepared route on their map and carry out the visual survey looking for evidence of change at each point. The evidence can be recorded on a piece of paper or, alternatively, on a prepared recording sheet with each of the numbered locations having its own 'change box' in which the evidence for change can be written or drawn. In addition, ask each pair to interview at least two people. Where possible this should include one shopkeeper and one shopper, but where only a small parade is being used (which is the preferred size) there may not be enough shopkeepers to go around. In this case ask the pair to interview two shoppers.

On return to class go through the points identified on the base map and discuss the evidence and nature of the changes observed with the whole class. Then make a list of the changes identified during the questionnaire survey distinguishing between shops and shopping parade, and shopkeepers and shoppers where appropriate. Then open up the discussion to consider the ideas for future change expressed in the questionnaires. This can lead on to why change occurs, whether all change is good, and whether anyone should control change (for example, planners).

Suggestion(s) for extensions

Ask local people such as pensioners, councillors or planners to visit the classroom to talk about the shops and the shopping parade in the past. Ask the children to tape record and edit interviews with these people with the aim of producing recorded evidence of the change in the shops.

The children could be provided with old photographs of the shopping parade or data from the 1891 census (who lived where, the size of family, the birth place, the job) or data from a Kelly's Directory (the name of the owner of the shop, the function of the shop) with which to compare the present and the past.

Suggestion(s) for support

To develop the concept of change, play Kim's Game where a tray of goods is shown to the children for thirty seconds. Then one item is removed and the children must identify the missing object. This can be modified by adding items or changing them in some way. Another way to do this is to use two playmats to make similar layouts with small differences, and ask the children to identify the changes made. The children can then make their own changes to the mats and ask their friend to identify the changes made.

Assessment opportunities

Observe targeted individuals to see if they can identify changes, the reasons for change and the need for control of change.

Opportunities for IT

The children could set up a database to record the current characteristics of the shops as a future reference. Useful information could include:

- shop name
- owner
- local or national chain
- function
- number of assistants
- size of the shop frontage
- types of wrapping material used
- forms of security
- type of rooms, windows, doors

Some databases also allow a picture field to be included so that other changes can be noted. These pictures can be scanned from a set of pictures on Kodak CD-ROM of the shopping area, made by the school.

Display ideas

A large scale collage of each shop could be assembled in the form of a shopping parade. Alternatively, a thematic collage of before and after features could be drawn using, for example, the old and new pillar and telephone boxes, old and new windows, styles of lettering, and old and new materials.

Other aspects of the Geography PoS covered

1b; 2a, b, c; 3a, b, d; 4; 5a, d; 10b.

Reference to photocopiable sheet

Photocopiable sheet 148 is used to prepare the pupils for the visit and to give them practice in identifying change.

LOOKING AFTER OUR SCHOOL GROUNDS

To understand how and why people seek to manage and sustain environments.

Groups of four or five within whole class.

20 minutes introduction; 25 minutes fieldwork; 15 minutes follow-up.

Previous skills/knowledge needed

The children will need to have some degree of aesthetic awareness. They should be willing to express themselves verbally in public. Finally, they should understand the concepts of ranking and sorting and be able to follow a map.

Key background information

The school grounds provide an invaluable resource for teaching. There is little doubt that a pleasant and stimulating school environment exerts a great influence on the behaviour of the children and on the perceptions of the school held by the pupils, staff and neighbours. There are many facets of the school grounds which can be addressed within the whole school curriculum, ranging from tidiness and anti-vandalism (including graffiti) measures, through to positive improvements and enhancements with the use of playground games, murals, tree and bush planting, pond-making and the provision of quiet areas.

The involvement of children in the design and management of school grounds is a positive force for the development of responsibility and ownership, and hopefully leads to the enhancement of self-esteem. Since much of the work involves co-operation with the community (local contractors or parents working on the project), an increased sense of community is another advantage of school grounds development.

Preparation

Make a collection of numbered photographs of attractive and unattractive features in rural and urban environments. Draw a large-scale map of the school grounds and make an A4 copy to give to each group for their fieldwork. On the map identify and number approximately six places where both 'nice' and 'nasty' features are observable. To do this you could use numbered crosses for the locations and site an explanatory key at the side. Link each place with a trail which should try to include the outside walls of the school, the playground, the garden, the playing field and a view of the outside of the school buildings.

For the support activity, draw a view of a large bare stretch of wall on an A4 sized piece of paper.

Resources needed

One copy of photocopiable sheet 149 per child, pictures

illustrating attractive and unattractive features of rural and urban localities; for each group: a copy of a large scale school grounds trail map (see 'Preparation'), a clipboard, a waterproof cover for the clipboard and a pencil. For the support activity, a photocopied drawing of a bare wall.

What to do

Start the lesson with a class discussion of people's tastes and what some people like and others dislike. You could discuss favourite football teams or television programmes and ask what it is the children particularly like or dislike about them. After a few contributions turn the discussion to factors which influence the opinions of the children. Include, for example, the role of parents, friends, pop stars and the media.

Divide the children into groups and circulate the collection of photographs. Ask each group of children to make two lists, one of the numbers of the photographic views they like and another of those they dislike. Discuss with each group why they liked some features and not others.

Next (as a whole class) move the discussion to focus on the classroom and ask the children which features they like and dislike about it. Ask them whether anything could be done to improve the classroom. Explain that you are going to take them in their groups out of the classroom into the school grounds, and that they are going to go to a number of places where they will be asked to record what features they like and what they dislike.

Take each group around the trail marked on the map and at each place ask the group to identify two nice and two nasty features. Instruct one child in each group to either draw a picture or write the name of the nice and nasty features on the base map.

On returning to the classroom the children use photocopiable sheet 149 to make an individual, personal list of the nice and nasty features of various parts of the school grounds (the walls, playground, garden, playing field, and view of the school), based on their group map. Having done this, focus on the nasty aspects and again, using photocopiable sheet 149, ask each child to record things that could be done by them, the class, school and parents, today, this week, term and year.

Suggestion(s) for extensions

Ask the children to identify their own good and bad places in the school grounds. They could also be asked to make their own base map. Ask the children to identify a small improvement task and work out the sequence of activities which would need to be followed, by whom, and including a time-scale.

Suggestion(s) for support

Using a drawing of a bare school wall, ask the children to design a mural reflecting the life of the school. An alternative would be to ask them to design a small area of the playground with games to play. Then ask them how this improves the area.

Assessment opportunities

Listen to the children during the class discussion of the television programmes and football teams they like and dislike; also listen to the group discussions about the photographs and to the reasons given for liking and disliking places. Then, look at the suggestions made by individual children on how to improve the school grounds.

Both through the group discussions and individual suggestions, look especially for evidence of an awareness of personal responsibility, a willingness to become involved in school ground improvements, and an awareness that some things can be done immediately while others need more planning and a longer time-scale.

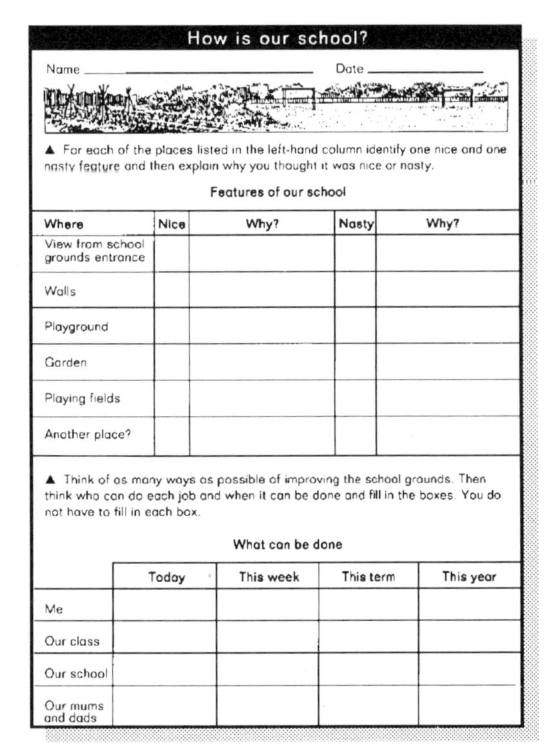

How is our school?

Name ______________ Date ______________

▲ For each of the places listed in the left-hand column identify one nice and one nasty feature and then explain why you thought it was nice or nasty.

Features of our school

Where	Nice	Why?	Nasty	Why?
View from school grounds entrance				
Walls				
Playground				
Garden				
Playing fields				
Another place?				

▲ Think of as many ways as possible of improving the school grounds. Then think who can do each job and when it can be done and fill in the boxes. You do not have to fill in each box.

What can be done

	Today	This week	This term	This year
Me				
Our class				
Our school				
Our mums and dads				

Opportunities for IT

The children could use a word processor to write a description of each of the places that they like or dislike and the reasons for their choices. They could then add their ideas for how things could be improved. Children could add pictures to their work by scanning your photographs or by using pictures from a Kodak CD-ROM made in advance.

The children could plot this information onto a map of the school, drawn using a drawing package. They could create a suitable key for identifying good and bad points about the locations.

Display ideas

A large scale map of the school grounds with drawings and/or photographs of the nice and nasty features mounted on red (nice) and blue (nasty) card can be made. In addition, ideas for the mural can be added as can a large plan of the playground games.

Other aspects of the Geography PoS covered

2a, b, c; 3a, b, d, e; 4; 10a.

Reference to photocopiable sheet

Photocopiable sheet 149 is divided into two parts. The upper part 'Features of our school' asks the children to tabulate a list of nice and nasty features of the walls, playground, garden, playing fields and view of the school from the entrance to the grounds. In addition they are asked to give reasons for their choices.

The lower part 'What can be done?' is an action plan which asks the children to identify things that can be done to improve the school grounds by different people and over different time spans.

BUILDING A RESERVOIR

To consolidate the fact that change in the environment has good and bad effects.

Seven groups of four to six children within class.

20 minutes discussion and map analysis; 15 minutes in groups deciding on responses; 30 minutes public enquiry.

Previous skills/knowledge needed

The children should be able to read maps and be familiar with map symbols, grid squares and co-ordinates. They should also be able to empathise with other people.

Key background information

All human beings and societies need water to drink, wash, grow food and use in industry for cooling, cleaning and other processes. Traditionally water came from springs and then as they dried up (mainly due to the fall of the water table) wells were dug down into the ground (see rivers). As demand for water has continued to grow as a result of population increase, the invention of new equipment and industries (washing machines, car manufacturers) and irrigation of fields, the water authorities have had to look elsewhere for water. They looked to the wet areas of countries (in Wales areas such as the Cambrian Mountains). Here they built dams making reservoirs which store water. This water was then piped to towns and cities.

Not all reservoirs are built to store water, some are built to supply hydroelectricity, others to stop rivers flooding and some to provide places for people to canoe, sail and fish. Since they are very expensive to build most reservoirs are now multi-purpose, that is they often fulfill all of the above functions at the same time.

This apparently 'good' idea has had many associated problems and illustrates that, generally, there is always a drawback to every good idea. What is good for some people is bad for others. For example, a Welsh farmer might not view the construction of a reservoir in his valley in the same way as an inhabitant of Liverpool who would gain cheap and reliable water from it.

When a reservoir is built there are many consequences:

▲ The pre-existing valley is flooded and thousands of people may be forced from their homes. Villages and towns are abandoned, churches and graveyards are lost. Many people may have lived for generations in the valley bottoms which are often sites of the best quality land for farming. Communication routes such as roads, railways and telephone lines are flooded.

▲ Loss of important sites: sites of special environmental value such as bogs, woodlands, meadows and nesting places are lost. Sites of archaeological value are flooded and lost.

▲ Loss of fertile land and use of reservoir: the reservoir stops rivers flooding downstream and catches most of the material carried by the river behind the dam; therefore rich soil is no longer spread across the flood plain and the soil becomes less fertile. So, not only are the people in the valley affected, but farmers further downstream. Sediment collects behind the dam and over the years the reservoir fills up and ceases to function.

▲ Creation of 'natural' disasters: some reservoirs cause earthquakes where the weight of the water causes the ground to buckle slightly. Water from reservoirs can seep up into the soil on the slopes above the reservoir and cause it to slip into the water causing a massive tidal wave which smashes through the dam and can cause terrible flooding downstream.

Preparation

Invite a guest to come into your class and act as a 'Public Enquiry Committee Chairperson'. Collect a set of photographs of old declining inner city areas of housing and factories and a contrasting set of a new town. In addition a set of photographs of dams and reservoirs should be collected.

Resources needed

A set of photographs of inner city areas and a contrasting set of photographs of a new town, some photographs of large dams and reservoirs, a set of blue pencils for colouring, copies of photocopiable sheet 150 for each child.

What to do

Tell the children about the plan of a water company to build a dam and reservoir across a river valley so that a nearby New Town can be provided with more water. The New Town will provide homes for 25 000 people from a nearby run-down city where there are few jobs and most of the homes are deteriorating. Show them the photographs of declining urban areas and of new urban developments. Then show the pictures of a modern dam and reservoir.

Give the children copies of photocopiable sheet 150 showing the map of Floodville and the River Flashy. Explain that the area to be dammed and flooded is on the River Flashy near the village of Floodville. The dam (Dry Days Dam) should be identified as should the extent of the area to be flooded which can be lightly coloured in blue by the children.

Now discuss the map in terms of the geography of what is there.

▲ The importance of the River Flashy (as a habitat and a setting for Damp Hall) should be noted, the fact that it flows from north to south, and that it runs across a wide flat flood plain. Note the place name evidence of the village of Floodville (flood which is self-explanatory, and ville which is Anglo-Saxon for a town or village).

▲ Discuss the biological features of Lost Marsh including how important marshes can be as habitats for animals (especially birds) and plants. Talk about how they can be very wet and dangerous which means farmers drain them so that animals do not get lost and they can grow crops there. Note the name of Frogs Farm and that frogs need water and boggy areas.

▲ Talk about Widehurst Wood explaining that it has both deciduous and coniferous trees as can be evidenced by the two different tree symbols used on the map. Note the uneven shape to the woodland which indicates that it has developed naturally over a long period of time. Hurst (in Widehurst) is another old word for wood or forest.

▲ Draw attention to the coniferous symbols of Bleak Forest with its straight edges and trees planted in regimented lines. This is a plantation as opposed to a natural woodland and has been planted to produce timber for the paper, building and mining industries.

▲ Note the 'non-ancient' settlements including the four farms, Floodville village and Damp Hall (National Trust). Also note the evidence of a Roman Villa and the cutlasses which represent a famous battle in 1066. Note the importance of Monks Quarry and discuss its possible uses (rock used for hard core for roads, foundations or concrete). Finally note the importance of the communication links in the area. There is a road (A532), a railway with a station, several bridges, a number of footpaths and a length of electricity pylons.

Introduce the idea of role-play to consider the likely effects of the reservoir on the existing area. Divide the class into seven groups, each of which will examine the proposals from the point of view of a particular group of people. The interested parties are:

▲ the tenants association in the old city representing people who are to be rehoused in the New Town which needs the extra water;

▲ the management of the motor car factory which is planned for the New Town and needs the extra water to work;

▲ the National Farmers' Union which represents the four farmers whose farms will be flooded by the reservoir;
▲ the mayor of the village of Floodville;
▲ the Secretary of the County Historical Society, Nature Conservation and Ramblers Association;
▲ the County Council which is responsible for providing transport, industry and employment in this area;
▲ the Regional Water Authority.

One person should be selected from each group to act as its spokesperson. Give the groups fifteen minutes to discuss their views about the proposed reservoir. Tell them that they will then be invited to a Public Enquiry where the plan for the reservoir will be discussed and a decision made as to whether it should be allowed. After the fifteen minutes call the groups to order and set up the Public Enquiry. This requires that the classroom be reorganised as follows: a panel of three people at the front who are the Committee, the rest of the class facing the Committee, at the side a seat and table from where each representative will address the Public Enquiry.

It would add realism to the enquiry if someone with authority or expertise could be invited to join two children as part of the Committee. Possible people could be a planner or a representative of the local council or water company. Alternatively, the Headteacher or Chair of Governors could be invited to arbitrate. If this is not possible then a committee comprising of two children and the class teacher could be constituted. The children involved with the Committee should not have been involved in the group discussions, but should have formed their own individual group to consider all the points of view.

During the enquiry each group should be allowed to put their point of view for a maximum of two and a half minutes. At the end of the presentations the Public Enquiry Committee should be given two or three minutes to reach their decision, and then the Chair of the Committee given another five minutes to justify their decision to the Public Enquiry.

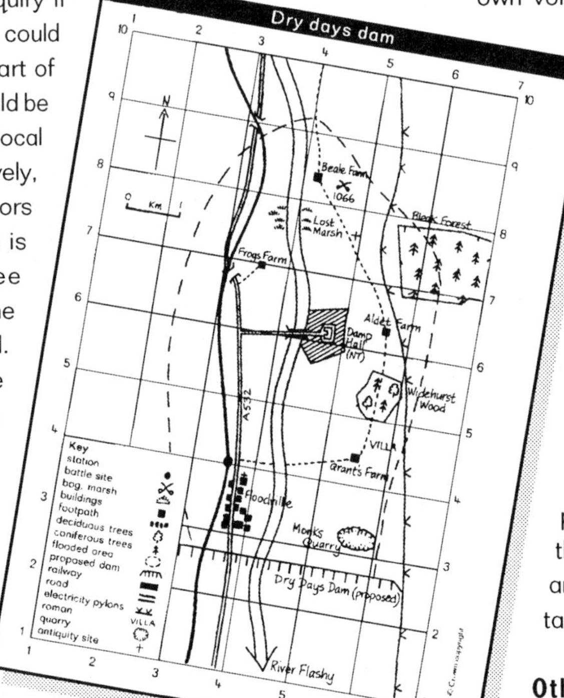

Suggestion(s) for extensions

Children capable of doing so could make a formal table of impacts which should include the accurate measurement of the lengths of road and railway flooded and the area of forest and village affected. The children could use four- or six-figure grid references to locate the features affected by the flooding in their table of impacts.

Suggestion(s) for support

Ask the children to draw pictures of individual features affected by the flooding such as the quarry, a farm, the railway station and to write a sentence explaining why this is a bad thing. These can then be used on the display.

Assessment opportunities

During the proceedings it should be possible to distinguish between those children who see everything from one point of view and those who can see contrasting views. It should also be possible to distinguish between children who can only see the direct effects of the reservoir and those who can see much more complex, indirect effects.

Opportunities for IT

The children could work in groups to produce an electronic presentation of the enquiry using a multimedia authoring package. Each group could be responsible for producing the pages about their particular aspect of the reservoir proposal to include text, pictures, maps and diagrams and even their own voices recorded using a microphone connected to a computer.

Older or more able children may be able to use software such as CLAREs Topographer which can make a three-dimensional picture from a map drawn by the children.

Display ideas

A large wall map of the area and a model of the area before and after the building of the dam could form the basis of a display. Include the photographs and pictures used at the introduction of the activity and any drawings done by children who tackled the support activity.

Other aspects of the Geography PoS covered

1b; 3a, d, e; 5a, c; 7a; 9b, c.

Reference to the photocopiable sheet

Photocopiable sheet 150 is a map of the valley to be flooded. Features generally have Ordnance Survey symbols. It is important that the children note the key and also the north point and scale. All of these can be used to increase the precision of the activity, especially with regard to language and vocabulary. The grid squares may also be used to add accuracy. All of the features located on the map should provide interesting discussion points across a range of themes and topics.

Assessment

The activities in chapters one to six have suggestions for formative assessment included with them. Some of the photocopiable sheets related to these activities are also suitable for summative assessment. These sheets have the assessment icon ✍ tagged onto them.

This chapter contains supplementary assessment activities aimed specifically at a summative outcome. The activities have been designed to complement those in the first six chapters of the book and they relate to photocopiable sheets 151 to 157.

Each activity includes an explanation of its context and how it might best be introduced to the children, a note on how it relates to the Programme of Study and suggestions on the desired outcome. Each one can be completed by children individually.

Much of geographical learning at Key Stage 2 is through the children's local area and therefore teaching needs to be tailored to that area. Summative assessment activities should be viewed in the light of wider geographical work the children have been involved in.

RONNY THE WATER DROP

Explanation

This activity is a cloze procedure in which children choose words from the bottom of the sheet and fit them in to the spaces provided. The text emphasises the fact that water travels from high areas to eventually flow out to sea at sea level. The activity determines whether children know the vocabulary which is associated with the different stages and landforms of rivers, as well as the terms erode, transported and deposited.

Reference to PoS

Thematic studies (Rivers) 7a, b.

Desired outcome

The children should be able to place the words in the following order:

spring > stream > channel > tributary > erode > banks > transported > valley > waterfall > meanders > deposited > river > mouth > source

When analysing children's work check whether any inaccurate answers do at least make some sense.

RIVER FEATURES

Explanation

The children identify which of twelve letters (R is included twice) labels which river feature and then complete the key on the left-hand side of the sheet. These labels represent the common parts of a river which children might be expected to know by the end of Key Stage 2. The completed key will spell the name of a river, and the children can have some additional fun in trying to locate this river. They then colour brown places on the picture where they think the river will be eroding and yellow places where they think the river will be depositing material.

Reference to PoS

Thematic studies (Rivers) 8a, b.

Desired outcome

The children should end up with the following result:

R = source I = tributary V = delta E = gorge
R = spring S = flood plain U = meander
K = sea H = waterfall O = stream N = mouth
A = valley. The River Sukhona is in Russia to the east of St. Petersburg.

Children should colour the banks of the streams and the outside of the meanders brown and the insides of the meanders and the delta yellow.

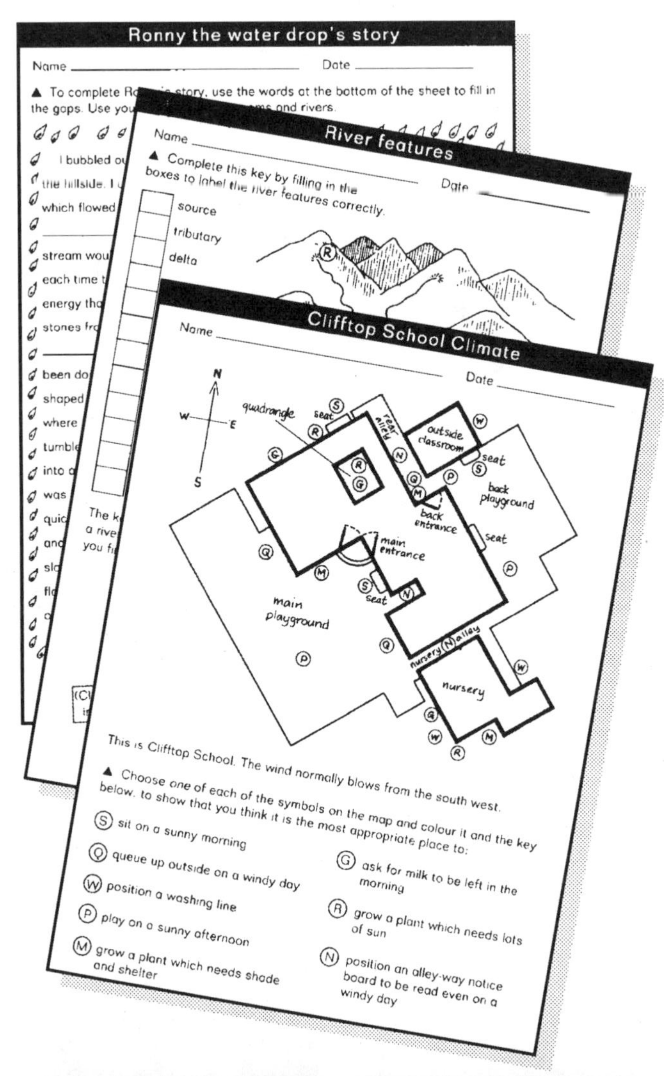

CLIFFTOP SCHOOL CLIMATE

Explanation

The children have to locate where they would site eight different weather sensitive activities or objects. They are provided with three choices for each of the activities or objects and they colour in the one which they think is most appropriate, given the information about the direction of the prevailing (normal) wind. You may need to remind the children that the sun rises in the east and appears to us to move through the southern sky, to eventually set in the west.

Reference to PoS

Thematic studies (Weather) 8a.

Desired outcome

The following are the most appropriate choices:

▲ S – seat beside the outside classroom (directly facing the morning sun);

▲ Q – rear alley (sheltered from the prevailing wind);

▲ W – to south west of nursery (in the prevailing wind and facing south);
▲ P – main playground (is in the afternoon sun);
▲ M – back entrance (in shady north-facing position and therefore cool);
▲ G – quadrangle (in shade and shelter);
▲ R – southern corner of nursery (facing due south);
▲ N – rear alley (not in direct line with prevailing wind and therefore not a wind-tunnel).

You could ask the children to make written justifications of their choices.

OUR SEASONAL SCHOOL

Explanation

The children are encouraged to consider how there are subtle changes from season to season in their school. They write a brief comment for each season in the boxes on the photocopiable sheet, to show that they are aware of seasonal variation with reference to how people in the school dress, the places they work, the activities which take place in the school, and such specifics as how they *think* the school fuel bill might vary through the year.

Reference to PoS

Thematic studies (Weather) 8a, b.

Desired outcome

The important outcome is that the children demonstrate an understanding of the pattern of the seasons and that they demonstrate awareness that activities are more likely to take place outside the school buildings in the late spring, summer and early autumn, than in the winter months.

VILLAGE, TOWN, CITY

Explanation

The children decide on one village, one town and one city which they know well (preferably in their region or another region containing a locality being studied). They write the settlement names in the relevant columns at the head of the photocopiable sheet and then tick which services are present in each of the locations. They then write an analysis, on a separate sheet of paper, describing what their tick chart tells them about the three settlements.

Reference to PoS

Thematic studies (Settlement) 9a.

Desired outcome

Hopefully children will recognise that there are more services present in larger settlements and that there is a loose hierarchy of services identifiable. This hierarchy is very loose, for instance, the smallest of villages may still retain a railway station. The children's written responses to the question at the bottom of the sheet should assist your assesssment of their understanding.

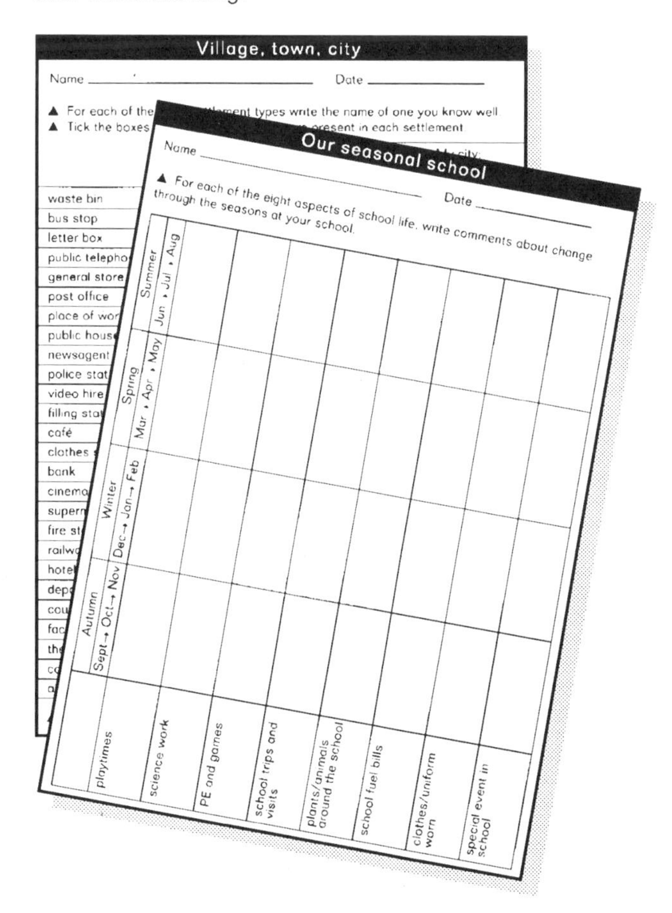

Village, town, city

Name ______ Date ______

▲ For each of the ... types write the name of one you know well
▲ Tick the boxes ... present in each settlement

waste bin
bus stop
letter box
public telepho...
general store
post office
place of wor...
public hous...
newsagent
police stat...
video hire
filling sta...
café
clothes ...
bank
cinema
super...
fire st...
railw...
hote...

Our seasonal school

Name ______ Date ______

▲ For each of the eight aspects of school life, write comments about change through the seasons at your school.

	playtimes	science work	PE and games	school trips and visits	plants/animals around the school	school fuel bills	clothes/uniform worn	special event in school
Summer Jun • Jul • Aug								
Spring Mar • Apr • May								
Winter Dec → Jan → Feb								
Autumn Sept → Oct → Nov								

WHERE IN DRIBBLEFORD

Explanation

The children have to locate where they might most likely find six different settlement land uses. They are provided with three choices for each of the land-use types and they colour in the one which they think is most appropriate given the information about the direction of the prevailing (normal) wind. Talk to the children about how the wind can carry smells and noise. It might also be useful to discuss how water was very important to early industry and how access to the transport network is so important to modern industries. Discuss the orientation of the compass rose on the map.

Reference to PoS

Thematic studies (Settlement) 9b.

Desired outcome

The following are the most appropriate choices:

▲ C – crossroads in the centre of town (town may originally have grown as a market town);

▲ I – north-western part, by the river (old industries often located where water was easily accessible for industrial processes);

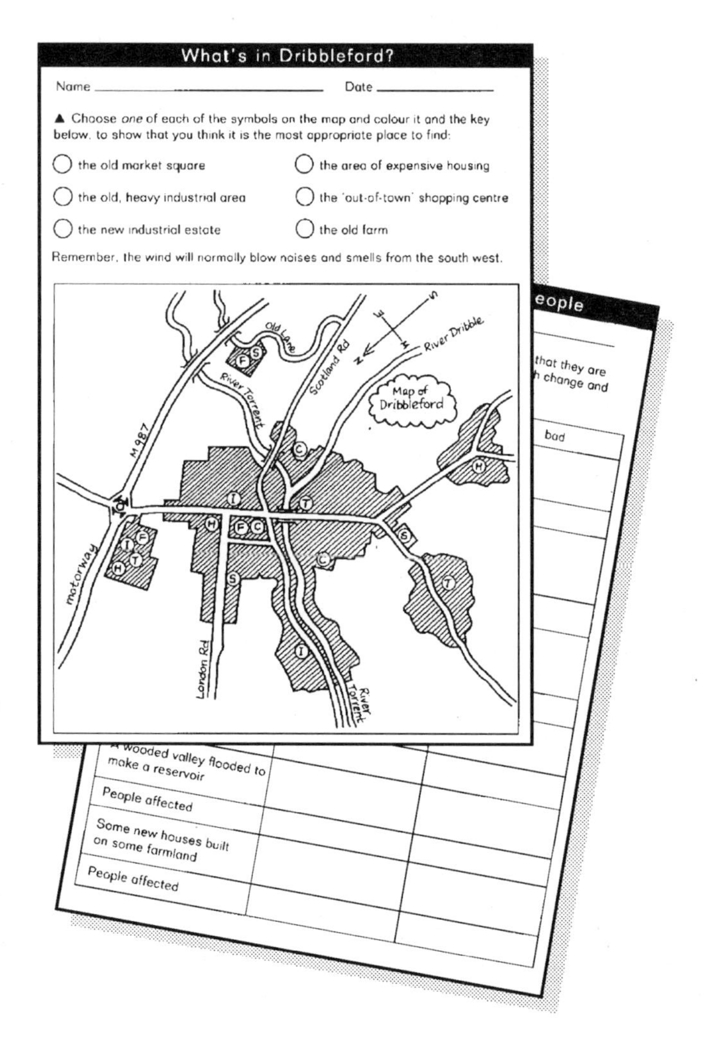

What's in Dribbleford?

Name ______________ Date ______________

▲ Choose *one* of each of the symbols on the map and colour it and the key below, to show that you think it is the most appropriate place to find:

- ◯ the old market square
- ◯ the area of expensive housing
- ◯ the old, heavy industrial area
- ◯ the 'out-of-town' shopping centre
- ◯ the new industrial estate
- ◯ the old farm

Remember, the wind will normally blow noises and smells from the south west.

eople

that they are
h change and

bad

wooded valley flooded to make a reservoir

People affected

Some new houses built on some farmland

People affected

▲ T – area near motorway junction (modern industry needs good access to the motorway and planners find ways to avoid lorries passing through towns);

▲ H – area to south of town (many people like to live out of the town itself and will choose to live away from and up wind from industry and noisy motorways);

▲ S – area on south-western edge of town (shopping centres need a lot of land and tend to locate near junctions of roads going to residential areas);

▲ F – on old lane (farm would have been there before motorway was built and is on an old route in a river valley).

Look at the children's answers carefully and discuss them as children may have good justifications for choosing alternative locations.

GOOD OR BAD?

Explanation

The children imagine that the five land-use changes are issues near to where they live (some of them may well be). The children have to write one good thing that they can see in each change and one bad thing. They are also encouraged to consider which groups of people are affected by such changes.

Reference to PoS

Thematic studies (Settlement) 9c;
(Environmental change) 10a.

Desired outcome

Look for an understanding of the positive and negative aspects of these changes in land use. Good answers will include evidence that the child can genuinely see both sides of the argument and that the child understands that virtually all development changes will benefit some people but may adversely affect others.

Photocopiables

The pages in this section can be photocopied for use in the classroom or school which has purchased this book, and do not need to be declared in any return in respect of any photocopying licence.

They comprise a varied selection of both pupil and teacher resources, including pupil worksheets, resource material and record sheets to be completed by the teacher or children. Most of the photocopiable pages are related to individual activities in the book; the name of the activity is indicated at the top of the sheet, together with a page reference indicating where the lesson plan for that activity can be found.

Individual pages are discussed in detail within each lesson plan, accompanied by ideas for adaptation where appropriate – of course, each sheet can be adapted to suit your own needs and those of your class. Sheets can also be coloured, laminated, mounted on to card, enlarged and so on where appropriate.

Pupil worksheets and record sheets have spaces provided for children's names and for noting the date on which each sheet was used. This means that, if so required, they can be included easily within any pupil assessment portfolio.

Photocopiable sheets 151 to 157 are to be used for the purposes of summative assessment and accompany the activities in the Assessment chapter.

Weather around our school (see page 14)

Weather around our school

Name ______________________ Date ______________

Location 1...	
Aspects of weather we are finding out about	**Comment/measurement**
Temperature	
Light (eg. artificial light, natural light, some natural light, strong natural light).	

Location 2...	
Aspects of weather we are finding out about	**Comment/measurement**
Temperature	
Light (eg. artificial light, natural light, some natural light, strong natural light).	

Rhymes of reason (see page 16)

Geography list poems

Name ______________________________ Date ________________

▲ Poem 1 is a list poem made of words which are all to do with traffic in London. Poems 2 and 3 need you to finish them. Poem 2 is about the weather on the highest mountain in the world, poem 3 is about the River Rhine.
▲ Write in the title to each of the poems.

Poem 1.

Title ....

Marble Arch
Beeping horns
Notting Hill Gate
Red double-deckers
Waterloo
Whooshing tube trains
Escalators
Circle, Northern, Jubilee
Traffic jams
Parking meters
Baker Street
Fraying tempers
Smoking exhausts
Taxi cab
River boatmen
Landing jetties
Island Gardens
Capital

Poem 2.

Title ....

Highest mountain
Scary feeling
Summit blizzard...

Poem 3.

Title ....

Swiss stream
Mountain torrents
Growing slowly...

 (see page 18)

Measure and map

Name ______________________________ Date ____________________

You are going to draw a map showing the edges of an imaginary playground. The numbers in the table are measurements in centimetres.

▲ Using a ruler and a set-square (to help you get exact right-angles) mark points at each distance mentioned in the table from the correct point along the map line. The two sides of the line have been labelled 'A' and 'B' to help you. Point 6 has already been done.

A	2.0	3.0	4.0	5.0	6.0	5.0	6.0	6.0	7.0	6.0	5.0	6.0	5.0	4.0	4.0
	1	**2**	**3**	**4**	**5**	**6**	**7**	**8**	**9**	**10**	**11**	**12**	**13**	**14**	**15**
B	1.0	3.0	5.0	7.0	9.0	9.0	9.0	9.0	8.5	8.0	7.5	7.0	2.0	2.0	2.0

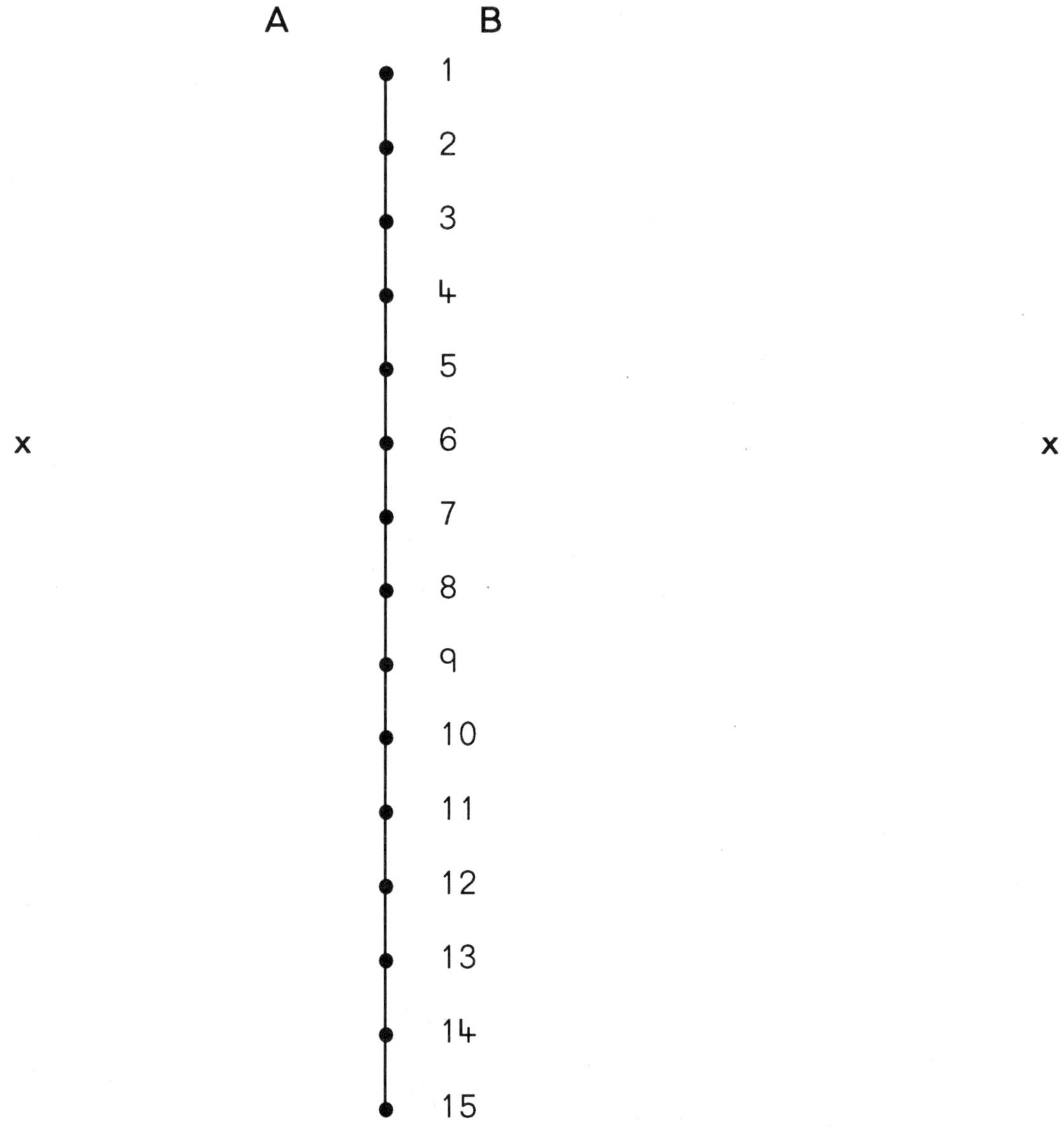

A B

1
2
3
4
5
x 6 x
7
8
9
10
11
12
13
14
15

'Let your fingers...' (see page 20)

'Let your fingers...'

Name ______________________ Date ______________

Type of directory: Area covered by directory:

	Title of section in directory	Name of company	Address	Copy of the entry
Doctor				
Supermarket				
Clothing shop				
Furniture shop				
Car repair				
Travel agent				

Issues (see page 21)

Issues questionnaire

Name ______________________________ Date ________________

Issue: ____

Statement 1: ____

Statement 2: ____

Statement 3: ____

Statement 4: ____

	Statement 1	Statement 2	Statement 3	Statement 4
Person 1				
Person 2				
Person 3				
Person 4				
Person 5				
Person 6				
Person 7				
Person 8				
Person 9				
Person 10				
Total score				

▲ Using the 'Scores' table below, give each person a score between 0 and 4 for each of the four statements that they comment on.

Scores	
Strongly disagree	0
Disagree	1
No opinion	2
Agree	3
Strongly agree	4

Total score for each column of 10 people

Between 0–7 = generally people strongly disagree
Between 8–15 = generally people disagree
Between 16–24 = generally people are mixed in views
Between 25–32 = generally people agree
Between 33–40 = generally people strongly agree

Using the 'Total score' table above, explain the result of your questionnaire:

____

____

____

____

Making maps at different scales (see page 24)

Making maps at different scales: 1

Name ______________________ Date ______________

Square 2
1cm on the map = 10m on the ground

0 10 20 30 40 50 60 70 80 90 100
scale in metres

My school

Square 1
1cm on the map = 2m on the ground

0 2 4 6 8 10 12 14 16 18 20
scale in metres

My classroom

Making maps at different scales (see page 24)

Making maps at different scales: 2

Name ______________________ Date ______________

Square 4
1cm on the map = 100m/1km on the ground

0 100 200 300 400 500 600 700 800 900 1000
scale in metres

My local area

Square 3
1cm on the map = 50m on the ground

0 50 100 150 200 250 300 350 400 450 500
scale in metres

My school and its surroundings

Symbols and keys – river basin (see page 26)

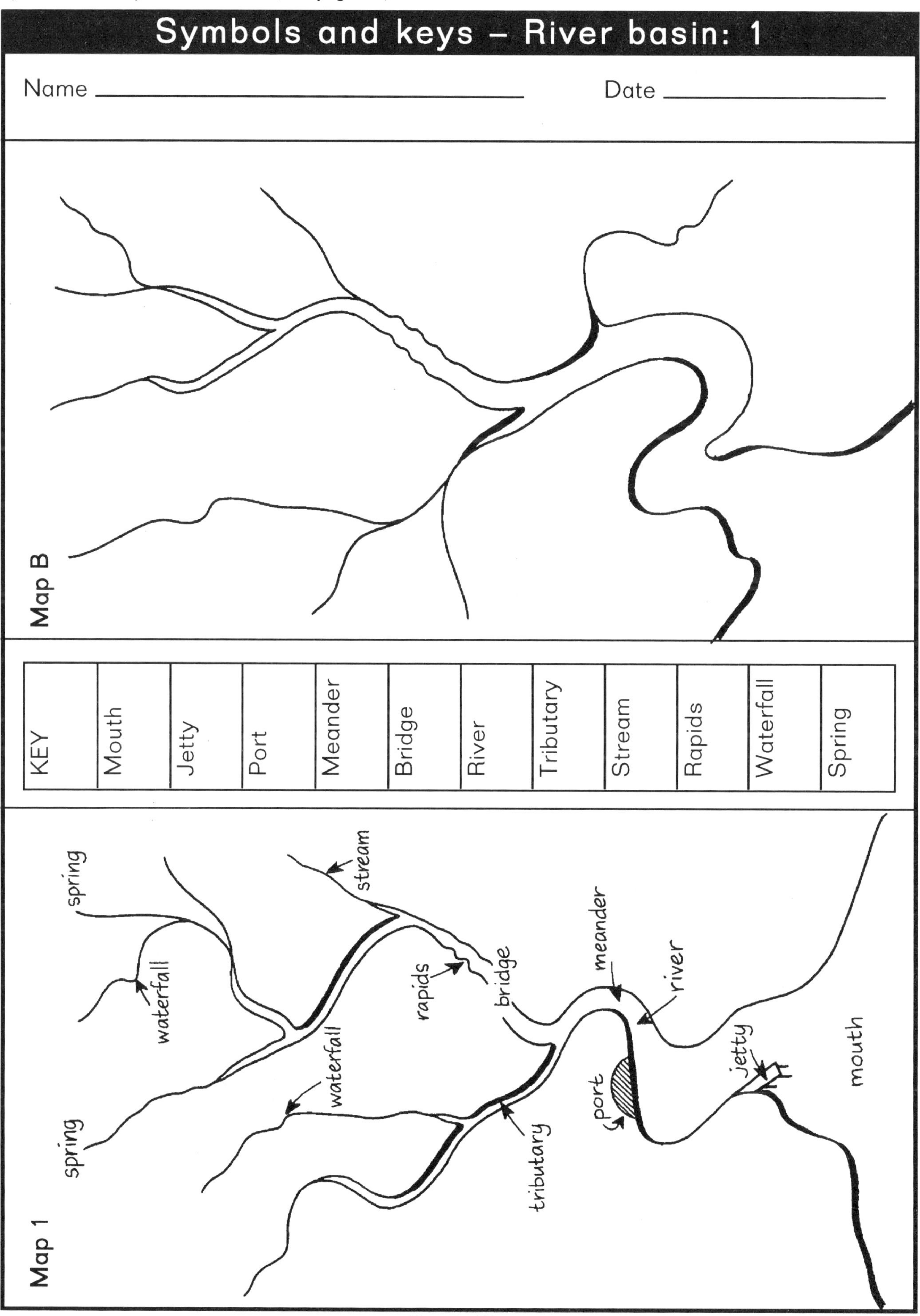

Symbols and keys – river basin (see page 26)

Symbols and keys – river basin: 2

Name ______________________ Date ______________

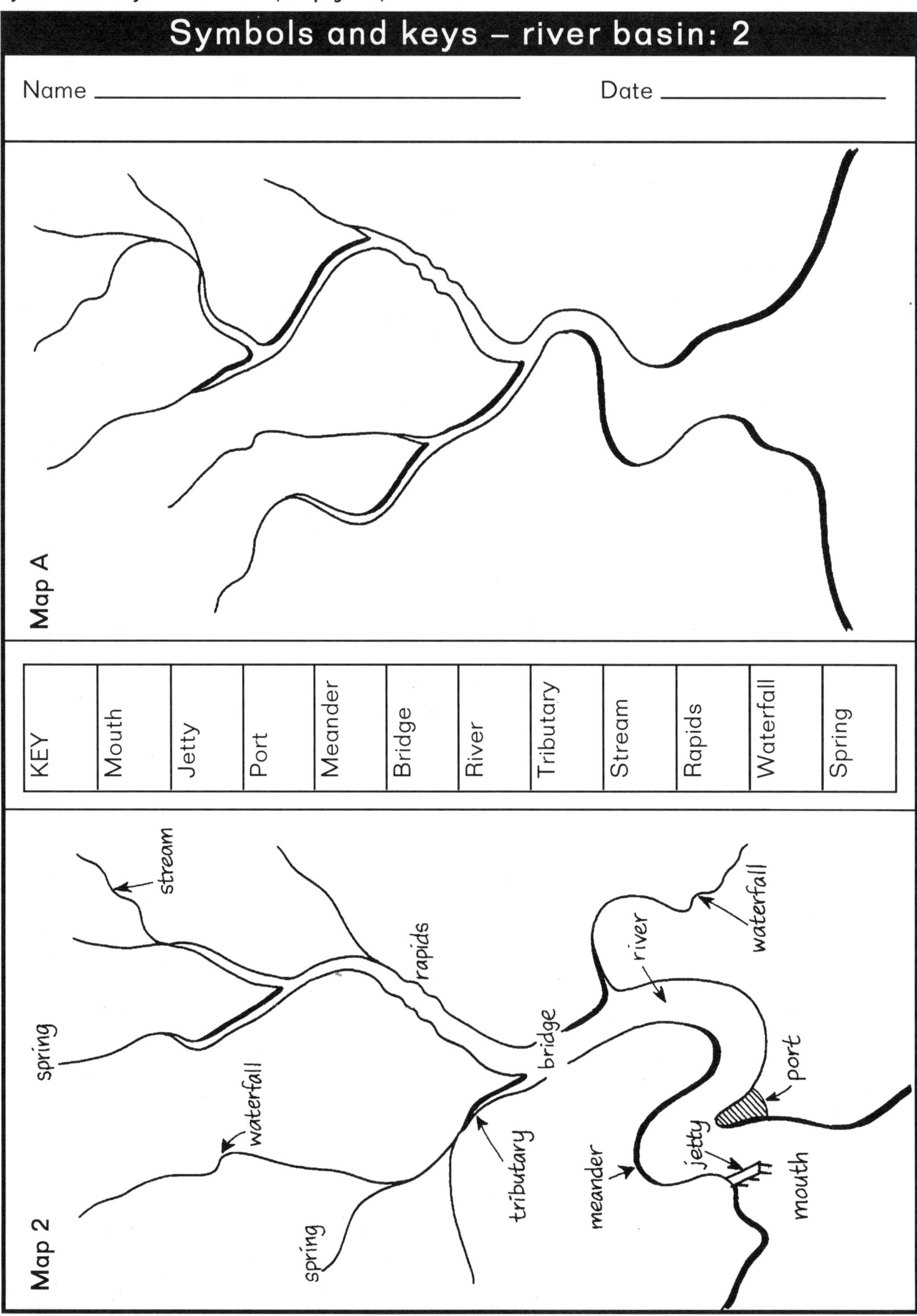

Mapping waste (see page 28)

Mapping waste

Name ______________________ Date ____________

Map of my school and its grounds

scale in metres

0 ______ m

Present in school grounds	Could be added in school grounds	
P	P	Paper recycling bins
G	G	Glass recycling bins
A	A	Aluminium/steel can recycling bins
R	R	Other recycling bins (plastic, for example)
C	C	Compost heap
I	I	Indoor wastepaper basket/bins
N	N	Indoor bins for other waste
O	O	Outdoor litter bins
D	D	Large 'industrial bins'
S	S	Places where paper is stored for reuse
L	L	Unwanted food for reuse by someone else
F	F	Clothes bins/collection points for reuse of clothing

Thematic globes (see page 30)

Thematic globes

▲ Use this sheet to help you design and make a thematic globe.

1 Blow up a balloon.

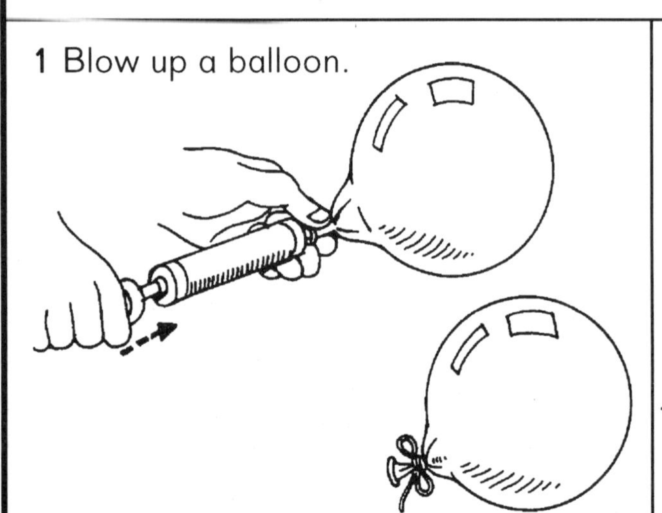

2 Get help to tie it off.

3 Stick layers of small pieces of paper onto the balloon using paste.

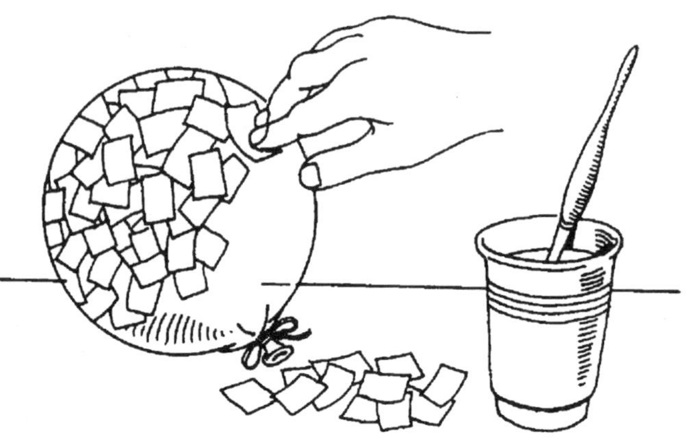

4 Mark on the world's continents with a pen. (Look carefully at a real globe.)

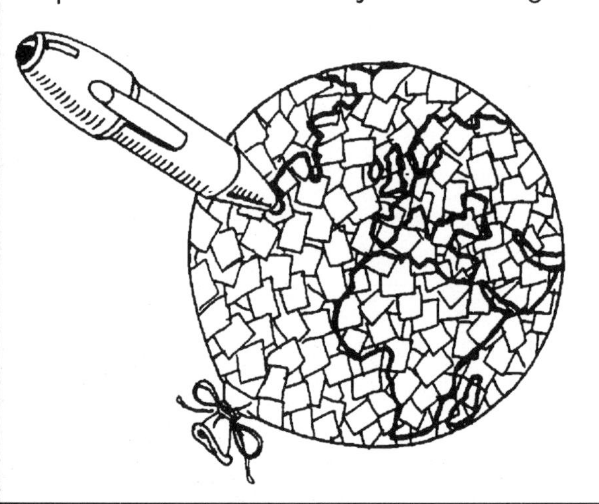

5 Now stick small pieces of green and blue paper on using paste to make the land and sea.

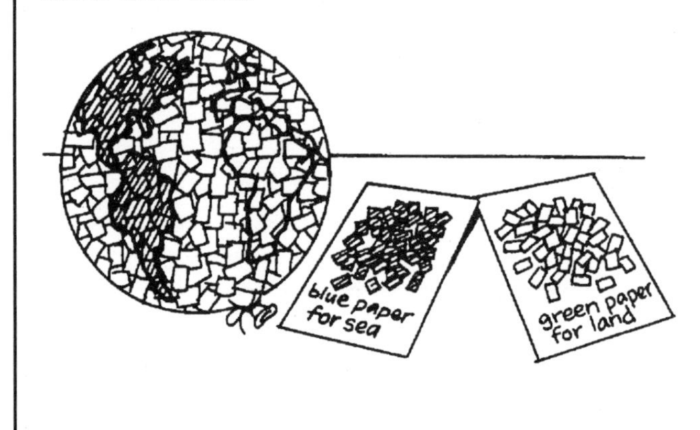

6 Draw the pictures connected with your theme.

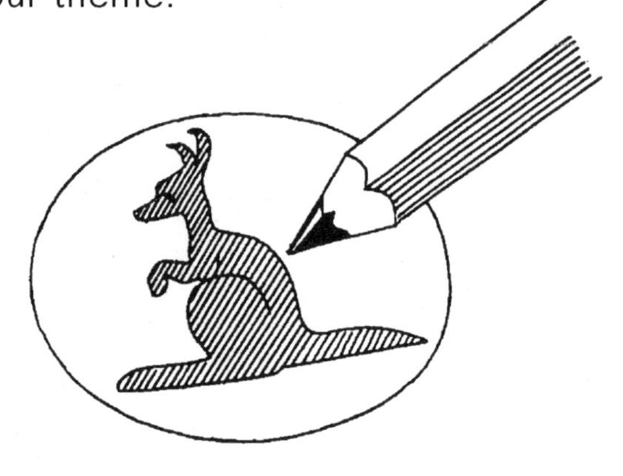

7 Stick them onto your papier mâché globe using glue.

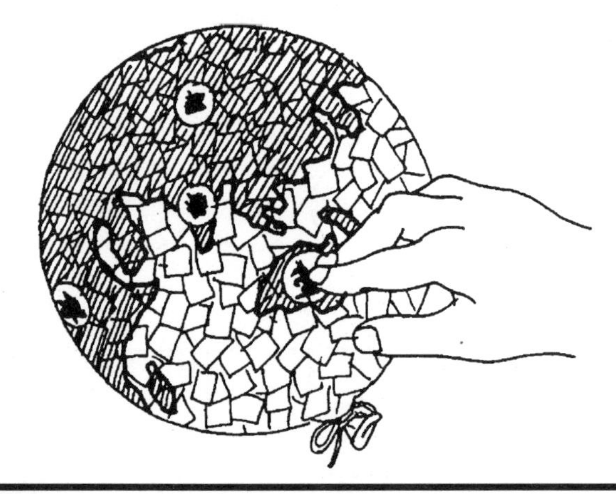

What's the weather doing? (see page 31)

What's the weather doing?

Name ______________________ Date ______________

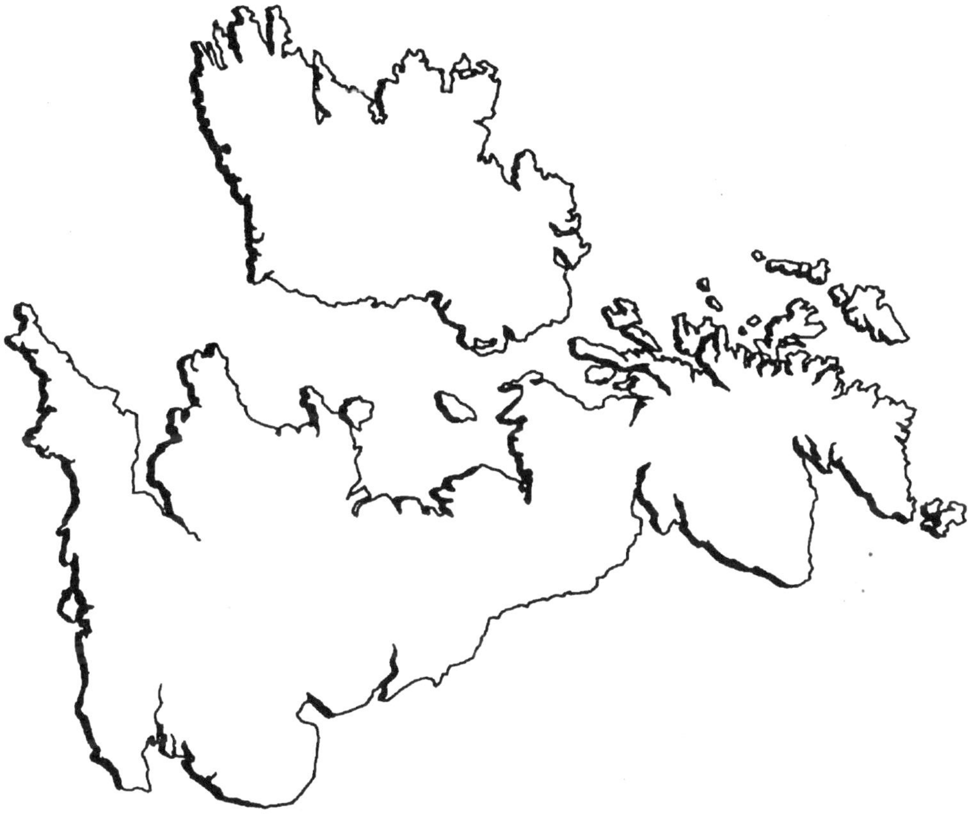

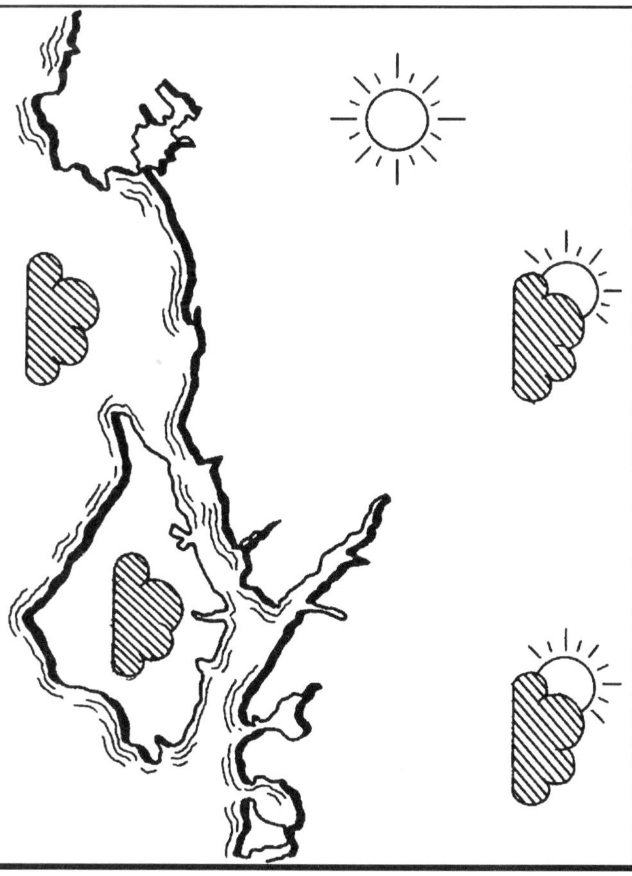

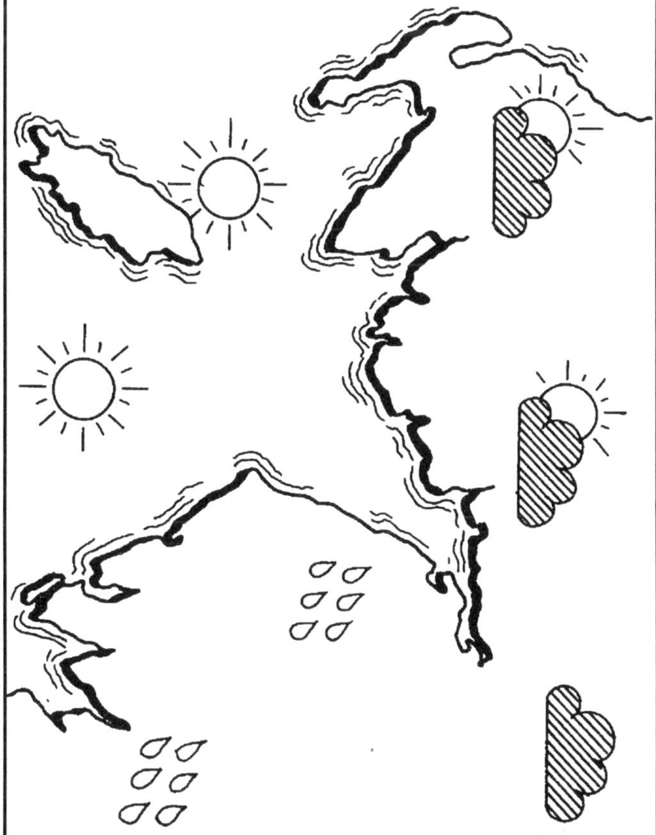

What's the weather doing? (see page 31)

What's the weather doing now?

Name ____________________ Date ____________

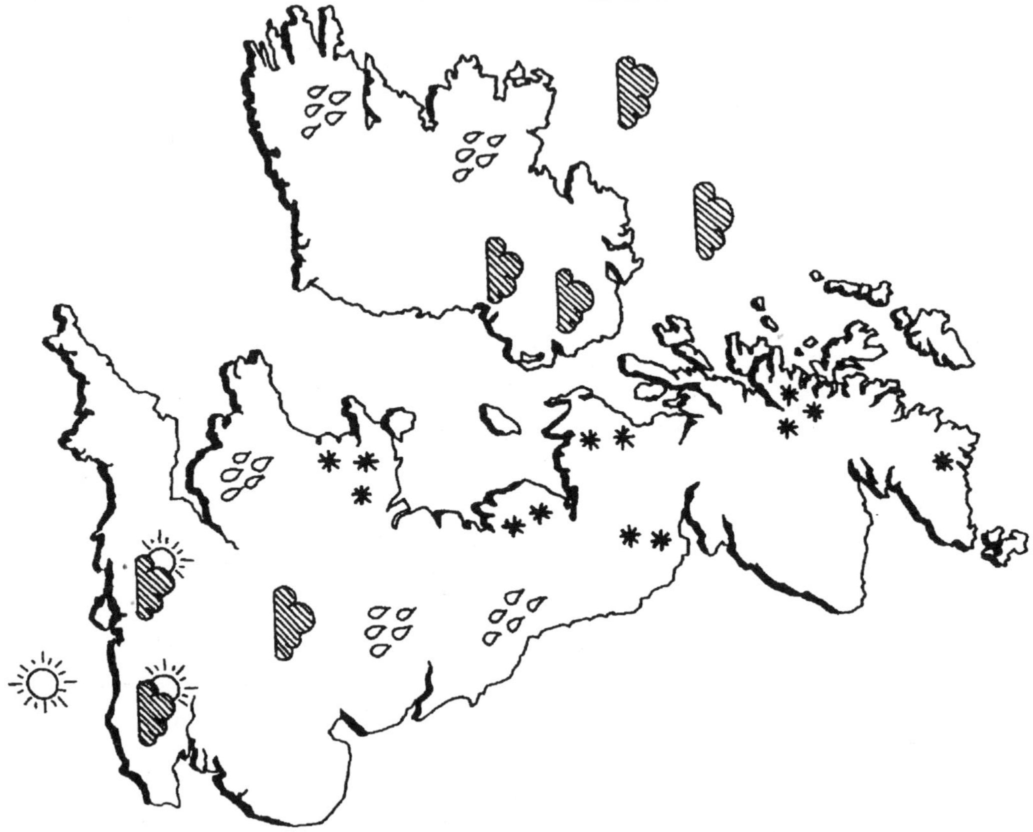

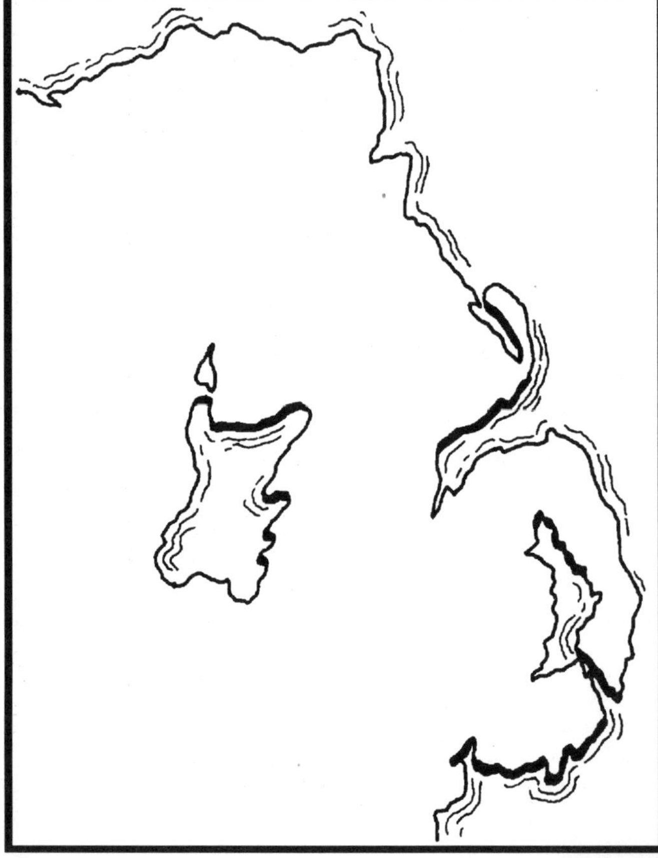

More houses needed (see page 33)

More houses needed: 1

Name ______________________ Date ______________

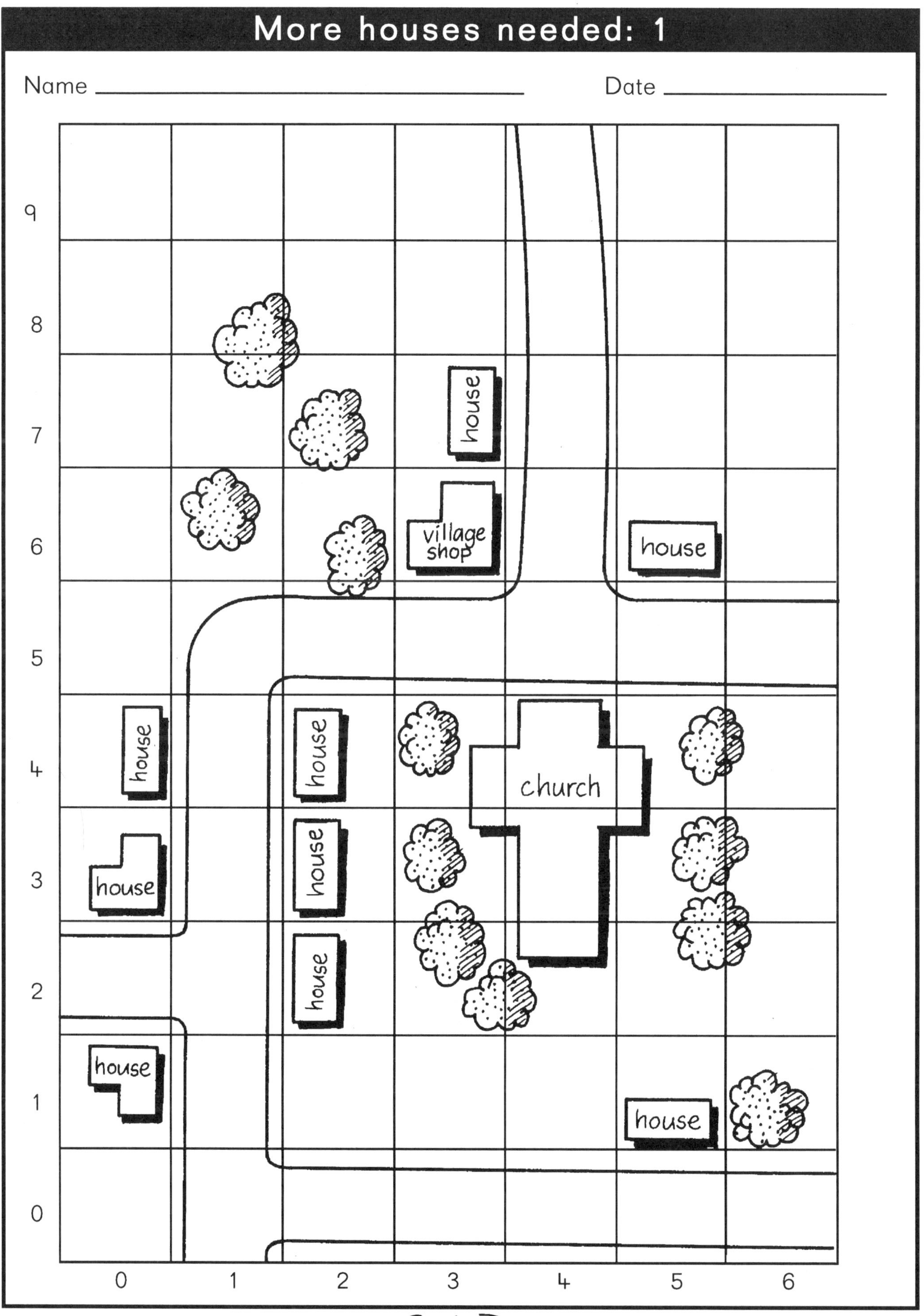

More houses needed: 2

Name ________________________ Date ________________

Village 'improvements'

It is your job to decide where new buildings are to be located in the village.

▲ Add the following on the map after careful thought.

	Grid reference		Grid reference
New road to cover at least 6 squares		11 new houses covering 1 square each	
New primary school to cover 5 squares			
2 new shops covering 1 square each		1 new telephone box	
		1 new electricity sub-station	

Will any trees be affected by your changes? If so, list the trees by giving their references here:

____

____

Will you be able to plant any new trees? If so, list which squares you will plant them in here:

____

____

Cities on the map

Name ______________________ Date ____________

KEY

Port □ Inland city ⬡ Airport ○ Tourist destination △

City	Port	Inland city	Airport	Tourist destination	Grid reference
Birmingham					
Cardiff					
Glasgow					
Oxford					
Norwich					
Plymouth					
Swansea					
York					
Newcastle					
Chester					
Southampton					
London					
Belfast					

River navigation (see page 37)

River navigation: 1

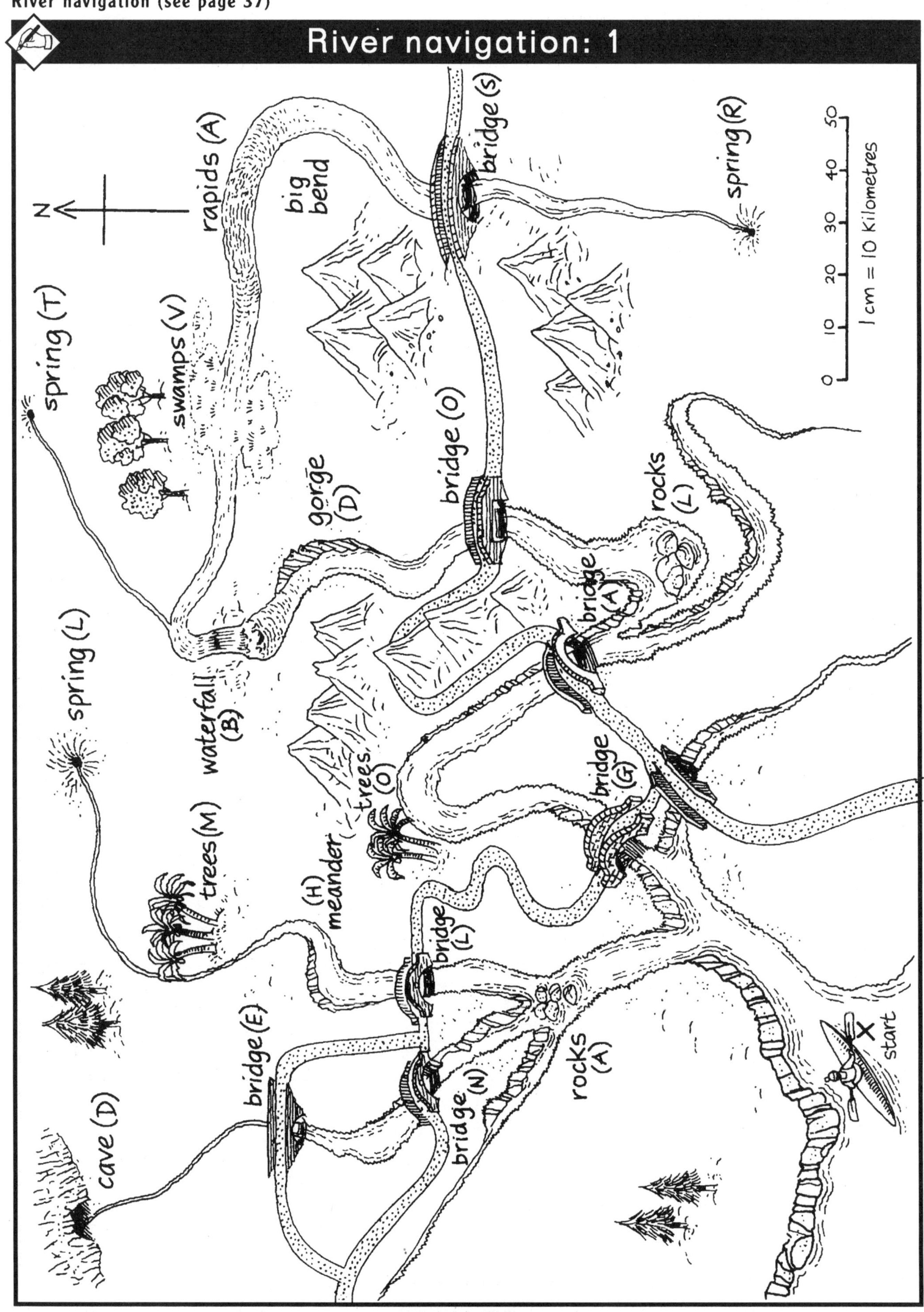

River navigation: 2

Name ______________________ Date ______________

You are going to find a piece of treasure at the end of a difficult journey inland from the mouth of a mysterious river. All your journeying will be by canoe.

▲ Follow these directions carefully and write the letters you find as you travel in the grid below to discover your prize.

Start at point 'X' and paddle 60km to the north east.
Collect your first letter.

Now paddle 40km north and then collect your second letter.

After paddling 70km to the south east
you will find your third letter.

You now must head to the north for 70km.
Pick up your next letter.

After just 20 kilometres canoeing in a north-westerly
direction you find your fifth letter.

Now turn east and travel for 80km to find the last but one letter.
Your last letter is 100km to the south.

N
W E

▲ Write down your seven treasure letters in the order you find them.

1	2	3	4	5	6	7

Environmental trail (see page 39)

Environmental trail

Name ________________________ Date ______________

▲ As you walk your classes trail write the answers to the questions about the building materials in this table.

The origin of a building material is the place where it originally came from (for example: wood – forest).

Place number	Building material	Origin of material	Place number	Building material	Origin of material
1			13		
2			14		
3			15		
4			16		
5			17		
6			18		
7			19		
8			20		
9			21		
10			22		
11			23		
12			24		

Places high and places low (see page 41)

Places high and places low

Name ______________________ Date ______________

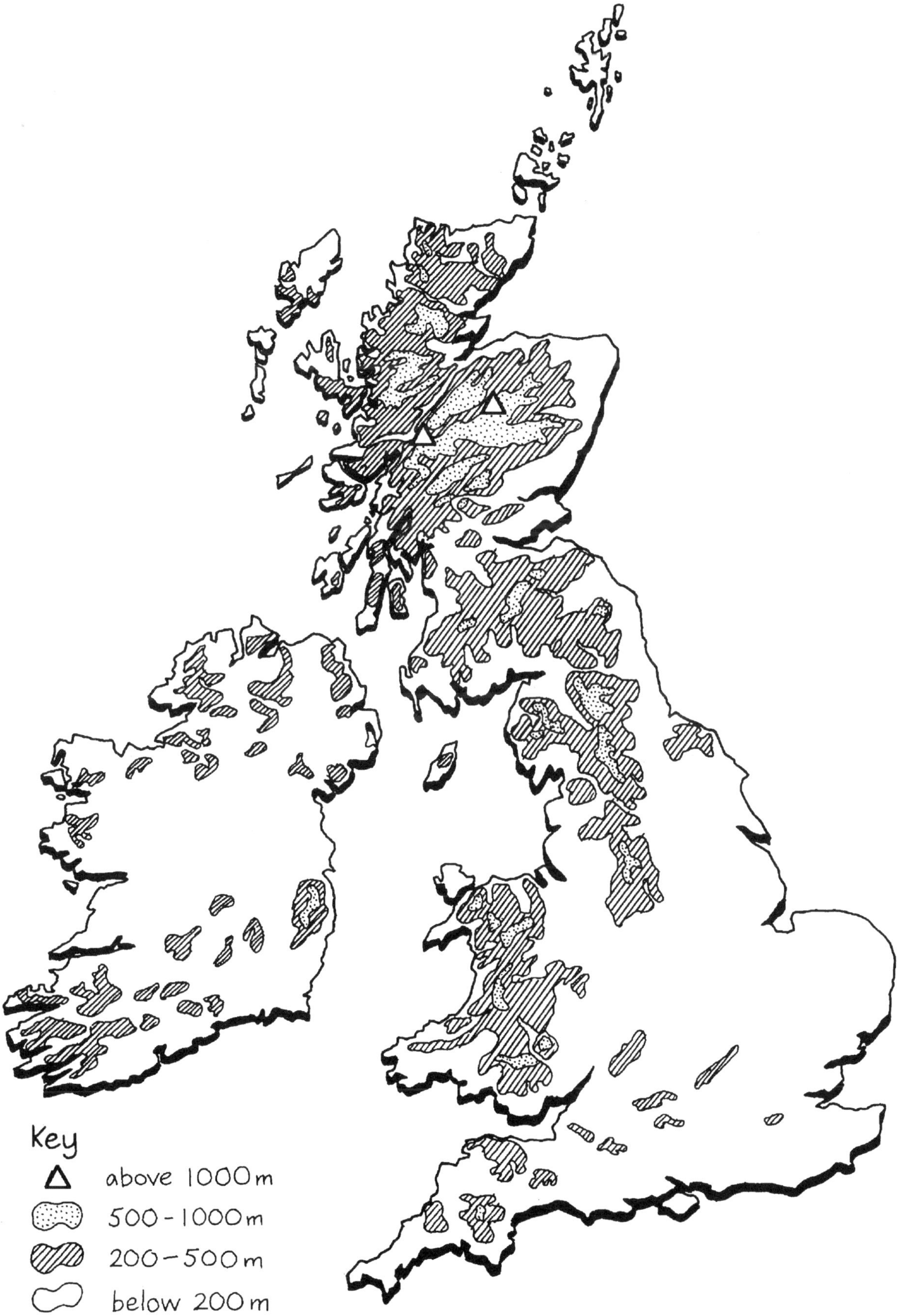

Key

△ above 1000m

500-1000m

200-500m

below 200m

How does the water get into the river?

▲ Cut out each of the sets of drawings for forests and towns. Put each of them into the correct order.

▲ Cut out the labels and put them with the correct pictures.

River parts (see page 48)

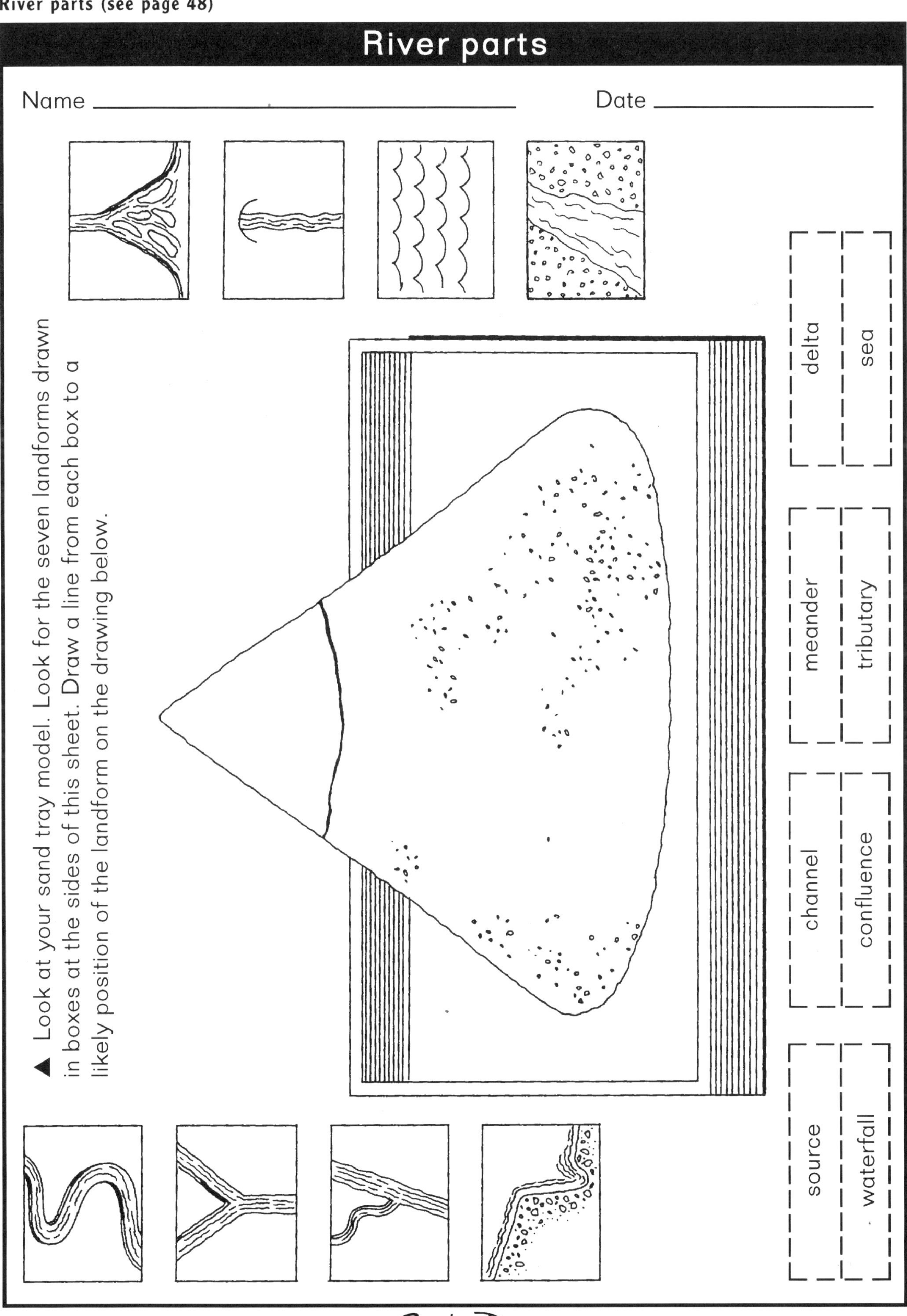

Where do rivers go? (see page 50)

The journey of the Nile

Name ______________________ Date ______________

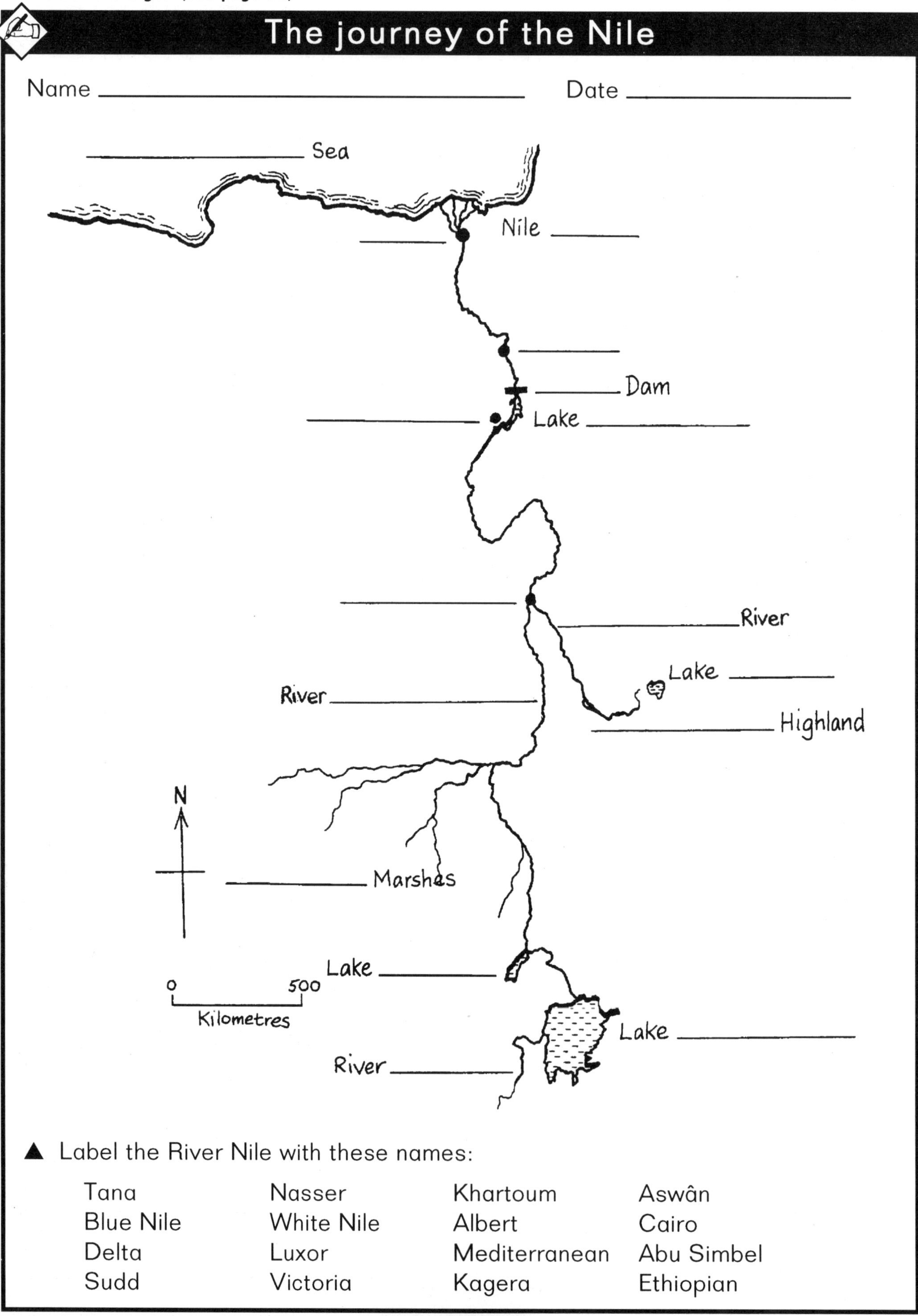

▲ Label the River Nile with these names:

Tana	Nasser	Khartoum	Aswân
Blue Nile	White Nile	Albert	Cairo
Delta	Luxor	Mediterranean	Abu Simbel
Sudd	Victoria	Kagera	Ethiopian

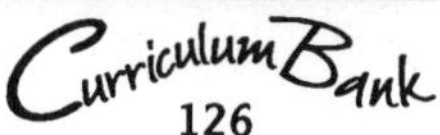

Rivers working (see page 54)

River erosion, transportation and deposition

Name ____________________ Date ____________

Experiment I: What is the effect of slope on river speed?

Slope	Speed – centimetres per second
steep	
medium	
gentle	

Speed
centimetres per second

gentle medium steep
slope

Experiment II: What is the effect of the amount of water on river speed?

Amount of water	Speed – centimetres per second
a lot	
some	
a little	

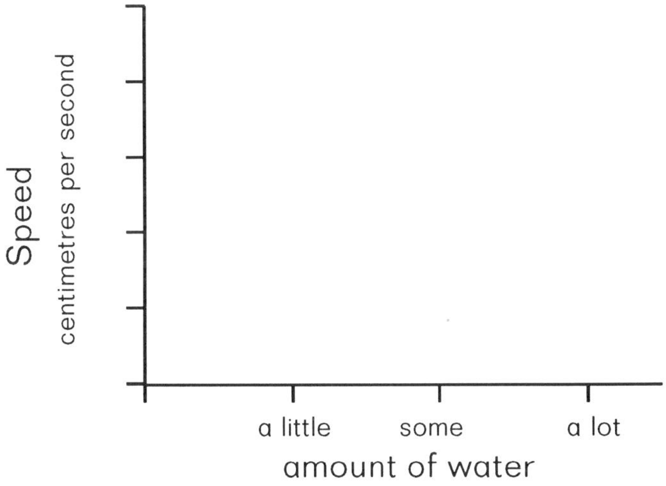

Speed
centimetres per second

a little some a lot
amount of water

Experiment III: What is the effect of river speed on the movement of pebbles?

Speed	Velocity in centimetres per second	stones moved		
		small	medium	large
fast				
medium				
slow				

River landforms (see page 57)

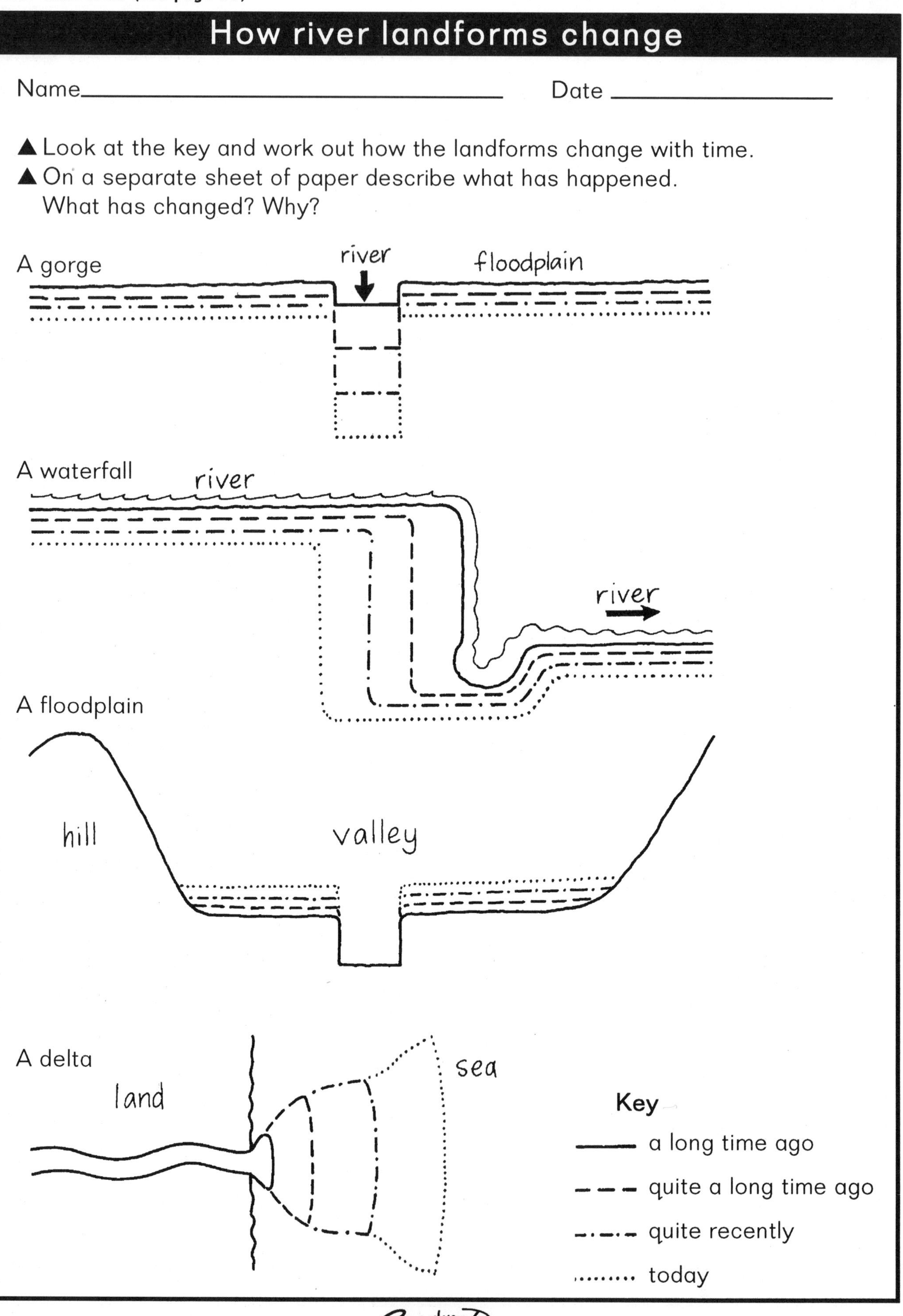

How river landforms change

Name____________________ Date ____________

▲ Look at the key and work out how the landforms change with time.

▲ On a separate sheet of paper describe what has happened. What has changed? Why?

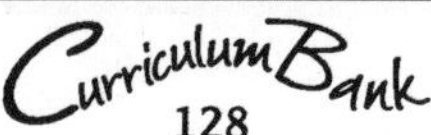

Keep safe by rivers (see page 60)

Dangers by rivers

Name ______________________________ Date ________________

All the children could be in danger of an accident.

▲ On a separate sheet of paper list the activity they are doing, why it is dangerous and what they can do to prevent these dangers.

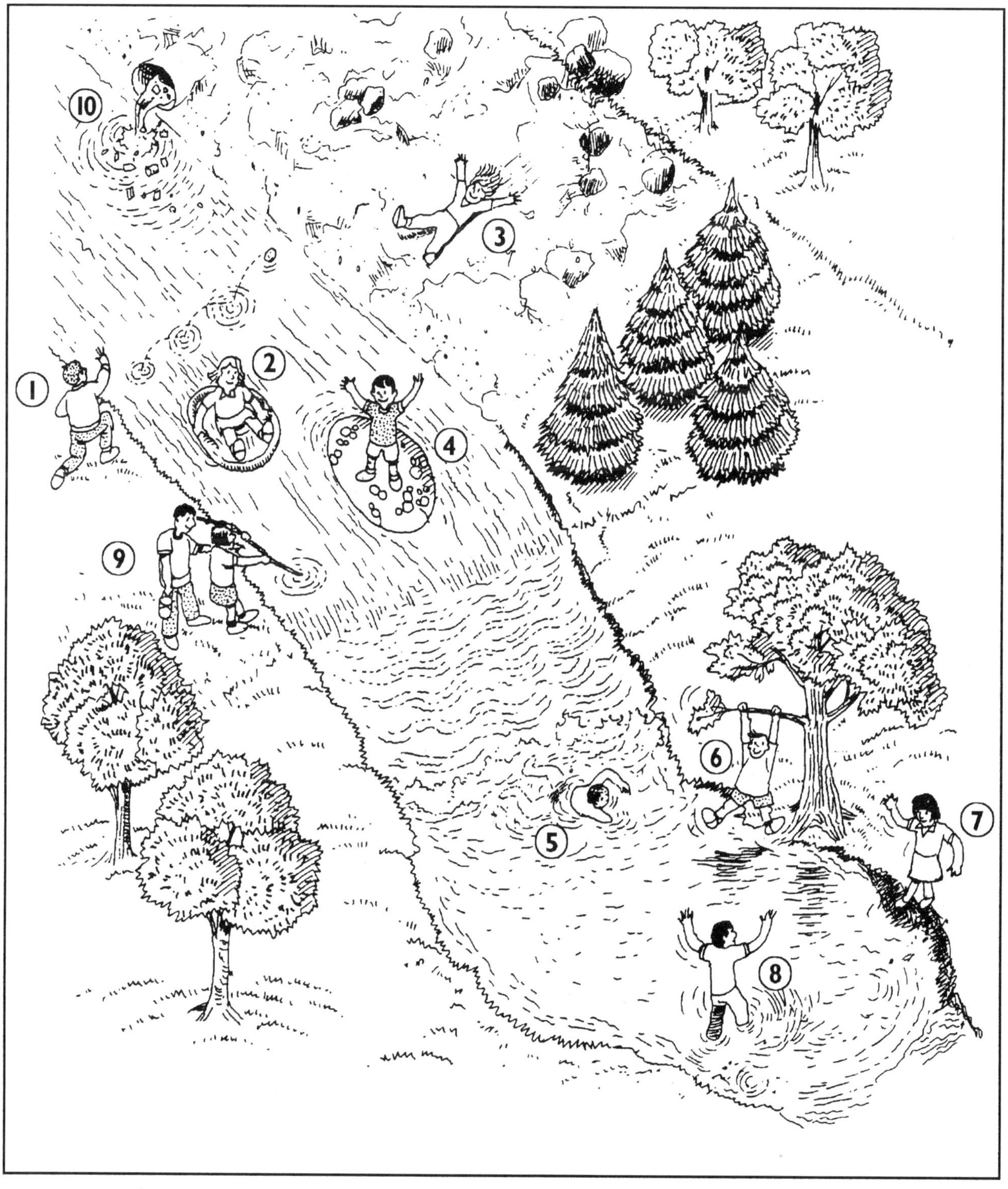

Weather measuring equipment

Name__________________________ Date __________________

▲ Name each weather instrument and fill in the missing words.

A __________

To measure the __________ you look at the scale which is marked in °__________. You must keep your__________ level with the top of the fluid. Always read a thermometer in the __________ and leave it for a few minutes before use. This thermometer gives a temperature of __________ °C.

An __________

This instrument measures the __________ of the __________. Always make sure that you hold it at __________ length and use it in an __________ space. The faster the cups go round the greater the __________ of the wind.

A __________ __________

You use this to measure __________. It should be set up __________ hours before a reading is taken. Rain drips into a __________ which then drips water into a collection beaker. These instruments should always be positioned on __________ __________. Always __________ them after taking a reading.

A __________ __________

This is also known as a __________ __________ indicator. It should be lined up in the right direction using a__________. The __________ blows the big flap so that the __________ points in the direction the wind is coming __________. This shows the wind as coming from the __________.

Measuring our weather (see page 64)

Weather data recording sheet

Name ______________________ Date ______________

		Rainfall	Wind speed	Wind direction	Temperature
Unit →		ml		(compass)	°C
Day	Date				
Tu					
W					
Th					
F					
Tu					
W					
Th					
F					
Tu					
W					
Th					
F					
Tu					
W					
Th					
F					

Two places

Name ______________________ Date ______________________

Sampling locations

1 ______________________ 2 ______________________

Before you have taken all your readings

Which location will have:

highest temperature ____________ lowest temperature ____________

highest wind speed ____________ lowest wind speed ____________

highest rainfall ____________ lowest rainfall ____________

brightest light levels ____________ dullest light levels ____________

In which direction do you think the wind will be blowing:

in location A ____________; in location B ____________ ?

Say why you expect these findings:

After you have taken all your readings

Were your findings correct? ______________________

What differences were there to your findings? ______________________

temperature ______________________

wind speed ______________________

rainfall ______________________

light levels ______________________

wind direction ______________________

Explain any differences:

Our local weather (see page 66)

Recording sheet

Name ______________________ Date ______________

		Location 1	Location 2
Tuesday	temperature		
	wind speed		
	wind direction		
	rainfall		
	light level		
Wednesday	temperature		
	wind speed		
	wind direction		
	rainfall		
	light level		
Thursday	temperature		
	wind speed		
	wind direction		
	rainfall		
	light level		
Friday	temperature		
	wind speed		
	wind direction		
	rainfall		
	light level		

Seasonal weather graphs (see page 69)

The seasons in our region

Name ____________________ Date ____________

Temperature

Jan Feb Mar Apr May Jun Jul Sep Oct Nov Dec

Sunshine

Jan Feb Mar Apr May Jun Jul Sep Oct Nov Dec

Precipitation

Jan Feb Mar Apr May Jun Jul Sep Oct Nov Dec

Seasons around the world (see page 71)

Climate map of the world

▲ Colour the key and then the map to show the five climatic zones.

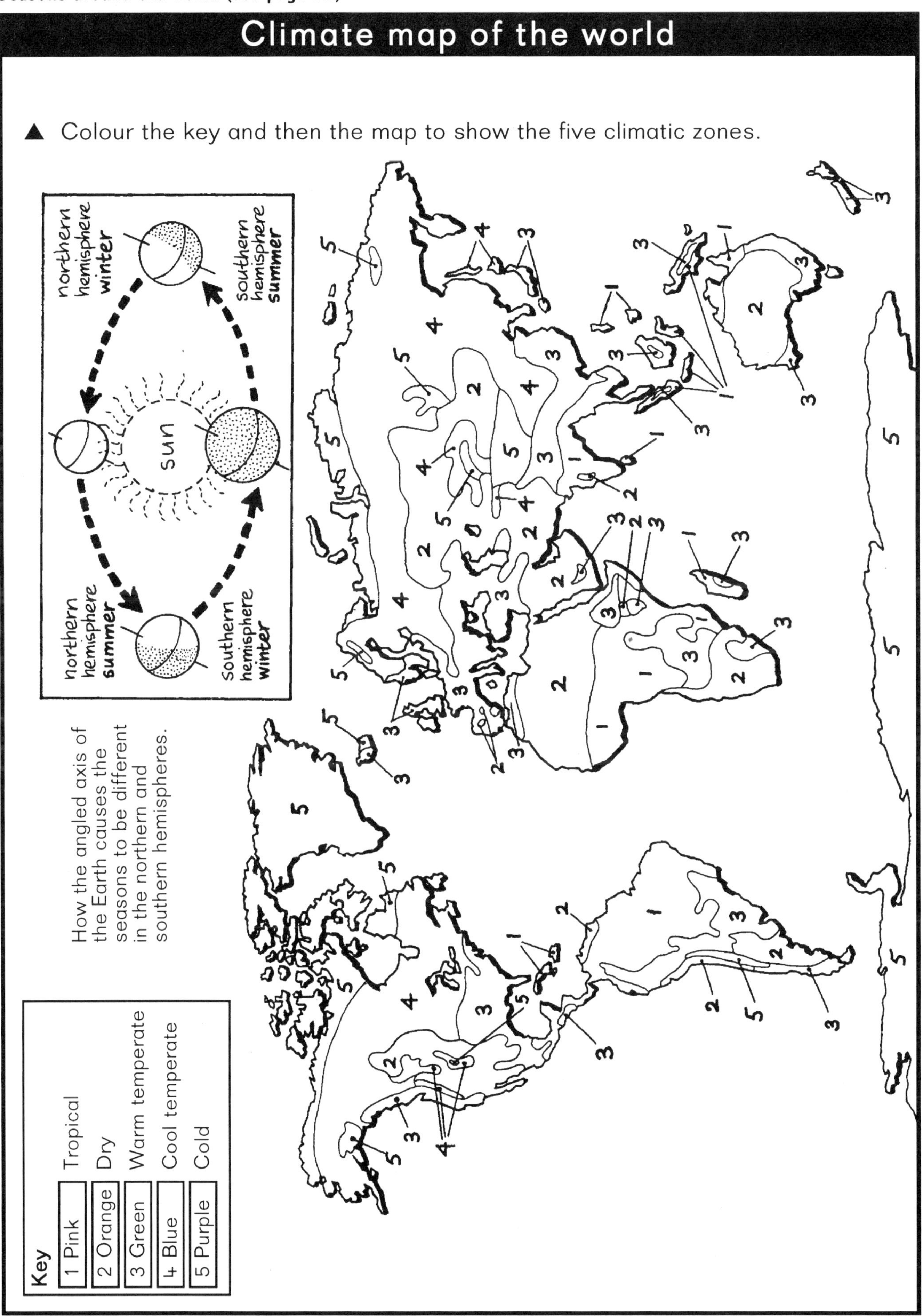

Seasons around the world (see page 71)

Seasons around the world

Name ______________________ Date ______________

	Name of place	Weather		Name of place	Weather	
Cold						
Cool temperate						
Warm temperate						
Dry						
Tropical						
		Summer	Winter		Summer	Winter

Our weather correspondent (see page 71)

Weather documentary planning sheet

Name ______________________ Date ______________

Programme planning team:

Weather type* – Hurricane/Monsoon rainfall/Hot, dry desert/Heavy snow

*ring the subject of this programme

World locations where this weather is found.

Explanation of the weather type.

Real examples of this type of weather being hazardous.

1	2

Village, town or city (see page 76)

Hamlet and city

Name ______________________ Date ______________

HAMLET

Name ______________ Scale of map used 1: __________

Area covered by hamlet in square centimetres ________ cm^2

Area covered by hamlet in square kilometres on the ground ________ km^2

CITY

Name ______________________ Scale of map used 1: __________

Area covered by city in square centimetres ________ cm^2

Area covered by city in square kilometres on the ground ________ km^2

Village or town

Name ______________________ Date ______________

VILLAGE

Name

____

Scale of map used 1: ______________

Area covered by village in square centimetres ____________ cm²

Area covered by village in square kilometres on the ground

______________ km²

TOWN

Name

____

Scale of map used 1: ______________

Area covered by town in square centimetres

______________ cm²

Area covered by town in square kilometres on the ground

______________ km²

Types of settlement (see page 78)

Types of settlement

Name ______________________ Date ______________

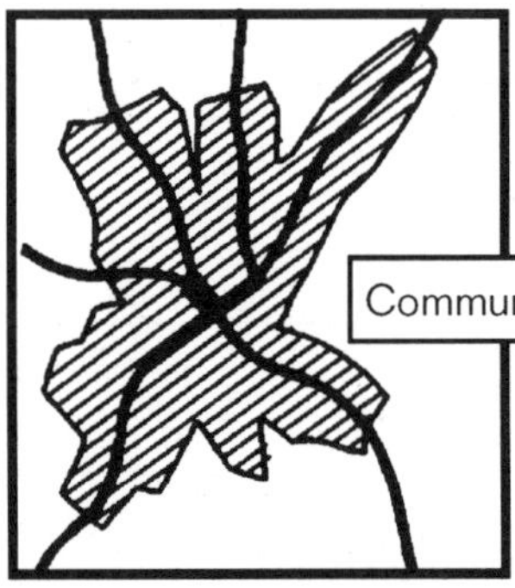

Communications-based settlement

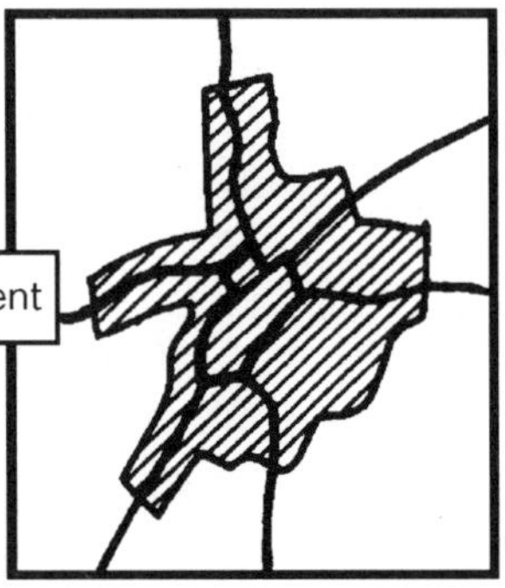

Market settlement

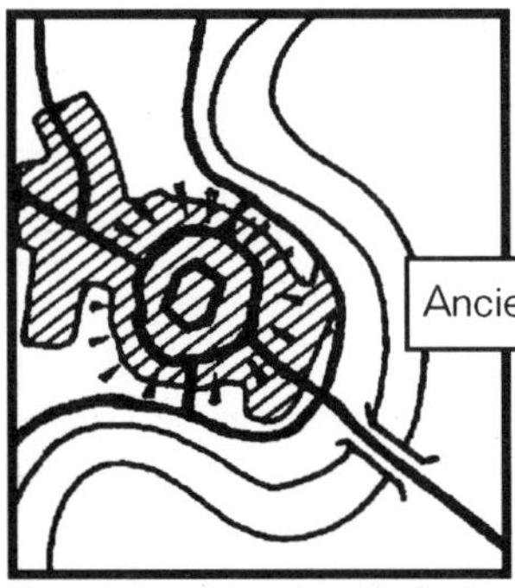

Ancient defensive settlement

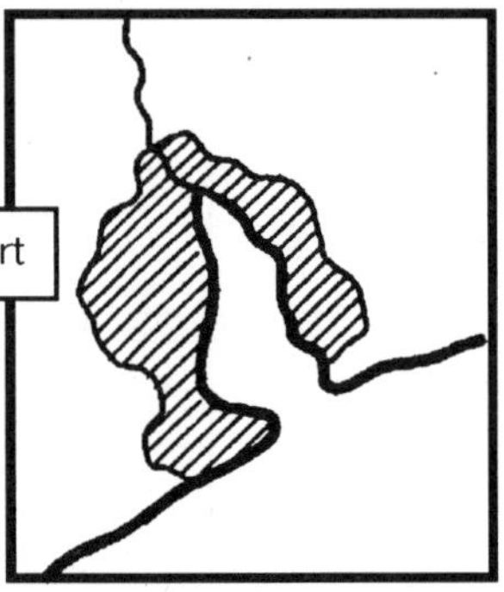

Port

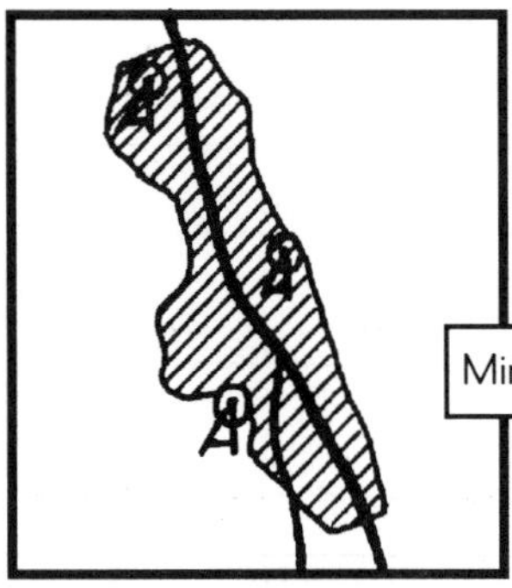

Mining settlement

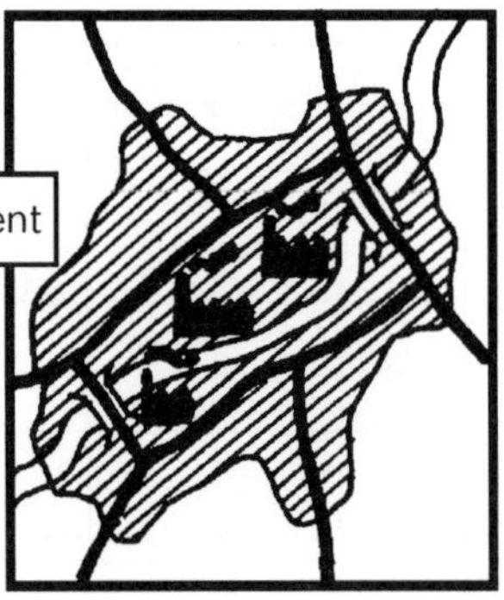

Manufacturing settlement

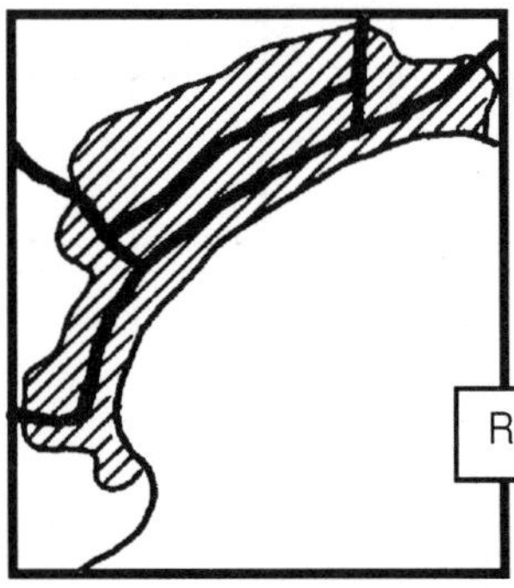

Resort

Name two communications-based settlements:

______________ village/town/city

______________ village/town/city

Name two market settlements:

______________ village/town/city

______________ village/town/city

Name two ancient defensive settlements:

______________ village/town/city

______________ village/town/city

Name two ports:

______________ village/town/city

______________ village/town/city

Name two mining settlements:

______________ village/town/city

______________ village/town/city

Name two manufacturing settlements:

______________ village/town/city

______________ village/town/city

Name two resorts:

______________ village/town/city

______________ village/town/city

Mapping land uses: 1

Name ____________________ Date ____________

Before and during our walk		After our walk	
Land-use categories	Surveying colour	Tally chart	Percentages of land-use in our square
1. Residential	☐		%
2. Retail	☐		%
3. Offices	☐		%
4. Educational	☐		%
5. Medical	☐		%
6. Manufacturing/Power supply	☐		%
7. Mining	☐		%
8. Indoor leisure	☐		%
9. Outdoor leisure	☐		%
10. Farming/Forestry	☐		%
11. Open countryside	☐		%
12. Transport	☐		%
13. Water not in another category	☐		%
14. Land/buildings not in use	☐		%

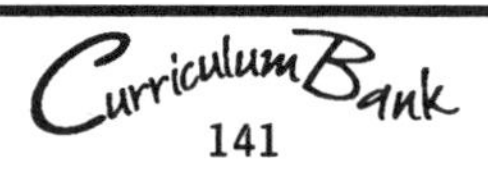

Mapping land uses: 2

Name ______________________________ Date ________________

▲ Place this grid over your completed map to calculate percentages of each land-use category.

Changing land uses (see page 82)

Changing land uses: 1

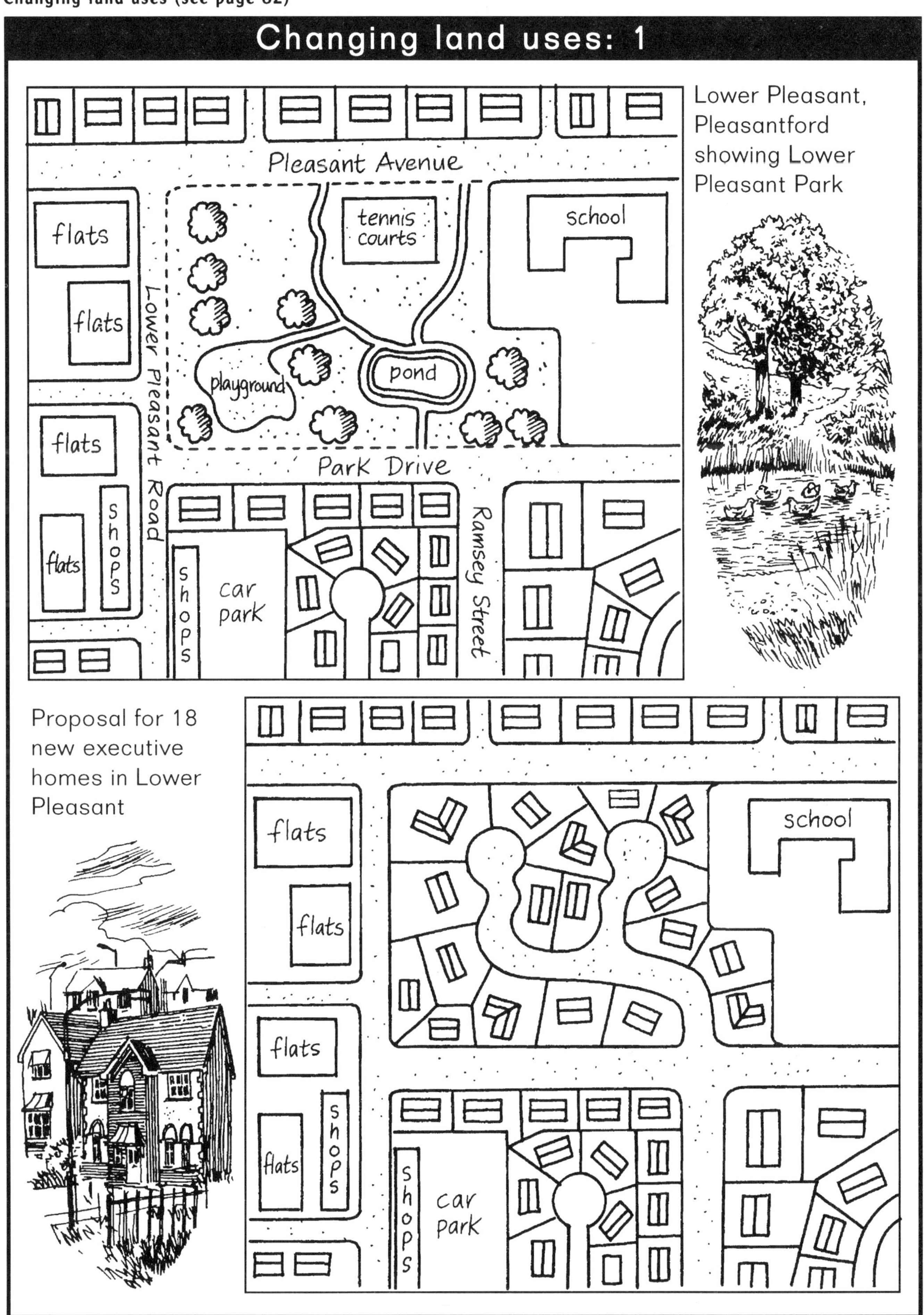

Changing land uses: 2

Conservationists

You are very unhappy that the park is to be sold for new housing. The park is the last area of green space in the community. All the other parks have been built on. The park has some very large and beautiful trees. The plan would knock all of these down and replace them with large modern houses. One of the trees is very old and you want it to be protected.

The area is very busy, with people and traffic. The park is the last area of quiet and calm. There are several species of birds nesting there. Foxes, moles and frogs have all recently been seen in the area. The flowers and shrubs are beautiful and the playing field and playground are used by local people.

Local people

You and your family have lived in the area for many years. You grew up here. The area has changed a lot. All the parks and green spaces have disappeared. There are lots of houses, flats and shops here now. Your children go to the local school. You use the playground and park a lot. You are worried that there will be nowhere for the children to play, except in the street.

You know that the plan is to build large houses. You could not afford to buy or rent these. You are unhappy with this and would rather see smaller houses or no houses at all.

Developers

It is your plan to buy the park from the local council and build 20 new, high quality houses. If you can get permission you can make lots of money. You will need to 'sell' your plan to the local people.

The park is used by the local people but it is also not a safe place to go near in the evening. There is a need for more housing in the area and this is the last piece of open space available to build them on. The housing will improve the way the area looks as the park is often untidy with litter and graffiti. You think that the new, high quality housing is just what the area needs.

Local councillors

New housing is needed by the community. There is a lot of homelessness in the area. Many of the flats are overcrowded. The council needs money to be able to improve the housing in the area. Selling the park to build new housing would bring money into the area. You know that the local people are not happy with the plan.

Some of you are shopkeepers. More people living in the area means more business. You are very keen for the project to go ahead. Some of you are worried that the local people will be upset if they lose their park.

More pupils – more space (see page 84)

More pupils – more space

Name ______________________ Date ______________

▲ Draw an accurate picture of what your design will look like.

▲ Answer the following questions on a separate sheet of paper:

1. What will your design look like from the outside?

2. What other learning areas will be affected by your design once it is finished.

3. Where will children using the classroom hang their coats?

4. Which toilets will children in the new classroom use?

5. How will children using the new classroom escape in the event of fire?

▲ Justify why you think your design is best.

Settlements in our region

Name ______________________ Date ______________

The main settlements in our region

▲ List the settlements you go to for each of the following:

The weekly shopping

To buy new furniture

A Sunday walk

To buy a new car

To see a sports event

For a good meal out

To visit a relative

To visit a museum

Noise near our school (see page 90)

Noise near our school

Name ______________________ Date ______________

Our Class Noise Survey

Road information	1	2	3	4	others
Type of road					
'A' road					
'B' road					
'C' road					
side road					
Road surface					
tarmac					
concrete					
cobbles					
other					
Roadside features					
walls/buildings both sides					
walls/buildings one side					
hedges/bushes/trees both sides					
hedges/bushes/trees one side					
open grass/flat land both sides					
open grass/flat land one side					
Other features					
bus stop in section					
traffic lights					
steep road					
other noise					
Traffic information					
Vehicles					
Number of vehicles in one minute					
bikes					
motor bikes					
cars					
vans					
lorries					
buses					
total number of vehicles					
Pollution information					
* *Noise level*					

* To record noise you can use words (like quiet or noisy), numbers (1–5), the distance you have to walk away from a cassette player before you cannot hear it, or the actual noise in decibels.

At the shops (see page 92)

At the shops

How is our school?

Name ______________________ Date ______________

▲ For each of the places listed in the left-hand column identify one nice and one nasty feature and then explain why you thought it was nice or nasty.

Features of our school

Where	Nice	Why?	Nasty	Why?
View from school grounds entrance				
Walls				
Playground				
Garden				
Playing fields				
Another place?				

▲ Think of as many ways as possible of improving the school grounds. Then think who can do each job and when it can be done and fill in the boxes. You do not have to fill in each box.

What can be done

	Today	This week	This term	This year
Me				
Our class				
Our school				
Our mums and dads				

Building a reservoir (see page 96)

Dry days dam

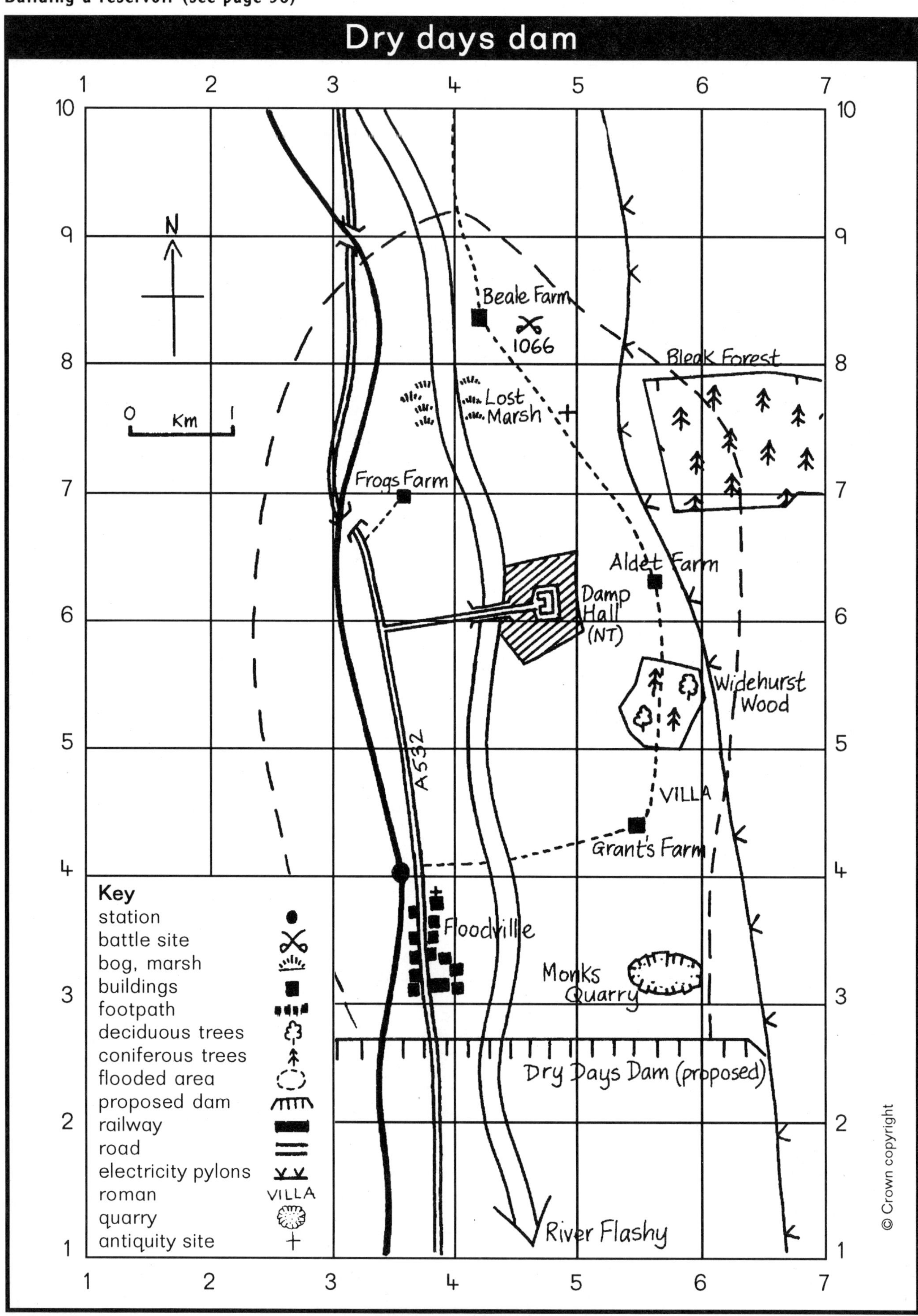

Ronny the water drop's story

Name ______________________ Date ______________

▲ To complete Ronny's story, use the words at the bottom of the sheet to fill in the gaps. Use your knowledge of streams and rivers.

I bubbled out of the ground at a __________ and then trickled down the hillside. I quickly joined lots more water to form a small __________ which flowed between boulders and began to cut itself a small __________ in the soft soil of the hillside. Every now and then another stream would join us. Each one of these was called a __________ and each time this happened we got bigger and bigger. We now had so much energy that we were able to __________ bits of soil and even small stones from the __________ and bed of the channel. We __________ this material down the hillside and because the stream had been doing this for a long time we quickly found ourselves in a deep V shaped __________. As we travelled down the hill we came to a place where the hard rock of the mountain came to the surface again. Suddenly we tumbled over the edge of this rock and fell down a __________ to splash into a pool below. Now we were quite big and the steepness of the slope was lessening. We twisted and turned in large __________, rushing quickly round the outside and moving slowly on the inside. The bits of sand and soil eroded from higher up the mountain were __________ in this slower water. We were now a mighty __________ which eventually flowed out to sea at its __________. We had had a lot of adventures on our journey from the river's __________ at the top of the mountain.

transported	tributary	spring	source
stream	deposited	waterfall	banks
erode	channel	river	meanders
	mouth		valley

River features (see page 100)

River features

Name ______________________ Date ____________

▲ Complete this key by filling in the boxes to label the river features correctly.

	source
	tributary
	delta
	gorge
	spring
	flood plain
	meander
	sea
	waterfall
	stream
	mouth
	valley

The key will now spell a river's name. Can you find it in an atlas?

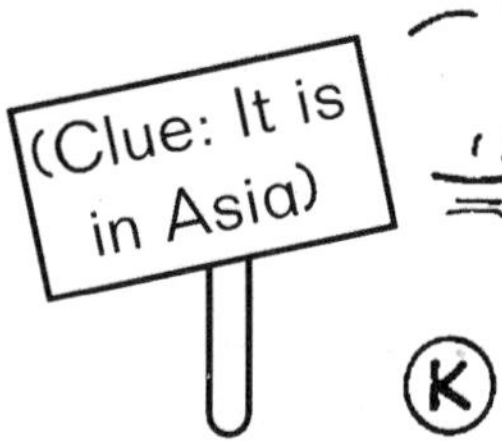

R A O H I E U S K V N R

(Clue: It is in Asia)

▲ Colour places *brown* where you think there is erosion, and places *yellow* where you think there is deposition.

Clifftop School Climate

Name ______________________ Date ____________

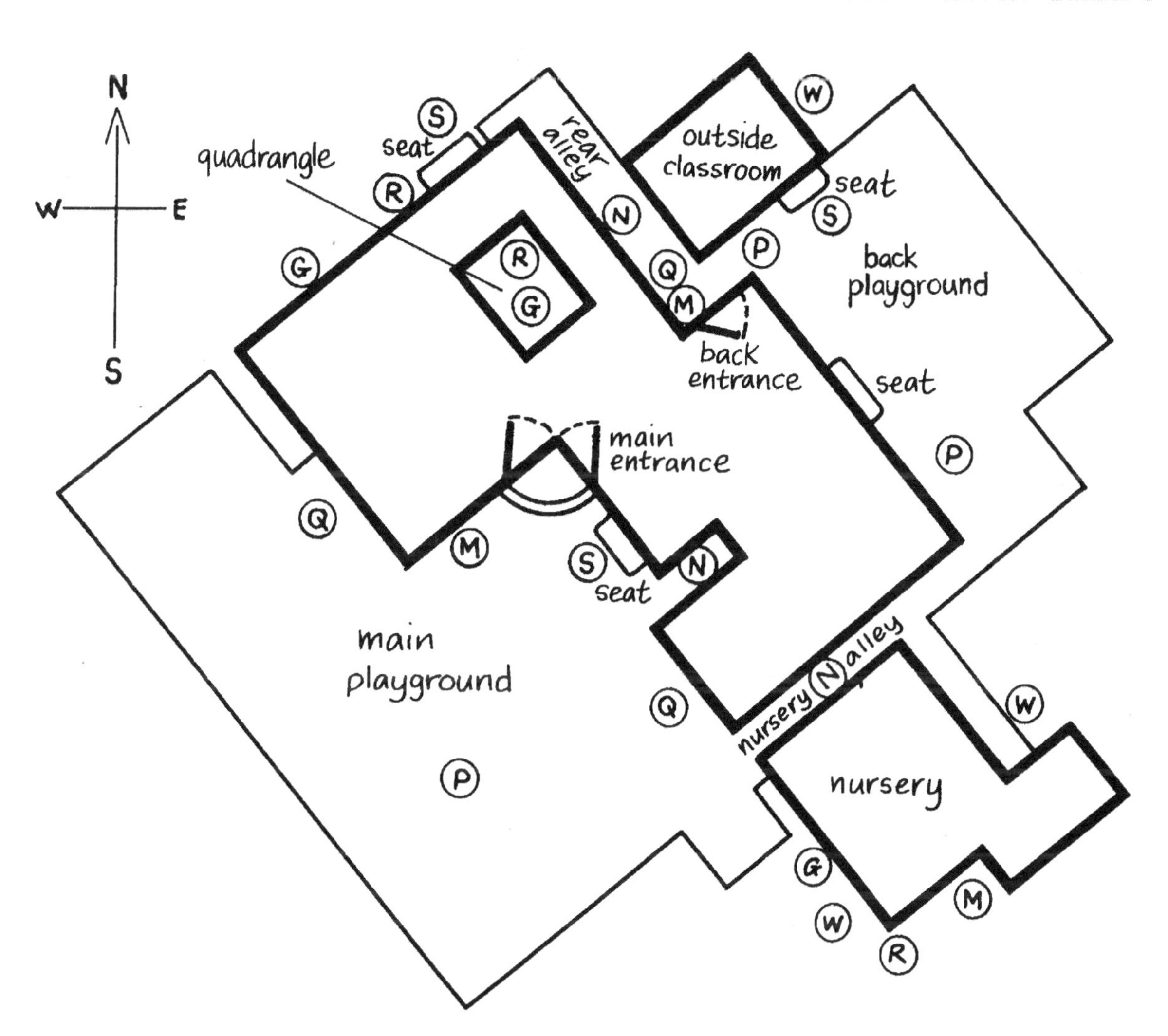

This is Clifftop School. The wind normally blows from the south west.

▲ Choose *one* of each of the symbols on the map and colour it and the key below, to show that you think it is the most appropriate place to:

- (S) sit on a sunny morning
- (Q) queue up outside on a windy day
- (W) position a washing line
- (P) play on a sunny afternoon
- (M) grow a plant which needs shade and shelter
- (G) ask for milk to be left in the morning
- (R) grow a plant which needs lots of sun
- (N) position an alley-way notice board to be read even on a windy day

Our seasonal school (see page 101)

Our seasonal school

Name ______________________________ Date ____________________

▲ For each of the eight aspects of school life, write comments about change through the seasons at your school.

	Autumn Sept→ Oct→ Nov	Winter Dec→ Jan→ Feb	Spring Mar→ Apr→ May	Summer Jun→ Jul→ Aug
playtimes				
science work				
PE and games				
school trips and visits				
plants/animals around the school				
school fuel bills				
clothes/uniform worn				
special event in school				

Village, town, city (see page 101)

Village, town, city

Name ______________________ Date ______________

▲ For each of the three settlement types write the name of one you know well.
▲ Tick the boxes to show which services are present in each settlement.

	My village:	My town:	My city:
waste bin			
bus stop			
letter box			
public telephone			
general store			
post office			
place of worship			
public house			
newsagent			
police station			
video hire			
filling station			
café			
clothes shop			
bank			
cinema			
supermarket			
fire station			
railway station			
hotel			
department store			
council offices			
factory			
theatre			
concert hall			
airport			

▲ Now explain what your tick chart tells you about the three settlements.

Where in Dribbleford (see page 102)

What's in Dribbleford?

Name ______________________________ Date ________________

▲ Choose *one* of each of the symbols on the map and colour it and the key below, to show that you think it is the most appropriate place to find:

- ◯ the old market square
- ◯ the old, heavy industrial area
- ◯ the new industrial estate
- ◯ the area of expensive housing
- ◯ the 'out-of-town' shopping centre
- ◯ the old farm

Remember, the wind will normally blow noises and smells from the south west.

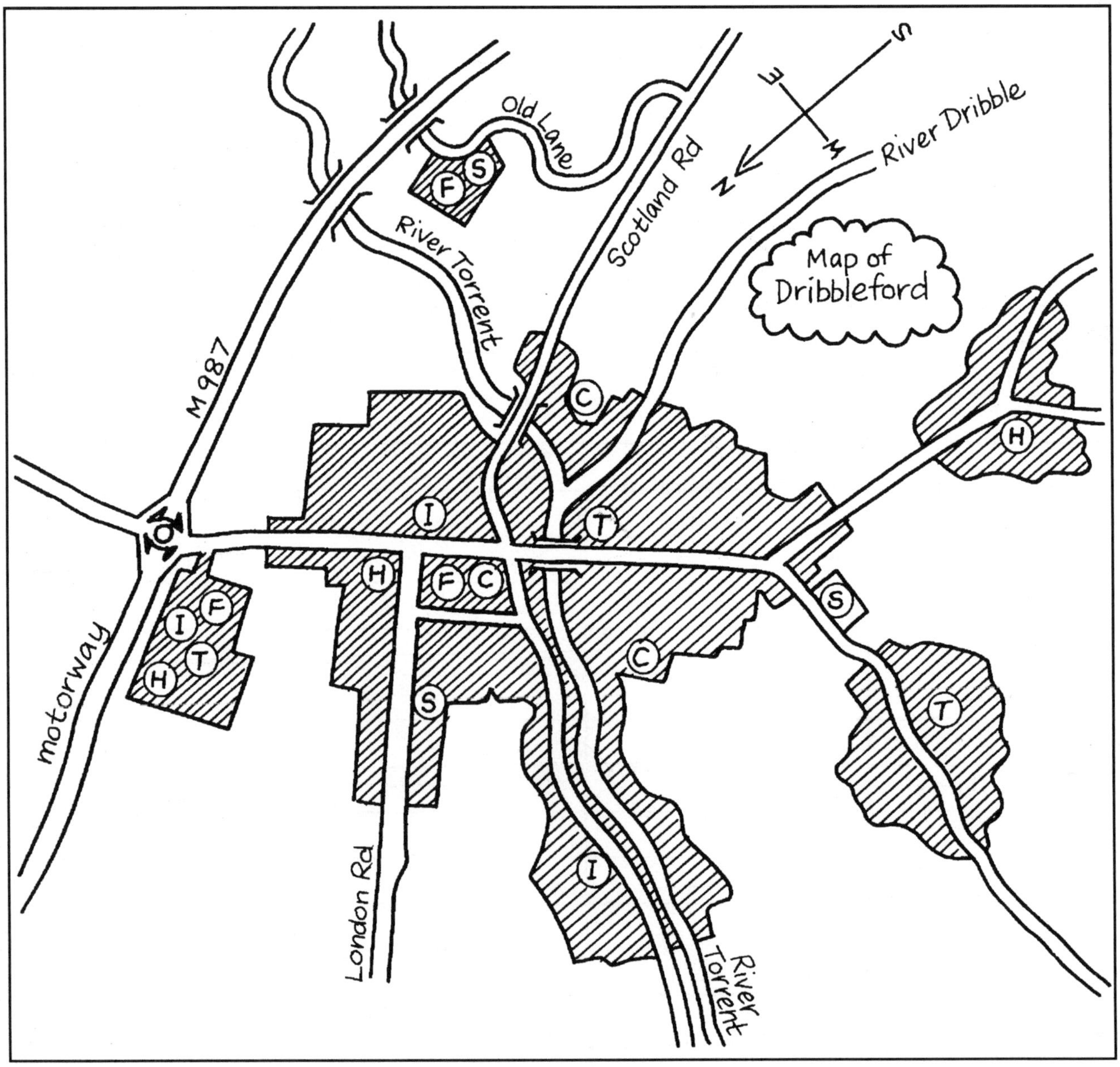
Map of Dribbleford
Old Lane
Scotland Rd
River Dribble
River Torrent
M987
motorway
London Rd
River Torrent
N
S
E
W
F
S
C
I
T
H
F
C
S
I
F
T
H
C
S
H
T
I

Good or bad (see page 102)

The good, the bad... and the people

Name ______________________ Date ______________

▲ Think about each of these changes in land use and imagine that they are happening near where you live. Write one good thing about each change and one bad thing. Mention groups of people who might be affected.

Changes	good	bad
A new main road using part of a park		
People affected		
Some farmland dug up to make a waste disposal site		
People affected		
The side of a mountain blasted to make a quarry		
People affected		
A shopping centre built on an area of old housing		
People affected		
A wooded valley flooded to make a reservoir		
People affected		
Some new houses built on some farmland		
People affected		

INFORMATION TECHNOLOGY WITHIN GEOGRAPHY

Main IT Focus

The main emphasis for the development of IT within these activities is on communicating and handling information.

Geography provides teachers with opportunities to use IT both to develop children's IT capability through communicating and handling information and to enrich their geographical knowledge and understanding. New software related to the National Curriculum geography themes appears regularly, particularly in the area of CD-ROMs. The Internet provides a rich resource base for information and pictures about weather, localities and environmental issues around the world. It also provides the opportunity to swap data with schools in contrasting localities.

Spreadsheets

Spreadsheets are an ideal way for children to record, tabulate and interrogate data in geography. A spreadsheet is simply a matrix of 'cells' which are identified by letters, along the top axis and numbers down the left-hand axis. (These letters and numbers can be replaced by labels.) Data can be entered directly into any one of the cells and consists of words or numbers.

Most spreadsheets contain a set of formulae for basic statistical work including means, ranges, maximum and minimum values. Some have the facility to plot graphs, pie charts and scattergraphs. They can also sort data into numerical or alphabetical order.

Mapping software

Most Local Education Authorities hold a licence for Ordnance Survey (OS) maps which extends to school use. There are several different formats of maps, but the most useful are the 'Land Line' series which gives a map which can be scaled up and down using appropriate software. The map is ideal for local study work as it shows each house, field, and even the position of the street furniture. Many LEAs have arrangements for getting access to these maps for a minimal handling charge. As the maps can also be purchased directly from the Ordnance Survey schools can also get access to contrasting UK locality maps which lie outside of their LEA.

Once you have the maps you will need suitable software for printing and manipulating them on your computer. The available software ranges from a simple map importer which allows you to import the maps into a drawing package, such as DRAW for RISCOS computers, to a fully working mapping package such as *Aegis 2* from the Advisory Unit for Computers in Education. This allows sections of map to be printed out at suitable scales for the age of the children.

Drawing software

This is particularly useful in geography for creating maps and plans which can be scaled up and down easily. Such software may be a dedicated drawing package, like *Draw for RISCOS computers*, as part of a suite of software such as *Claris Works* or be included within a word processor such as *Word for Windows*.

Drawing packages have a range of features to aid the drawing of regular shapes. One is a background grid which can be set to specific units; this assists the drawing of lines of specific lengths or for use in scale drawings. The option to *'snap to grid'* ensures that a line will automatically join up to the grid dot. This is useful for drawing plans of rooms/ buildings and drawing vertical and horizontal lines.

Other features allow specific shapes such as rectangles and circles to be drawn, as well as freehand lines and irregular closed shapes. Children need to know how to draw lines, change their colour and thickness, re-size simple shapes, rotate and copy them. Most drawing packages allow shapes to be filled with colour, lines to be drawn in different colours and text to be added, with the full range of text fonts and styles.

It may be helpful for the teacher to provide a file which contains the initial map or plan to which children can add their own information or designs. This will involve them in retrieving data from the disk. The teacher could also provide a toolbox of useful shapes or pictures (trees, buildings) so that when the child needs a tree, for example, they simply duplicate one from the toolbox and drag it to the required position, possibly re-sizing it to fit the scale they are using. It is also possible to 'import' pictures from clip art and CD-ROMS to use within the drawing.

By using these facilities children can make a complex map or plan from several different lines and shapes, called objects. These objects can be 'grouped' to make a single object. If the children had drawn a plan of the school, once completed with all the objects grouped, it can be scaled up or down with all parts scaled at the same proportion.

Many of the packages available to handle Ordnance survey digital maps have map editors which can be used in a similar way to help draw your own simple maps.

Multimedia authoriing software

This software is a recent addition for most schools but is proving to be a very versatile medium. It combines many of the features of a word processor or desktop publishing package but its main difference is that the different pages of a child's work can be linked together.

The software is able to handle a range of different information including text, pictures from art and drawing packages, digitised pictures from scanned images, ion cameras and video cameras, sounds from audio CDs or sound samples and moving pictures taken from a CD-ROM or captured using a video camera.

The grids on this page relate the activities in this book to specific areas of IT and to relevant software resources. Activities are referenced by page number rather than by name. (Bold page numbers indicate activities which have expanded IT content.) The software listed is a selection of programs generally available to primary schools, and is not intended as a recommended list. The software featured should be available from most good educational software retailers.

AREA OF IT	SOFTWARE	ACTIVITIES (PAGE NOS.)					
		CHAP 1	CHAP 2	CHAP 3	CHAP 4	CHAP 5	CHAP 6
Communicating Info	Word Processor	16,	31, 39	50, 60	73	76, 80	90, 92, 94, 96
Communicating info	DTP					80	90, 92, 96
Communicating info	Drawing software	**14**, 18,	24, **28**, 31, 33	44, 48, 60		80, 82	94
Communicating info	Art package			44, 60			
Communicating info	Mapping software	18	24, **28**, 31, 33	44			90, 94
Communicating Info	Authoring software		**28**	48	71, 73	84	96
Comm/Handling Info	KODAK CD-ROM					84	94
Information Handling	Database	**14**,	**35**, 41	57		78	92
Information handling	CD-ROM			48, 50	71	84	
Information handling	Spreadsheet	**14**, **21**	41	54	64, **66**, **69**	78	90
Information handling	Graphing software						90
Information handling	OS Map software		39				
Information handling	Internet		31		71	78	
Monitoring	Data-logging	**14**			64, **66**		

SOFTWARE TYPE	BBC/MASTER	RISCOS	NIMBUS/186	WINDOWS	MACINTOSH
Word Processor	*Pendown* *Folio*	*Pendown* *Desk Top Folio*	*All Write* *Write On*	*Word for Windows* *Kid Works 2* Creative Writer	*Kid Works 2* *Easy Works* Creative Writer
DTP	*Front Page Extra*	*Desk Top Folio* *Pendown DTP* *Impression Style*	*Front Page Extra* *NewSPAper*	*Creative Writer* *NewSPAper*	*Creative Writer*
Drawing Software		*Draw, Vector* *Art Works*		*Claris Works* *Oak Draw*	*Claris Works*
Multi-media Authoring		*Magpie* *Hyperstudio* *Genesis*		*Genesis* *Hyperstudio* *Illuminus*	*Hyperstudio*
Spreadsheet	*Grasshopper* *Pigeonhole*	*Grasshopper* *Advantage* *Key Count*	*Grasshopper*	*Excel starting Grid* *Claris Works* *Sparks*	*Claris Works*
Database	*Grass*	*Junior Pinpoint* *Find IT* *KeyNote*	*Grass*	*Sparks* *Claris Works* *Information Workshop*	*Claris Works* *Easy Works*
Graphing Software	*Datashow*	*Graph IT* *Data Plot*	*Datagraph*	*Datagraph* *Easy Works*	*Easy Works*
Mapping software		*Map Importer* *Aegis 2*		*Aegis 2*	
Data-logging	*Sense-it*	*Junior Insight*	*Investigate*	*Insight* Investigate	*Insight*
CD-ROM		*Children's Micropaedia* *Hutchinsons*		*Encarta 96* *Children's Micropaedia* *Grolier*	*Encarta 96* *Grolier*

Cross-curricular links

J. Thorpe

	ENGLISH	MATHEMATICS	SCIENCE	HISTORY	D & T	IT	ART	MUSIC	PE	RE
GEOGRAPHICAL SKILLS IN THE STUDY OF PLACES	Locational, directional and descriptive words and nouns. Reading skills using secondary sources. Writing directions.	Measuring time and distance, counting and graphicacy skills. Shape and space in the environment.	Scientific processes, observation, analysis and recording.	Geographical vocabulary's relevance to historical description. Historical sources to explain features.	Identifying design opportunities in the community. Design issues in the classroom.	Use of data logging equipment. Communications and media technologies as secondary sources.	Use visual appreciation. Aesthetic qualities of the environment. Recognise art from other cultures.	Sounds in environments. How music represents places in the world.	Vocabulary of movement. Improvement of spatial ability. Outdoor activity.	Religious stories. Visits to religious sites. Records (eg. parish records) as a data source.
THEMATIC MAPS	Reading maps, keys and directions. Labelling keys. Handwriting cartographic precision.	Shape and plan view. Measuring and scaling down. Grids and co-ordinates. Representing 3D shapes as 2D. Area in mapping.	Mapping the Earth as a planet in the solar system; its rotation and the poles, equator, prime meridian. Distribution map.	Using old maps as thematic maps; to gather information on places; to illustrate change through time.	The making and using of (thematic) maps, as a part of producing design proposals for environmental projects.	Using graphics and design programs to make maps. Using CD-ROM and other atlases and mapping programs.	Use control of tools/techniques when drawing maps. Aesthetic qualities of mapped images. Scaling up/down – an artistic skill.	Mapping sounds in the environment. Sound maps as thematic maps. Orchestra plans.	Representation of position in physical space. Use of apparatus plans in gymnastics.	Mapping world religions. Maps in the study of religious stories. Plans of religious buildings.
RIVERS	Speaking, listening, reading and writing using the vocabulary surrounding rivers.	Measuring stream widths. Using scale to calculate length of rivers from map. Timing speed of flow.	River as an environment. Solids and liquids in rivers. Electricity. Forces (friction).	The river as a settlement location, transport route, source of water and power and its change through history.	Designing and making bridges. Human designs for harnessing rivers.	Logging and handling data. Monitoring of events using IT.	Study of artists who have used rivers as a source of inspiration. Reflection of light on water.	River as a source of noise and inspiration. Composers using water sounds .	River as a leisure resource. Relevance of survival and water safety as in swimming.	Rivers as significant in religious stories and ceremony; and communication routes.
WEATHER	Weather words and poems. Written descriptions. Weather forecasts.	Using scales on instruments (including negative numbers).	Habitats. Electricity. Forces (friction). Sun – light source. Day and night. Seasons.	Effect of weather on people through history. Changing clothes/buildings. Weather and exploration.	Designing, making and evaluating weather-recording apparatus.	Logging and handling data. Monitoring of events using IT.	Studies of the sky at different times of day and weather and of artists' work on the weather.	The weather as inspiration for composing /performing/ singing.	Appreciation of the weather in outdoor activities. Weather as a dance stimulus.	Weather in religious stories.
SETTLEMENT	Place names and their make up. Ways in which we describe settlements. Reading guide books.	Counting systems and handling of data in traffic surveys. Shape and space in settlements.	Shelter as a requirement of a habitat. Materials used in construction. Electricity.	How settlements grow and evolve, Buildings, architecture and the built legacy of past societies.	Making models of settlements. Control mechanisms in settlements. Structures and aesthetics.	Logging and handling data. Collecting information on settlements around the world using the Internet and CD-ROM.	Analysis of architectural styles/traditions. Line, tone, shape, form and space in the depiction of townscapes.	Music from a range of cultures, city and different settlement groups. Places to hear music.	Study of leisure, sport and recreation facilities in different localities.	Places of worship in settlements. Ones which owe their location and origin to being religious sites.
ENVIRONMENTAL CHANGE	Presentation and role-play on environmental issues. Reading media coverage.	Handling statistics from surveys.	Life processes, green plants as organisms. Habitats.	Historical study to inform about the environment. Managing and sustaining environments for the future.	Designing, making and evaluating posters. Design issues in the environment.	Use of graphics, DTP, video and tape recordings in producing material to argue a case on the environment.	Poster design. Depiction of environments.	Music to represent issues in the environment.	Appreciation of sensitive areas during outdoor adventurous activity.	Connection between beliefs and stewardship of environment. Habitats (graveyards).